THE WEIGHT I CARRIED

THE WEIGHT I CARRIED

Hiking Through Grief and Healing
on the Appalachian Trail

STEVEN C. WRIGHT

With Tara Shoemaker Holdren

Carpenter's Son Publishing

The Weight I Carried: Hiking Through Grief and Healing on the Appalachian Trail
©2025 by Steven C. Wright

All rights reserved. No part of this book may be reproduced or transmitted in any form or by any means, electronic or mechanical, including photocopying, recording or by any information storage and retrieval system, without permission in writing from the copyright owner.

Scripture taken from the NEW KING JAMES VERSION®. Copyright© 1982 by Thomas Nelson, Inc. Used by permission. All rights reserved.

Published by Clovercroft Publishing, Franklin, Tennessee

Cover and Interior Design by Suzanne Lawing

Printed in the United States of America

ISBN: 978-1-968127-01-5 (print)

Disclaimer:
The advice, opinions, and suggestions herein are personally anecdotal and are in no way intended as a substitute for professional or medical consult. This is my story alone, and not intended to be doctrinal. Some of the names of real persons have been changed.

DEDICATION

For Sandy—
*my first great love,
the one whose courage, laughter,
and suffering cracked me wide open.
You were the mountain I could never summit.*

For my Dad—
*the man who carried me when I couldn't walk,
who bled for me and broke with me.
You taught me what strength looks like when it weeps.
I wish I could've said I was sorry sooner—
but this book, this trail, this healing—
is me saying it now, again and again.*

And for anyone who's ever battled the shadows in their mind—
*you are not alone. Your struggles are real.
Even in the silence, God is near.
Even in the ashes, hope is yours to choose.
The same God who walked me through fire walks beside you now.
You are not forgotten.
You are being led—step by step, breath by breath—away from the
darkness and toward the light.*

ACKNOWLEDGMENTS

This book wouldn't exist without the kindness, grit, and patience of a lot of people.

First, to my Mom—At my lowest, when I had forgotten my own worth, you looked me in the eye and asked me to say my name. When I finally spoke it aloud, you reminded me, without hesitation, that it belonged to a man who was going to change the world. I've never forgotten your words.

To Tara—my ghostwriter, my friend, the one who gave shape to my mess of memories. I came to you with no plan, no money—just a scattered story and a hope. You didn't flinch. You called it a ministry and gave yourself to it, fully. That kind of generosity is rare, and I'll never forget it.

More than a year later—two summers lost, countless nights burned—you were still in it with me. I had no notes. Just photos, pieces, and regret. I left things out. I tried to make myself look better than I was. But you held the line—helped me face the truth, even when it hurt. You made me brave enough to be honest. Thank you.

To Chad—Tara's husband—thank you for sharing her time, her presence, her energy. I know what it cost, and I'm so thankful.

To my daughter, Jocelyn—you've carried so much of this quietly. Running the behind-the-scenes that no one sees. You showed up in every way you could. I couldn't have done this without you.

To my son Tristan—my personal PT on speed dial—thank you for your patience, your knowledge, and your quiet understanding of my inability to quit. You never got frustrated, or gave up on me, even when my body was breaking. You always helped me find a way forward.

To my son-in-law, Tommy—thank you for being thoughtful and sharp. From Zoom meetings to reading contracts, you've had my back the whole way.

To Nancy—my sister—thank you for reading my words aloud until I could finally hear them. I didn't believe this story needed to be written until I heard you read it.

To Mary Lou—thank you for all the time and energy you put into helping shape this thing into what it became.

To Ian—thanks for the late-night texts and your clear-eyed honesty.

To Alex and Tiffany—thank you for covering the bases I didn't even know existed.

To those who sat around the table with me, read early pages, asked hard questions, or just kept telling me to finish—thank you. Your fingerprints are all over this.

To my family, my friends, and everyone who said this story mattered—I finally get it.

And I'm grateful.

—Steven C. Wright

·

CONTENTS

SECTION I
INTRODUCTION

Chapter 1:	Seventeen Deaths	17
Chapter 2:	Breakdown	21
Chapter 3:	Putting Out the Fleece	24

SECTION II
NOBO (NORTHBOUND)

Chapter 4:	Racing	29
Chapter 5:	Cold	37
Chapter 6:	The Kid Deserves a Chance	43
Chapter 7:	You Will Like It, I Guarantee It	48
Chapter 8:	Bear Tag	52
Chapter 9:	Becoming Camel	56
Chapter 10:	We're All F----d Up	59
Chapter 11:	Hurricane I	66
Chapter 12:	The Heart Is a Bone That Heals	71
Chapter 13:	The Smokies	80
Chapter 14:	Pink Crocs and Ponies (Hurricane II)	84
Chapter 15:	Norovirus	88
Chapter 16:	COVID and Convalescence	93

Chapter 17:	The Ephesians Effect	99
Chapter 18:	Berries and Shrooms	104
Chapter 19:	Cancer Is a Forbidden Word	107
Chapter 20:	Bees	110
Chapter 21:	Hitting 900	114

SECTION III
MAINE

Chapter 22:	Stories from Shaw's	121
Chapter 23:	100-Mile Wilderness	129
Chapter 24:	Jouster Down (The Shoulder Incident)	142
Chapter 25:	Katahdin	149
Chapter 26:	Bigelows and Broken Bones	154
Chapter 27:	Hurricane III	165

SECTION IV
SOBO (SOUTHBOUND) -ISH

Chapter 28:	Bye-Bye Tag-Along	173
Chapter 29:	Saddleback and Mahoosuc Notch X3	177
Chapter 30:	Soundtrack for Fraconia Notch	182
Chapter 31:	The Interview	190
Chapter 32:	Suffering	195
Chapter 33:	Rain Man Returns	208
Chapter 34:	Can You Hear Me Now?	213
Chapter 35:	Rain Without Rain Man	228
Chapter 36:	Defender of the Trail	236
Chapter 37:	A Happy Crew	243

Chapter 38:	On the Boardwalk	248
Chapter 39:	At Wits End	254
Chapter 40:	Bird on the Table, Birds on the Trail	259
Chapter 41:	Draggin' Horns	268
Chapter 42:	La La La (Port Clinton)	275
Chapter 43:	Old Friend, New Friend	281
Chapter 44:	Spared	289
Chapter 45:	Not Too Crabby	296

SECTION V
NOBO (AGAIN)

Chapter 46:	Colder	303
Chapter 47:	Hungry	317
Chapter 48:	A Purpose	326
Chapter 49:	The Church	337
Chapter 50:	Finish Line	341

SECTION I
INTRODUCTION

For we do not wrestle against flesh and blood, but against principalities, against powers, against the rulers of the darkness of this age, against spiritual hosts of wickedness in the heavenly places.
Ephesians 6:12 (NKJV)

CHAPTER 1:

SEVENTEEN DEATHS

I know I should start at the beginning, but where is that? Even as a boy I was building the life that has led me to this one, and as a young man those childhood events stuck with me. I married my high school girlfriend, Sandy, and really, we became adults together. Then in the middle of my life, I lost her to breast cancer, and those last moments of her suffering dominated my thoughts until I could no longer see anything but darkness. I was in trouble.

Therapy was good, but nine months on the Appalachian Trail were better.

This story is about how I went through hell to be the last thru-hiker to complete the trail in 2023, but in the process I managed to find healing for my body and mind. The trail has a way of doing that, and everyone on the trail has a reason for hiking it. You'd better have a good reason for hiking it, because it will test you. The wilderness is going to bite down, chew on you, and spit you back out. Your reason for being there has to be strong enough to get you through.

I had an excellent reason.

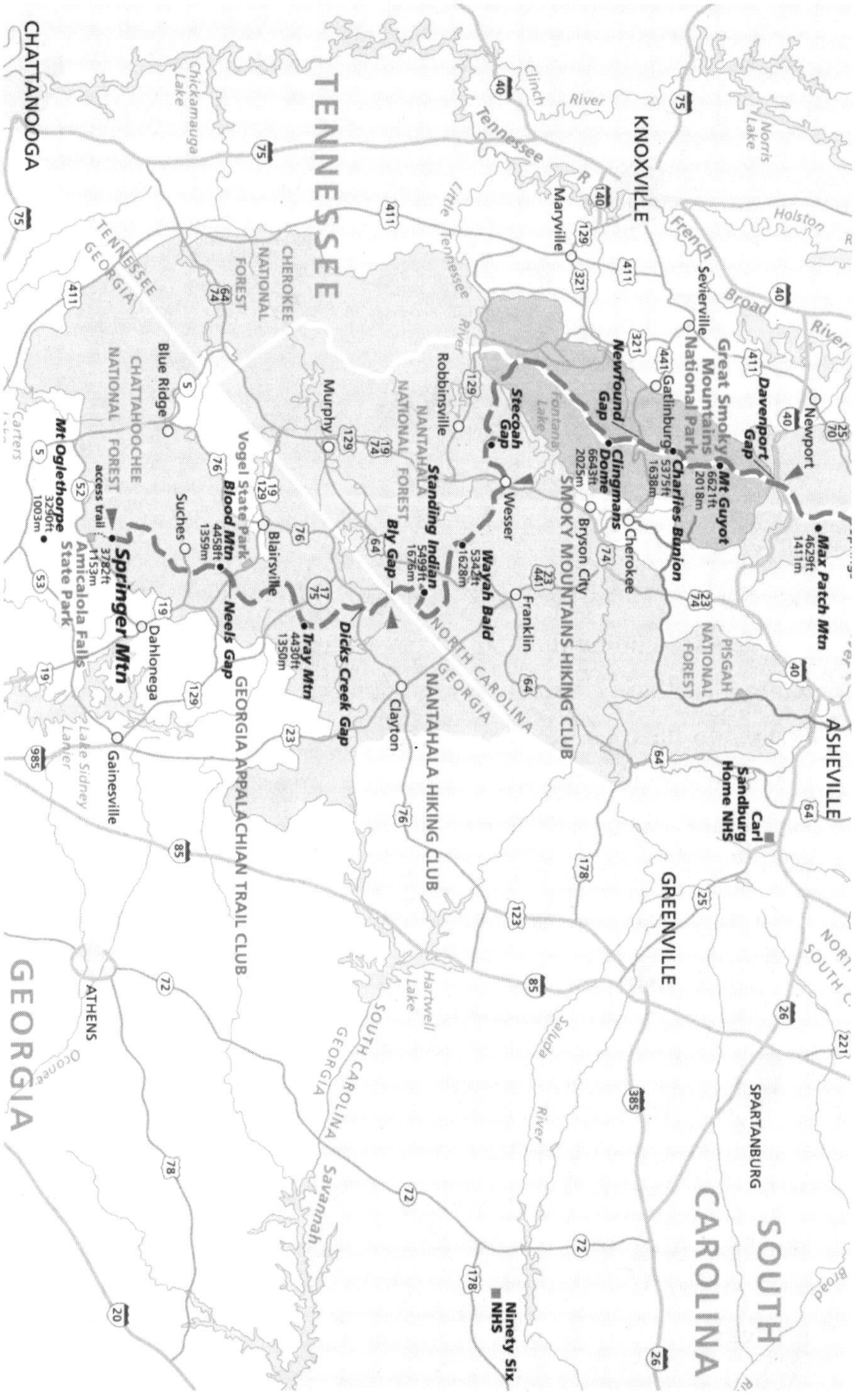

CHATTANOOGA
KNOXVILLE
ASHEVILLE
GREENVILLE
SPARTANBURG
ATHENS
TENNESSEE
GEORGIA
SOUTH CAROLINA
NORTH CAROLINA
Maryville
Sevierville
Gatlinburg
Newport
Great Smoky Mountains National Park
Davenport Gap
Max Patch Mtn
4629ft
1411m
Mt Guyot
6621ft
2018m
Charlies Bunion
5375ft
1638m
Newfound Gap
Clingmans Dome
6643ft
2025m
Cherokee
Bryson City
SMOKY MOUNTAINS HIKING CLUB
Fontana Lake
Stecoah Gap
Wesser
Robbinsville
Murphy
Franklin
Wayah Bald
5342ft
1628m
Standing Indian
5499ft
1676m
NANTAHALA NATIONAL FOREST
NANTAHALA HIKING CLUB
Bly Gap
Dicks Creek Gap
Clayton
Tray Mtn
4430ft
1350m
Blairsville
Vogel State Park
Blood Mtn
4458ft
1359m
Neels Gap
Suches
Springer Mtn
3782ft
1153m
access trail
Mt Oglethorpe
3290ft
1003m
Amicalola Falls State Park
Dahlonega
Gainesville
Blue Ridge
CHATTAHOOCHEE NATIONAL FOREST
CHEROKEE NATIONAL FOREST
PISGAH NATIONAL FOREST
GEORGIA APPALACHIAN TRAIL CLUB
Carl Sandburg Home NHS
Ninety Six NHS
Chickamauga Lake
Norris Lake
Hartwell Lake
Lake Sidney Lanier
Clinch River
Tennessee R
Little Tennessee River
Holston
French Broad River
Saluda River
Savannah
Oconee

I've had the privilege of being with 17 people as they passed from this life to the next. I mean, I'm counting the ones who were in my arms or I was holding their hand. There were probably between two or three hundred people whom I helped under dire circumstances, but I'm talking about the ones who passed while I was right there. Some were through a ministry that serves people who are dying but want to pray with somebody. It is a privilege to pray with someone when they are dying. It's one thing when someone is dying of a slow disease, and another when they are in an accident or trauma. If they are awake, sometimes it's terrible, and they just want someone to hold their hand. There were some for whom death I knew was imminent. I stayed as long as I could, but as soon as I left the hospital they died, and I feel bad about that. I do not include them in my total.

I don't feel that I am a great comforter, but something did happen that impacted my life, and it put a burden on my heart for this kind of ministry. Many years ago, I was driving along and came upon an accident. One car was crunched up like an accordion and the other was upside down. I ran to the group of people in the middle, and the driver of one of the cars had been pulled out and was lying down on the road. I could see right away he had a severe cut on his neck. He was bleeding badly, and I knew he was going to bleed to death. I immediately reached to put pressure on it.

"Don't touch him!" an EMT ordered, and grabbed my hand. "What the hell are you doing? You can't touch him. You don't know what you're doing."

Well, he was right, but I knew that unless someone put pressure on his neck this man was going to bleed to death.

"You're just going to get the shit sued out of you! What are you doing?" the EMT continued.

I listened. I pulled my hand away and watched this man die in front of me. I could have stopped it, but I listened to this EMT! I've thought of it over and over again. Why did I listen to that asshole? The next day I signed up for a class in lifesaving: choking, first aid, etc. I was overcome with guilt and a desire to be used by God in this way, and He did not disappoint. When I became a Christian, I heard a sermon one time on wanting to be used by God. "If you don't pray this prayer, you will never be used," said the preacher. That got my attention. "If you say 'God, use me,' He will. And it might not be in the circumstance you want."

I've found it to be true.

I learned that when you pray for God to use you, you must be very willing to do anything. If you're not, you will not be used. God does not cater to the easy way. His way is sometimes hard. You might have to crawl in a burning vehicle. You might have to crawl in a vehicle under water. You might have to bust open a window to get to the people. I had to do all of those things, and many more! After that man bled to death, I felt that I had failed, and I made my mind up that I didn't care if someone sued me because I was trying to do good. I just want to be used. So I lose my house over it? It doesn't make a difference. I want to be used by God.

You cannot go wrong when you are being used by God, even if you lose everything, including your life. So be prepared. It's isn't always pretty or easy. Just pray for God to use you, and I guarantee He will. My buddy Mookie, whom you'll read about later, was with me so many times when we came across burning or wrecked cars that he begged me to stop praying to be used.

Six times I prayed with people in a hospital bed.

Eleven times I prayed with people in some kind of trauma.

Now, in all those 17 people, I never saw anybody suffer like my wife did in her last moments. Believe me when I tell you that she died a painful death that was not like any other I had witnessed. It was vicious and cruel. She was not in a coma. She was fully aware of every bit of it. She suffered until her last breath.

CHAPTER 2:

BREAKDOWN

That's why my wife's death in 2018 hit me so hard. I was so angry with God. I knew that Satan was responsible for pain and death, but I also knew that this God I had loved and served all these years could have prevented Sandy's. Maybe I thought He owed me or something. I don't know why I would ever think I should have any privileges with God, but it didn't seem fair. Even now these words hurt me to say them.

In the end, it would take the whole 2,198 miles of the Appalachian Trail for me to be able to give this to God. But at the time of her death, I just could not. The images of Sandy in pain were on replay in my head, and I could not stop them. For five years, until I hiked the trail in 2023, I held God responsible. Those words would shock those who know me, that I could think that about God, but I'm being honest.

I worked at the local university. I was grieving and bitter, and it showed.

Finally a guy who worked with me stopped me at my truck after work and tried to give me a pamphlet to read. It was short, like about three paragraphs.

"I've noticed you aren't right, Steve," he said kindly. "I think you need to read this."

I didn't want any part of it. He didn't know the first thing about how I was feeling and had no right to tell me what I did or didn't need. He tried several times, but I kept refusing him.

At last he said, "Let me tell you a story."

He asked me if I had heard about the football players who had drowned. I had read about it in the paper. The one kid started drowning and the other one went out to save him. The first kid dragged him under, and they both drowned. Their team went on to win the state championship that year with all the players wearing black armbands in a tribute to their lost friends. I had heard about it all right.

"That was my son," he said, the one who had gone in to save his friend. It had cost this boy his life. "I lost my son, but also then my wife, my house, and I ended up bankrupt." He told me how dealing with this grief had cost him everything.

Well, then he had my attention. I took the pamphlet. It was called *Attitude* by Chuck Swindall, and it changed my outlook completely. He wrote about how your outlook on life is the single most important factor, above circumstances or even success. Our attitudes are the only thing we can control, the only "string" we have to play. I realized that what was happening in my mind was controlling my life, and I had to figure out how to change it.

Armed with these paragraphs, it was clear I needed help. I quit working. It was so unfulfilling anyway, and I could barely get myself going in the morning at this point. I decided to go to a hospital and face the facts: I was in trouble and needed help. I was ashamed, but too desperate to care at that point. They immediately checked me into the wing for people on suicide watch. The room was bare, the air stale, and I was absolutely going even more crazy in there. So as soon as someone came in and the door was open, I bolted. Instead, I made arrangements to see a counselor, and she gradually, session by session, got some of the many tentacles of my screwed-up thinking and feeling back under control.

Finally, in one session she asked me, "What do you like to do? What makes you happy?"

"Hiking," I said without a thought.

"Well," she said, "why don't you go do that?"

Why indeed. Well, I was broke, for one thing. We had used every dime to try experimental treatments and somehow save Sandy's life. But Sandy's own words about the trail came back to me.

One evening, I had been sitting with her, and she started speculating about who might be a good next wife for me. She had grown so thin and white; her frailty was like a stubborn visitor we could not get rid of. Full of spunk though and as practical as ever, she came up with three names for me.

She said, "You know, Steve, I think you should still do the AT. I think"—she paused for extra effect—"maybe you could meet your next wife there."

I didn't want to hear anything about another wife, I can tell you that. But her words returned to me now with some fresh pain. Before we had our kids, Jocelyn and then Tristan, it had always been our dream to do the Appalachian Trail together. But you know, life starts happening pretty fast. We always loved hiking as a family, but we were busy with soccer and dance and work and a hundred other things. After the kids were older, Sandy was less interested in sleeping on the ground, for sure.

I wasn't looking for another wife. I mean, it would have been nice for someone, anyone, to fill the hole she left behind. But mostly I didn't want our old dream to go unrealized. Could I do it? Did God want me to do it?

CHAPTER 3:

PUTTING OUT THE FLEECE

By this time, it was 2019. I decided to start training at least. While I was working in Malibu, California, I started trail running with my pack, and I strained my Achilles tendon. Then the nationwide shutdown for COVID happened on March 13, 2020, the day before I was supposed to leave for the trail. Then in 2021, and in 2022, I was trying to sell my house to make sure I had the money to do the hike, but the sale fell through. Then in 2023, I tore my labrum in my shoulder on February 6 while lifting a new window into a house. I was worried I wouldn't be able to do the hike (I would have to leave mid-March again). I decided to ask God for a sign. Since I was already hurt, I needed to know He wanted me on the trail. So I put out the fleece.

What does that mean, you ask?

In Judges 6:36-40, Gideon wants to know whether he will be able to rescue Israel, so he puts out some fleece and makes this deal with God. If he wakes up in the morning and the fleece is wet with dew, then he will know that God will help him save Israel. If it's dry, then God won't. So he puts out the fleece. Sure enough, the next morning, it's wringing wet. The funny part is that Gideon is still pretty nervous about it, and he wants to make sure it isn't just a coincidence that the fleece was wet. Maybe it was just a dewy kind of night, you know? So he goes back to God and he says (I'm paraphrasing), "Hey, don't be angry with me, but I just want to make sure you are with me. This time, I'll put out the fleece and if it's dry, even though there's dew all around it on the grass, then I'll know for sure you are in favor of me going in to save Israel." Sure enough, the fleece is dry, and the dew is all around. Gideon has his sign from God.

My fleece was a GoFundMe page. The typical cost to do the Appalachian Trail is $10K. If I could raise the money to go on the hike, I would do it. Then I would hike to raise money for the Sloan Kettering laboratory that studies triple negative breast cancer. They had worked with Sandy, and in fact, her tumors are still there for the purpose of their research. My daughter Jocelyn helped me make the page, and we waited.

In a week we had the $10K. I was like, well, okay then, God. I'm going to do the AT.

So I started prepping for the trail, for real this time at the ripe age of 64. Suddenly, I found myself so excited, the first excitement I had felt about anything since Sandy's death.

SECTION II
NOBO (NORTHBOUND)

Yea, though I walk through the valley of the shadow of death,
I will fear no evil;
For You are with me;
Your rod and Your staff, they comfort me.
Psalm 23:4 (NKJV)

CHAPTER 4:

RACING

The skies open up in a torrential downpour as my daughter Jocelyn and I start up the trail toward Amicalola Falls in Dawsonville, Georgia. Many years earlier I had read a book by Earl Shaffer, *Walking with Spring,* and Amicalola Falls is where he started his hike. *Welcome to the AT,* I think.

Thanks to the thunderstorms, water pours like a beautiful and translucent veil over the pinched-up face of the rocks. The rocks go up like stairs for the feet of giants, and I feel so small, so exposed on the little wooden bridge at the foot of the falls.

Jocelyn hikes about five miles in with me, but then has to head off the trail for her ride back to Atlanta. Both of us understand what this hike is for and what it means for us.

"I'll see you in Maine," she says with a sniffle. She's videotaping me as I walk away into the woods, and I hear her say, "There he goes!"

The fog is thick, and the rain is still coming down in sheets as she gets smaller and smaller behind me. I consider going to a hut that some hikers had told me about just six miles in. It's raining so hard that I'm tempted. The whole group who has started with me ends

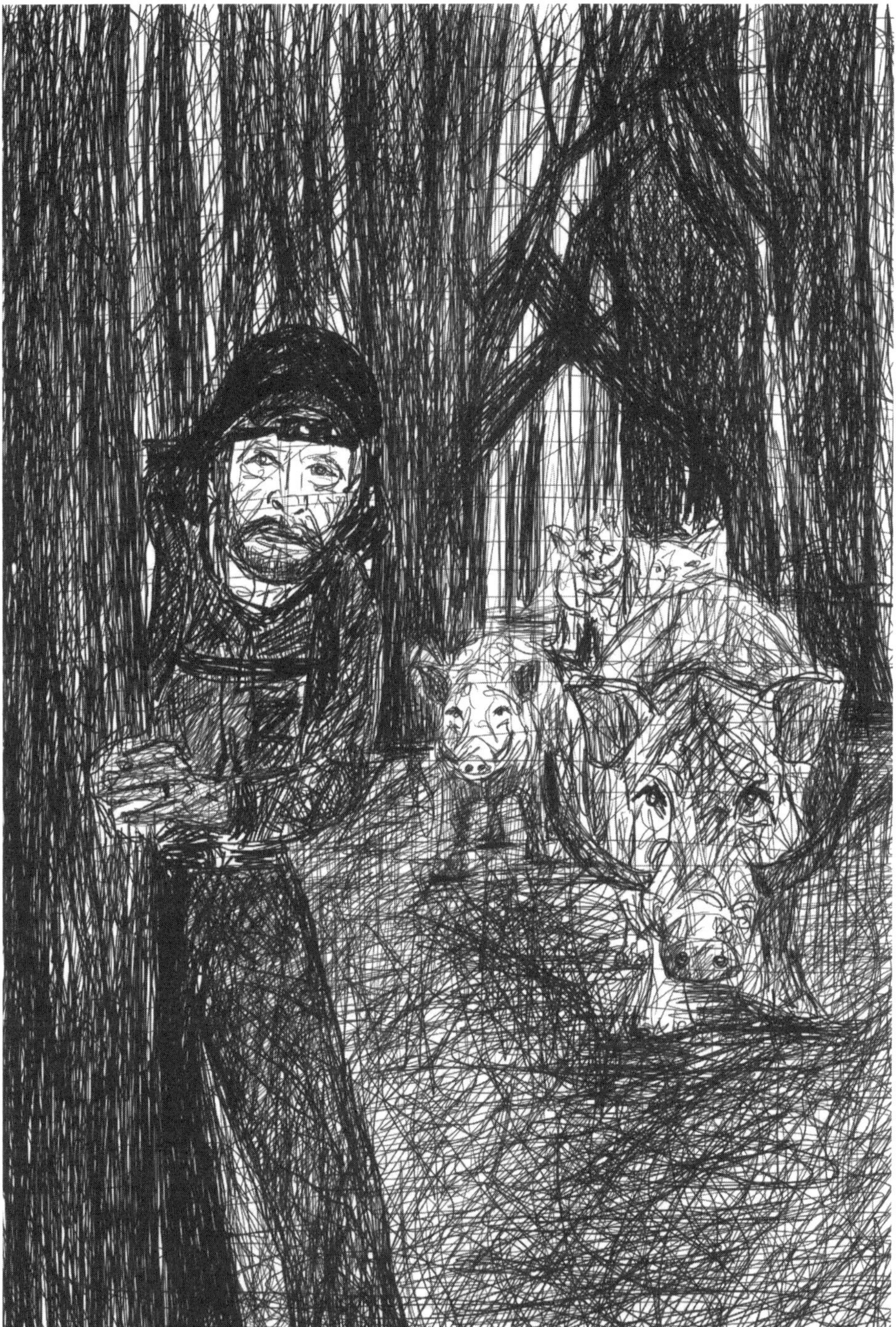

up going there, but I think, *Aw, screw it, I might as well get used to the rain.*

I hike and hike and get to the approach trail, the official start of the AT. In the dark, I manage to hike right past the shelter. I was looking out for it, but I'm not really using my app correctly at this point, and I miss it. Whatever. I want to test my tent for leaks, so here I go. I check my watch. It's 9:30 at night, and I have hiked several miles in the dark with my red light on in my head lamp because of the fog. When I look back up, it looks like there's a bear right in front of me. *This trail has a lot of adventure already*, I think, pleased. But even with my damaged hearing, I start hearing noises around me, all around me. Cubs with their mother? *I'm in trouble.*

I can tell, whatever it is, it's walking toward me.

It stops about 20 feet in front of me. It puts a massive head down, and roots up a giant stump out of the ground in one motion. My brain finally pieces together the clues: *a wild boar.*

I can make out all these littler pigs to my right. There is nothing to my left. The big boar doesn't seem to care that I'm there, and maybe that's because I am using the red light. The smaller pigs are running 130-140 pounds, and they are about 10 – 15 feet away. I count maybe 30 or 40 of them. The big boar seems content with the grubs it has just discovered under the stump. I am frozen in place, but I put one hand on the trunk of a nearby tree on my left. Just like always, I figure if I get in trouble, I can get up that tree real quick.

Now, I am an expert tree-climber. On the Appalachian Trail, I will climb no fewer than 75 trees, just to get a better photograph. My tree-climbing has gotten me out of trouble plenty of times. One time though, it got me into big trouble.

It was hot, even in Rhode Island, and I didn't want to be there. The year was 1968, and I was nine years old, but I was about to start third grade in the city of Providence. Is the math not math-ing? No, my mother, in all her wisdom, didn't send me to school late. The truth is that already I had failed first grade and repeated it. I was hopelessly behind, unable to pay attention to anything the teachers told me. I learned to sit on my hands, my hands literally under my ass, in order to keep in the chair. It was impossible. It would be no different at my new school, and I knew it.

We were there so my dad could get dialysis at the veteran's hospital. He was a good man, but he was an alcoholic. He had never actually laid a hand on me, but I can't say the same for my older brothers. Two of my older brothers, George and Drexel, were serving in Vietnam at the time. They were done with school probably around tenth grade, and I glued myself to the television every night listening to the war news. Someday, I would be there with them.

My family, really, was super close. We were flat broke, always, but it was basically a happy home. I had seven brothers and sisters, and four of them eventually went blind later in life because of a congenital defect that resulted in retina pigmentosa macular degeneration. That was a trying thing for our family. My oldest sister Mary Ann was already married, so she was out of the house when we were in Providence, and George and Drexel were in Vietnam, so at home now were just Tammy, me, Wally, Nancy, and Bonnie. My sister Nancy got married at 18, just after she graduated high school.

Like I said, we were flat broke. So that meant that in the summer and fall we all worked picking tomatoes for two different farmers. Our whole family, all the siblings who were left anyway, went into the field, except Tammy, because she was so young. I liked picking tomatoes, to tell you the truth. It was fun. I got to be with Wally, Nancy, and Bonnie. We also worked side by side with black and Hispanic kids, who were funny, and we all got along and had a good time. I was not particularly good at picking tomatoes though. I would end up talking a lot and would get in the wrong row. I might have been just a little too young, but anyway, I loved it.

But there were no tomatoes to pick here in Providence. I was alone in the school lot with a single tree in the middle of it. Enter James. I will not learn his name till much later, but for now he is a welcome distraction.

"Want to race?" he asks. He means up the tree.

"Sure," I say.

Back in Pennsylvania, we had a hedgerow of big trees right behind our house. In no time, I could be up 60 feet and looking down at the world. At nine, I am the fastest tree climber of all my friends back home, and I am confident I can beat James. The tree has smooth bark, and no branches down low. Even at first glance, I know I can take him.

James has some trouble getting to the first branch, so I actually reach down and grab his shirt to help him out. Then I smoke him. I'm pretty high up and triumphant above him. Only then do I realize that a crowd has gathered around the perimeter of the lot. They are, in fact, all black kids, and James too is black, a detail I hadn't registered before. Based on my time in the tomato field, the color of his skin made no difference to me, and I stupidly assumed it made no difference to other people either. Turns out, it made a huge difference. Apparently, my victory over James is an offense in some way, and the crowd is there to avenge his loss. They begin chucking rocks, hard, and they are landing them, even as high up as I am. I take a few hits before I figure, That's enough

"Don't get down," says James. "They'll kill you."

Well, I'm a country kid, and that seems a little harsh. Surely James is exaggerating.

"No, man, I'm serious. They'll kill you." His eyes are luminous and earnest.

Another few rocks hit their mark. I was dead anyway, wasn't I? Sooner or later the rocks would do their work, and I figure getting down can't be much worse.

I am wrong. By the time I shimmy to the ground, they are in a large circle. Like I'm an absurd kind of bowling pin, they begin pushing me around the perimeter, and the circle gets smaller and smaller. Finally, the shoving launches me across the circle, side to side, and I fall to the ground. *Well, they will be satisfied now,* I think.

Far from satisfied, their feral excitement at having a downed victim only intensifies the attack. At ground level, I feel the first stomps like cannonballs dropped from great heights. On my legs, wrists, hands—each stomp is breaking bones. My fingers snap like twigs, then my wrists. To this day I don't know what shoes they were wearing, but they weren't any kind of sneaker I ever knew of. They had sharp heels like dress shoes or even boots, and the heels left behind bloody gashes. I take kicks to the ribs (which break), back, and then to my face and head. Finally, after a kick to my right ear, I go blissfully unconscious.

As my feet had hit the ground at the base of the tree, James had taken off at a sprint to find a cop. When he returned with the cop, he undoubtably saved my life. The boys took off running, and I was taken to a hospital.

When I come to, James and his mom are there by my bed.

"Hey, what's your name?" James asks. They hadn't even known what name to write on my chart. I mumble "Steven" through my broken face. The pain everywhere is excruciating. Breathing hurts. Talking hurts. Thinking hurts.

"Where do you live?" James's mom asks. I didn't know. I probably could have gotten there from the school yard, but at the moment the brain fog from my concussion was preventing me from having much clarity. Eventually, the nurses put out a notice, and my parents were looking for me, so I was identified and reunited with them. I was, however, also deaf in my right ear for the rest of my life. But, while there would not be voices, music, or the sound of birds in that ear, there would be a persistent locust-style buzz that would nearly drive me insane sometimes.

So, I was lucky to hear the hogs, and probably I should have heard them sooner than I did. I stand with my hand on that tree, watching them for a half hour. Then they finally go down over the bank. I wait another 15 minutes before I take another step. I go another five minutes in the opposite direction of the pigs before I pick a camping place. I'm not hungry yet, somehow. But I make dinner anyway, rice and beans. I eat a few bites and then roll the bag up and put it back in my pack. I hang the pack up in a tree and go to sleep.

I'm soaked, lying there. The inside of my tent is wet. Because I've had my gear since 2019, it's already a little old, but it seems like everything is working. I sleep well.

When I wake up, it's almost daylight, and it has stopped raining. Everything is wet. When I get my bag down, I notice gray juice from the beans and rice has leaked all over the inside of my pack. I must have stabbed the food pouch with my spork before rolling it up for the night. Awesome. Rice everywhere. I'm a freaking magnet for a bear now.

But I'm not a stranger to being hunted, in some ways. There were other close calls in Providence. There was a bully who would pick on us and chase us around. I was so fast, though, he couldn't catch me. But he could always catch my friends, and I would never desert them. I got the shit kicked out of me so many times because I hung out with slow guys. Now whenever my older brother Wally showed up, those guys ran like sissies, because he was tall and had big muscles. He was over six feet, and a few years older than they were. Wally and I were the closest. He was always in trouble like me. At first when we were little, it was like with any little brother, he didn't want me hanging around. By the time we got into our teens, though, I think I won him over. We actually hung out. And after I graduated and started working full time at my brother Drexel's construction company, Wally and I were still the closest. I really liked being with all my brothers, and I was good at construction. I could do everything from siding to framing and even remodeling a bathroom. Everything was a competition with me, so I pushed myself to go faster and do my work better than anybody. I could work all day with my brothers and turn around and go right back out with them that night. I tell you, when you've got a brother and a friend in the same guy, you've really got something there. Blood is thick, thick as molasses. It's sticky. Wally always stuck by me, and I stuck by him.

CHAPTER 5:

COLD

With no rain, I'm flying over the trail today. I have come into the hike with the torn labrum and a torn Achillies on the mend, and I'm hurting a little. It rains on and off, and I make 15.4 miles. I can tell the air is changing, though, and that night I can finally see some stars. It's a blessing for tomorrow's hike, I think.

But the next morning the temperature is in the 20s. By now I'm at 3,600 feet and everything is frozen. It doesn't matter if you're in Georgia; it gets cold at 3,600 feet. And honestly, as I go along I am blown away by the mountains in Georgia. I don't know why, but I didn't expect them to be so magnificent. It's a beautiful state with so much to offer. I was actually not too far from where they filmed *Deliverance* at one point.

The forecast was for down around zero for that second night. I could hardly believe it. There were about 22 people from Florida when we started out and one guy from Chicago. He was hiking a little slower than me, and I never saw him again. I'd run into the guys from Florida here and there, and they were not really prepared for these temperatures. They were frozen. About half of them quit that very day. But it was a good thing they walked. It was even colder the next night.

On that next night, a dad and his young boy are camping near me, and I can hear the boy crying in the night. I go over and offer him my Mountain Wear puffy coat and my mittens. He gladly accepts, and the dad thanks me again and again. Their plan was to do the trail and the boy was going to do a report on his experience while the dad did homeschool lessons with him. I am warm enough with my Smartwool long underwear and hoodie and socks. My sleeping bag was doing its job. In the morning, they quit.

It broke my heart to think of that dad, trying to do this special thing with his son. My dad's alcoholism stole so many things from us. I was sure that everything that had happened to me in Rhode Island was his fault, because he was the reason we were there.

Two years after I got beaten up, we were still in Providence. With the exception of my hearing, I had recovered physically from the beating, but school was still not going well for me. I'm sure today I would have been labeled with some alphabet letters that include some D's ... ADD? ADHD? Back then it didn't matter. All that mattered was between being deaf in one ear and trying to sit on my hands, I was not successful. I had failed the fifth grade.

I refused to do it again. What was the point of school anyway? As I said, my plan was first to be a mountain man like in the movies, but I figured in real life I'd probably go join the army and fight in Vietnam with my two older brothers. My mother and father vetoed this, even if it had been legal to send a 12-year-old to war. My father's health had continued to decline. As the argument about school heated up, my temper got the best of me, and I uttered a sentence that would confirm from that moment forward that I was absolutely the worst human on earth—ungrateful, cruel, unredeemable, and definitely unlovable.

I told my father I wished he were dead.

Now, my father was no saint, as I mentioned before. The whole reason he needed the dialysis was because he was an alcoholic. Why was he an alcoholic? As an adult I'm guessing he was using it to dull the memories of his own service in the military during WWII. Here was a man who fought in Germany, but would never tell us anything about it. In fact, he instructed all of his friends (which of course I tried to pry information out of) not to say anything about it either. He said none of us needed to know what he had experienced, and he stuck to it. The vet hospital which provided his life-saving dialysis was in Providence, and that was really the only reason we had moved here. I had heard my parents' conversations about his health on numerous occasions while I played my little games under the kitchen table. I had roads and men and cars, and while I was fully absorbed in my imaginative scenarios under there, I was also listening. At one point he had commented to my mother that maybe we would be better off without him. Instead of meeting that thought with immediate compassion and concern, my self-absorbed little boy brain seized upon the idea and secretly agreed with him.

And then I said it out loud. The impact was visible on his face. It crumbled in a way I had never seen a man's face break before. He put his head down and wept. I had never seen my father ever cry actual tears, but there they were. My mother reached over and slapped me, hard, across the face. My dad left the room, but I sat there mad as a hornet, just beginning to grasp the magnitude of what I had done. Later, she called me back to the kitchen. By this time my father was gone, who knows where.

"You have to apologize to him," she said. Her voice was stern, and her eyes were flinty with something else besides the command. I didn't argue with her.

"Listen to me," she said. "What's your name?"

Duh, I thought. "Steven."

"No, what's your full name?"

"Steven Wright." Where was this going?

"What's your *full name*?" she demanded. Her eyes bored into me.

"*Steven Curtis Wright*," I recited firmly.

"All my life I prayed to God that one of my sons would change the world." She was stiff, intense, challenging me to doubt her or mock her. I had no intention of doing either. "You," she said with a little stab at my shoulder and a little bit of spit at the side of her mouth, "are that son. You are going to change the world. Do you hear me? You are going to change the world."

We sat in silence, and finally I left the room. What in the world did she mean? And worse, what did it mean on the heels of the thing I had just done to my father? Was I a hero or a villain? How was I going to change the world when I couldn't even pass fifth grade? My sneakers were scuffed up, my jeans ragged, my attitude was as defective as my hearing. I was dumbfounded. At least, I could honor my promise to apologize to my dad.

But, I couldn't. I don't honestly know why. I wanted to. But the wound I had inflicted had already begun its slow destruction on the man. All the fight went out of him and sadness was left in its place. Once, he took me out fishing to a bay in Providence where we plugged the wriggling bloodworms firmly onto our hooks. I knew he was waiting for me to apologize, but I couldn't. It was like a big apple was stuck in my mouth, and I couldn't get past it to say the words. He had clearly lost his will to fight anymore, and it was clearly my fault. Nothing I ever said would change that, or repair the lesions of shame that infected me.

Just 10 days later, he died. I had killed him. I had used words instead of a knife, but I had watched as they cut right through him, and he couldn't recover from that. As the people filed by his casket at the funeral home during the viewing hours, I could not meet their eyes. Did they know I was responsible for his death? Their pitying glances assured me they did.

I skipped out as soon as I could and hung out on the sidewalk outside. I thought back to when I was released from the hospital after getting beat up. My father had wanted to teach me to fight. Sick as he was, he could not do much. About a week after the incident, he put me in the car. We pulled up to a gritty-looking gym. With fingers that still would not do what I needed them to do, and ribs that still protested every time I tried to move, I peered through the car window wondering what in the world we were doing here. Then my father came around to my side of the car, opened the door, and scooped me up into his arms.

I still do not know how he had the strength to lift me.

He had a port in his arm that was used to hook him up to dialysis. Somehow, in the process of carrying me, the port ripped away, and blood began to flow down his arm. We made quite a sight, a feeble white man with blood running down his arm, cradling a scrawny nine-year-old kid with a swollen face and black eyes.

"Man, you're bleeding bad," said one of the trainers.

My dad completely ignored this observation. "This is what they did to my son," he said. "Can you train him?"

"You know, there's a white gym right down the road," said the trainer. But it turned out this trainer was a veteran, and so was my dad, and that was all my dad needed to know. We drove home in silence, and I just stared at him as he stared at the road and the blood just poured out of his arm. What? What could he be thinking about like that?

It took a full two months before I could get in the ring to do anything at all. And I did learn to defend myself. But it was that moment, my dad using every bit of strength he could muster to hold me in his arms as the blood drenched his clothes, that replayed over and over in my head as I stood there on the sidewalk during his viewing. That was how much he loved me, and I had said the words that killed him, and never even apologized.

One of my teachers came by, and I remember she spoke to me, but I was completely numb. My mother's own pronouncement over my life did not console me. In fact, it made it worse. I would obviously disappoint her, and my own cruelty trumped any impulse to do good no matter how you sliced it up. It was also clear that her prayers were going to be wasted on someone like me. Prayer, in general, was obviously a waste. And based on the evidence, I was eager to conclude that there was no saving God who could bring my father back, or my innocence. My life as a stone-cold atheist could begin in earnest, and I was done apologizing for anything. It was all going to hell anyway, so why not live it up?

And that's exactly what I did.

CHAPTER 6:

THE KID DESERVES A CHANCE

I decided to make my own rules about what was right and wrong. We were poor, so stealing didn't seem wrong to me. It was just a way to even out the playing field a little bit. Unfortunately, the law didn't agree with me, and I was on probation in two places because I had been in trouble in Providence and in Greenville, Rhode Island, where we lived for a little while just outside of the city.

My attitude wasn't helping my mom cope with my dad's death at all. There she was, broke, with all these kids, and all of them except Bonnie weren't turning out so well. She just couldn't handle it. She was a deeply religious woman, but it wasn't enough to carry her through. Little did I know at the time how much I would be able to empathize with her!

Anyway, she went somewhere to recover. I don't really know where, and at the time I didn't want to ask. In my world, what mattered was that we were back home in Millville, Pennsylvania. All the other siblings had found relatives to live with, except me. Could you blame them? At the age of 12, I was already a total screwup. My oldest sister, Mary Ann, talked the school district in Millville to let me go into sixth grade as long as I maintained a C average. Mary Ann was like the second mom of our family. But no one wanted to welcome a dangerous, troubled kid like me into their home. I totally understood; I didn't like me either. Finally a distant relative, Jack, took me in. He was a super talented musician and maybe he could understand a little bit about being a rebel. He and his wife, Connie, lived in a duplex with two kids, a boy Terry and a little girl Trisha.

My sister Nancy is about seven years older than me. She always had a very pure and simple faith in God and was like Mary in the Bible to me. She drops me off at Jack's, and I can tell right away that something is wrong with Connie. They are about to have supper, so we all sit around the table. I'm right next to Connie, Trisha and Terry are across from me, and Jack is on my right.

"I'll go get the chicken out of the oven," says Jack, and goes into the kitchen. In a flash, Connie turns to me and latches on, her nails digging into my left arm. Her face contorts in anger, but she's crying and muttering. Luckily, she's muttering into the ear that still works.

"If you do anything to my daughter, I'll send you away so fast," she says almost incoherently. "If you try to talk my son into drugs, I swear I'll …"

Jack comes back in. "What the f--k is going on?"

Immediately, I decide to cover for Connie. How can I blame her? I wouldn't want me mixing with my kids either. With her claws still in my arm, I laugh a little. "She's just telling me the rules about the laundry and shit," I say.

Jack looks, but doesn't comment. Dinner proceeds but the tension is thicker than the heat. It's stifling. I think, on top of everything else I've done, now I'm going to destroy this marriage. Clearly, here was more proof that there was no God. I just got out of one shithole, and now I'm in a worse place. I make up my mind right there that I'm going to run away.

That night, I get right to it. I strip the bed and begin ripping the sheets to lower myself out of the third-story window and take off into the night. I can hear Jack and Connie fighting below me in the kitchen.

"First of all, you will not preach that Jehovah Witness cult shit to him," says Jack. Connie had just converted, and it was already an issue between them.

"Why would you let that hoodlum in here with your own kids?" yells Connie. "You value him more than you value your own kids." I keep ripping. I'd need a long rope to get down.

Jack says, "I've known this kid since he was little. He's a good kid, Connie, and he deserves a chance."

I stop, mid-rip.

"If he touches or even speaks to our daughter, I'll leave. I'll take the kids and leave."

Jack waits a beat. "Connie, I believe in this kid. Everything is going to be okay."

It was like I was frozen in place. Jack believed in me. He was sticking up for me. I dropped the ripped sheets and found a way to put them in the trash. No way was I going to let Jack down now.

And I didn't. I started sixth grade, and I was without blemish. Perfect. Not because I wanted to please God, but with all my heart I wanted Jack to be right about me.

By Christmastime, Mom was back, and we were together again. I was the last one to get back to the family, but I didn't stop to wonder why. Mom grilled me about what had happened with Connie, but I just couldn't rat her out. Connie was justified in her fear that I would be trouble. But I was super proud of not screwing up again! I continued to do what I could in school, and I got my C's, but it was rough. My teacher, Mr. Boyles, was tough on me. I would get in trouble for fidgeting, and have to stand in the corner with my hands out, holding buckets. Other people would have the same punishment, but no one else had to hold the buckets except me. He was trying to break me, I think. It didn't work!

Then seventh grade started, and our school was a small school that had the junior and high school combined. Luckily, my English teacher looked like Olivia Newton John. I was totally in love with her. I thought that informing her of my devotion every day would help me pass, but it didn't. She pushed me, and I probably learned more from her than anyone else. My science teacher, Mr. Bower, was the only one who could control me. He was also my basketball coach in senior high. I loved basketball!

And I was fast, so fast. My gym teacher Bill Anderson saw me lap the whole soccer team during an unofficial practice around the field. He timed me, and I was faster than the fastest kid in the district. He offered to drive me to a nearby town to participate in that school's track team, if I wanted. But, because we had no money and to keep me out of trouble, my mom had arranged for me to work as a janitor in the next little town over, about five miles away. Since I couldn't run track, I ran to my job every night, and then ran home when I was done. Two huge hills were on the way, and I would compete with myself to run them faster and faster each day. I won the approval of the guy I worked for there, because I tried so hard each night. I worked there from sixth to ninth grade. Then my brother Drexel started a construction company, and I worked both places in eighth grade.

Athletics saved me, in a way, because I just wanted someone to tell me that I was doing a good job. I mean, my mom would tell me that all the time, but I needed to hear it from someone who didn't have to say it.

But remember, I was just doing right by me, by my own standards and in my own strength, without regard for God's standards. So to me, it still seemed fair to steal, because we were so poor. My buddy Eddie and I liked bacon and eggs, so we started stealing chickens.

We stole as many as 14, stuffing at least two at a time under my sweatshirt, and then riding away on Eddie's motorcycle. I got the shit clawed out of my stomach on those raids. We tried to get a little piglet too, but he squealed too loudly and gave us away. When we got caught, Eddie took the rap for it and didn't rat me out. Man, I could write a whole book on Eddie! My buddy Mookie and I had a pretty good racket going too. He and I would steal cigarettes and then sell them at school. At night we stole beer, and then we all drank it, even on weekdays. I learned if you don't think about things too hard, then they can't bother you. At least not till later.

CHAPTER 7:

YOU WILL LIKE IT, I GUARANTEE IT

After only three days on the Appalachian Trail, it's already down to just me and my memories. All of the 22 hikers that started with me have quit. But I am here, putting one foot in front of the other until I get where I need to go.

I should explain how I got the idea to do the trail in the first place.

One day my teacher, Mr. Van Horn, met me in the hallway right before class.

"Steven, I got good news. I got this book for you." His deep baritone voice was so kind. He was a theater director too, so he sounded like a narrator in a movie. But, he had said the word "book," and already my face probably showed my reaction to putting "good news" and "book" in the same sentence.

He continued, "Now don't say anything. You have to read it. This is going to be a grade for you."

"I hate reading, Mr. Van Horn. I can't do it."

"I knew you would say that, but it's on hiking, and I know you like hiking." Well, that was true. "Everybody else in class is reading something else, but you're going to read this. You will like it. I guarantee it." Twenty years later the education world would call this "differentiation" and show teachers how to accommodate for different kinds of learners. Turns out it's something good teachers knew how to do all along.

The poor guy. I liked him, and again, I really just wanted to please him. I said, "I'll read it just for you, but I'm not going to enjoy it." I gave him a little laugh.

He laughed right back, his deep on-stage comedy chuckle. "Yes, you will." With a twinkle in his eye, he left me and walked into the room.

I took it home. That was one of the only books I ever took home, and it was on a Friday. I was set to meet my new girlfriend Sandy at the basketball game later, but I thought, *Well, I'll read the first chapter.* It was going to take months probably, so I may as well get started. *At least I'll be able to tell him I did it without completely lying.* I flopped onto my bed and opened it. Right then, my mom yells up from downstairs that it's time to eat. I tell her I'll be down in 15 minutes, that I had to read one chapter.

"You're reading?" she yells back, and her voice goes up in disbelief.

"Yeah," I yell back. "I got to do it or else I'm going to flunk again." I knew that would work. Plus, it was true.

"You take all the time you want! Your supper will be on the table. We'll eat without you." My left ear could still hear pretty well, and I heard her walk away from the bottom of the stairs. So, I had bought myself 15 minutes.

The book was a version of *Walking with Spring* by Earl Shaffer, the first man to walk the Appalachian Trail. The trail was completed in 1952, and Earl had returned from WWII nursing his own wounds of grief and horror. He had lost his best friend in the war in a violent way that haunted him afterward. During my own time on the trail, I would meet so many veterans searching for their own healing from post-traumatic stress disorder (PTSD). The trail does that. Your body and mind are pushed to the limit, and the sheer power of nature works on you like a grindstone. I think most people find what they need there, in the dirt, the rocks, and the pristine mountain views. Your body and mind have no choice but to distill the mess of your life down to an essential core. You have no choice but to face it.

Of course, the book was all about nature, which I loved. I wanted nothing more than to be a "mountain man" and live off the land. The guy took wrong turns, faced the grueling climbs, and all the while he was wrestling with his grief and guilt. I could relate. A day did not go by that I didn't remind myself that I had all but killed my own father, and I had continued to heap bitterness on the guilt. Even though I was cruising along now, with my new interest in Sandy and my jobs and my athletics to keep me busy, I was still holding on to the guilt and self-loathing like a dirty little jewel I kept buried underneath all I thought and did. Earl seemed to share what I felt, and I could not put the book down. I was so shocked at my own discovery: I actually liked to read something! I wasn't hungry for supper at all.

I read for four more hours.

Mom finally came up with my dinner and put it on the dresser with two glasses of water. She was smiling. In my whole life I had only ever read the Bible and *To Build a Fire* by Jack London, where the guy freezes to death in the Yukon. She was just as shocked as I was. The two glasses of water were so that I could stay as long as I wanted to. I wasn't having too many problems with the words, and I already had several chapters down.

Finally, I got a call from Sandy. Whoops.

"I haven't heard from you all night. Is something wrong?" In order to call me, in those days, she had to go to a friend's house and use the phone.

"No, I'm reading a book!" I just knew she would understand. "I'm reading a book about hiking. Mr. Van Horn gave it to me. He said I had to read it or I'd flunk." I admitted that he may have been kidding about flunking. I told her the whole story.

"Just call me tomorrow," she said. "I want you to keep reading!"

And I did. Finally, when it was dark, my mom did come up and get me to give my eyes a break. I walked around the room and stretched, and it felt good because my back was killing me. Then I was right back to it. First it was midnight, then 2:00 in the morning, then 4:00, and then the sun came up. I absolutely could not believe this was happening to me.

"Did you read all night?" My mom stood in the doorway.

"Yep! I'm almost done with this book!"

She clapped her hands together and shut the door. By 8:30 I was done. I read the whole thing! My first thought was *Sandy has to read this*. She was just as proud of me as my mom, and she loved the book too.

"Someday I want to hike the Appalachian Trail," I told her.

"Me too," she said. And our pact was sealed.

CHAPTER 8:

BEAR TAG

So far, the trail was everything I thought it would be, even on these frosty mornings.

I ran into a guy named Frostbite. He got his name that morning because his water reservoir in his backpack had a leak in it. He thought he was just sweating, but in zero-degree weather, the pack froze to his back. He was wearing a ball cap and didn't think about it when his ears and the tip of his nose went numb. He ended up with frostbite, and also a pretty cool trail name.

I wore my Filson wool hat, with my ball cap over that, and then my hoodie. I can't see with a hoodie on unless I have a ball cap. Drives me crazy. I also wore a winter grade Smartwool gaiter. I loved that, and it protected my face. Between the three hats, the gaiter, my Feathered Friends Flicker 20-degree quilt sleeping bag, and my insulated sleeping pad, I was like a Pop-Tart in a toaster at night.

Too bad my hands didn't work as well in the cold as my tent. I couldn't take many pictures when it was this cold because I had frostbitten my fingers once when I was working outside in Wellsboro, Pennsylvania. It's cold as hell out there. It got my three fingers on my left hand, and two on my right, and from then on they just had

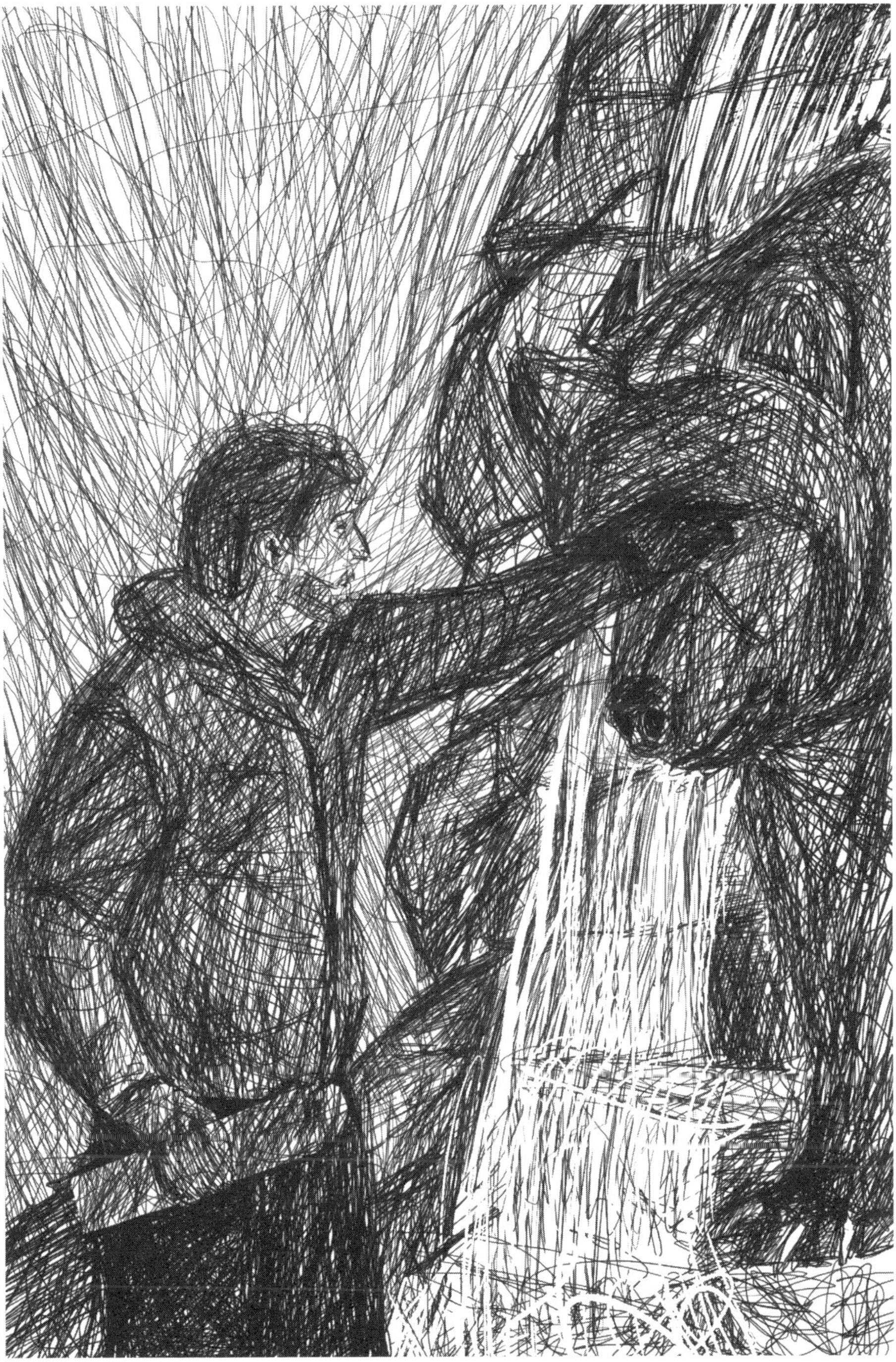

no circulation on their own. They can't make their own heat, so to speak. I have to keep them in my mittens or in my pockets.

I catch up to a whole new crew and celebrate St. Patrick's Day in town with them.

When you're in town, usually you've got to resupply. However, I still didn't need to. I had so much extra food with me because "hiker hunger" hadn't hit me yet for some reason. At first, I tried to force myself to eat, but then I didn't hike as well, so I gave it up. I figured it would happen, and when it did, man, did I get it.

One morning I wake up at 3:30 a.m. Can't sleep. So I figure, I'll get going. I finish my breakfast and need to refill my water for coffee later. I head over to the waterfall just off the trail. I was going to just refill without taking off the pack, but there were some huge rocks, and I didn't know how I was going to maneuver around and get the full bottles back in the side pockets. Off comes the pack. I also can't juggle all three water bottles, so I put two down and get closer to the water, picking my way using my red light to check my footing. The cold is still intense, freezing the mist in the air and making fog. I'm carrying my water bottle in my right hand, and I step forward with my right foot. My left foot is off the ground as I'm extending toward the waterfall. I reach out with my left hand to steady myself against a rock.

It is not a rock.

Slowly, before I actually touch it, I put together the details of hair, and the slope of the flank, and figure out it's a big ass bear, sitting down. He must have been asleep, and now I've awakened him. He turns to the left, but I'm on his right, with my hand almost touching him. I retract the hand slowly, and he looks me directly in the face.

I am blinding him with the red light. I assume. He stares, I balance, and the seconds stretch to minutes. I'm quite sure touching him will not be the right move, but I'm starting to wobble. I try to ease my left foot back to the ground. I slip a little, and by then I'm pretty sure he has figured out what I am, and I start backing away. I am terrified and actually excited at the same time.

I decide, well, I don't think you want to eat me or you would have by now, so I'm going to get a picture. And if you do eat me, at least I'll have a picture. In the end, my video just shows him running away. Well, at least I know my ticker works. Turns out hiking with a good shot of adrenaline makes you smoke those next miles.

CHAPTER 9:

BECOMING CAMEL

My plan was to get down to a road, get a ride into town, eat something wonderful, shower, and then get back to the trail in time to hike another five miles. That way I can avoid taking a zero day. At the road, there is a lady and a young guy there. I had run into the guy before several times on the trail. The lady's name is Veto from Halifax. She got her trail name because every time someone suggested a name for her, she vetoed it. As we talk, they reveal that they had passed a guy who had fallen and broken his ankle. He was really hurting, and needed some help to get off the mountain. Veto had tried to help, but she couldn't, and neither one of them wanted to miss the shuttle into town. We decide that I can take my pack off, and run up and help this guy get down, while they hold the shuttle for us all.

Now it was only nine in the morning, but I was already in for 13 miles that day. I drop the pack and start my run up the mountain. When you take your pack off, you feel so light! But I was still huffing when I finally reached them. Another guy was already helping him down, but in order to do that, they both had taken off their packs and left them behind. So I run up even further and grab the packs, probably 30 pounds each, putting one on the front and one on the back, and then run downhill to catch back up to them. When we all get to the bottom, the shuttle is waiting there like the cavalry to take us into town. We go to the hostel, and the young man goes to get his foot checked.

He was 33, and this had been his third attempt at the AT. The other two times he had broken a bone also, and this attempt would be a wash as well. He was brokenhearted and just couldn't take the defeat anymore. He decided to give up his dream of hiking the AT, and I understood how heartbreaking it would be. Little did I know how completely I would be able to relate to his experience. I still pray for that guy, because I just know how it would have crushed me to give it up.

The hostel was called Around the Bend. That's where I bought my first alpaca hoodie by Appalachian Gear Company. Then I sent my Smartwool hoodie home, because I just didn't want the extra weight. It was a good swap. That alpaca hoodie became one of my favorite pieces because it was cool in the summer and warm in the winter. It never got smelly.

One week down! I'm feeling better, stronger, and it was nice to have that little break. The next day I start to get a whiff of something, something different, down through the mountains. It smells like … steak? Hamburger? I check the map. Nothing. Nothing should be there. But sure enough, when I get down there, there is a herd of people. They turn out to be ex-hikers from 2018, all sizes and ages. The man responsible for the amazing smell of burgers was called Aquaman, because he drank so much water on the trail. Another guy was cutting up tomatoes and onions. They had cheese, salt and pepper, beer, and soda. It was a feast! The smell ignited hunger in me, and truthfully, I had hiker hunger for the rest of the trip. That burger tasted like a steak at a five-star restaurant. They had water for us to refill with or take along. They tried to stuff a beer in my pack but no way was I carrying that extra weight up a mountain. You know you have become a true hiker when you can't justify the extra 12 ounces so you can have a beer.

"Well," they said, "there's one alternative. You have to drink it." So, I got a belly full of beer and burger, two beers actually, before I got out of there. They wanted to know my trail name.

"I don't know," I said. "I ain't got one yet." They had suggested Billy Goat, but there already is a hiker called Billy Goat who's hiked the trail nine times, and he's still alive.

"Don't worry," the one guy said, "I'll give you one before you leave." *This ought to be good,* I thought. I laughed.

He told me to take the gallon of water they had there, and fill up my cup and all my bottles. "I'm the Aquaman," he says. "You gotta drink a lot of water when you're around me."

I said, "Aw, I don't carry water."

"What the hell?" he says. "Everybody carries water on the Appalachian Trail, you dumb ass."

"Well, I don't," I said. "I broke my back. I got two shoulders with torn rotators. I ain't carrying no water, unless I'm cooking."

"What are you, a f-----g camel?"

And then I had my trail name.

CHAPTER 10:

WE'RE ALL F-----D UP

Well, I'm sore, but I'm doing over 18 miles a day on the third week of my hike. I'm not pushing it, because my knee lets me know it doesn't like going downhill. I'm not in the Smoky Mountains yet, but I may as well be because everything is like 5,000 feet high. There is a series of guys ahead of me in army fatigues. There is quite a group of them, and I learn their captain's trail name is Witch Doctor. They have all served as marines in Afghanistan, and just like Eric Shaffer in *Walking with Spring* who was in WWII, they are there to let the trail do its healing work on their battered minds.

I hit it off with them. After about four days of running into them, they kind of adopted me. I was mostly alone all day, but at night they would look for me. This one guy's name was Tracker, and that guy really knew how to find somebody.

I asked him, "How the hell are you finding me?"

He said, "It's easy. You walk like nobody else I've ever seen. You kick your heels, and you have a hell of a turn out. You slam your right foot down." I looked down at my legs. I guessed that sounded about right. "Plus," he said, "you got a shoe that not many people have on the trail."

At that time I was hiking in my Topo boots. They have a wide toe box and a different kind of tread. I told him about my days trapping, where I would track animals down. We kept talking and hit it off.

Those military guys were quite the partying group too. I guess you need a little beer with your dirt sometimes when you're burying war memories, just like my dad was. Those guys could drink a lot of beer, smoke a lot of pot, and then go zooming up a hill. I would always have one beer with them.

"Everybody out here is f----d up," Witch Doctor said to me one day. "What's your f--k-up story?"

I told them I didn't like talking about it.

"Cause you've got to be f----d up to do this," they said.

I agreed that I was f----d up.

"Hey," yells Witch Doctor at the top of his lungs to the rest of the group, "Camel over here is f----d up! How about you guys?"

"I'm f----d up!" and another "I'm f----d up" and another and another broke out like popcorn cooking in a pan.

"And you're f----d up," says the Witch Doctor to end it, pointing to me. "You're in. You're in our group. You can't get away from us now."

So I told them about losing Sandy. And they understood.

Let me tell you how I met her.

"Did you see the new seventh grader?" My friend Artie asks me this in homeroom.

"No way. A seventh grader?" Was he nuts? Ninth-grade boys did not notice seventh-grade girls.

"I'm telling you she's hot." Artie wagged his head from side to side. "She does not look like a seventh grader." Artie, as a rule, was not a liar.

Later, Artie pointed to her in the hall. He had not exaggerated in the least. Her long brown hair was flipped on the sides in the popular style, and she carried herself with confidence, her arms out front wrapped around her books. She smiled an easy smile of big white teeth curved under full wide lips. Her name was Sandy Harding. No way was I going to let Artie have her.

I asked her to go to the community play with me, and she said yes.

Luckily, I wouldn't have to face her dad until a year later, when we finally were able to stop sneaking around. Her dad, Sam Harding, scared me. He was serious and gruff, and his jowls were taut as he rested his hands on his sturdy frame. I was tough enough and reckless enough to know how to talk to adults, though, so I schmoozed him the best I could. Eventually, he loved me, and I loved him. But back in ninth grade, I just tried to impress Sandy, being as cool as possible. We sat there awkwardly, trying to make small talk in the high school auditorium. I'm sure I tried to be funny. Somehow, by what I now know to be one of the most spectacular miracles of my life, Sandy became my girlfriend.

She helped me with my schoolwork and kept the pressure on for me to tone down my wild behavior.

When I was in tenth grade and she was in eighth, we were still having to sneak around to be together. By this time I had met her parents, and I just couldn't win them over. I couldn't blame them. We were grounded, I think, at this particular time, and I don't even remember why. Now our baseball field had an enormous bank right behind where the first baseline dugout was. It was probably 30 feet high, and steep. It was our one-year anniversary of being together, so we planned to meet down by the dugout. Down there behind the tall bank we couldn't be seen by the road. We were having a wonderful day and I thought, wow, it would really impress her if I rode my bike down the bank to her.

You can see by now, I frequently have ideas that seem good at the time, but turn out to be not so good. She is out maybe 30 feet away from the bank watching, and I start down over. All the little bumps are magnified as my bike picks up speed. So far so good. At the bottom, though, the immediate contact with level ground sends me flying over the handlebars, and I just instinctively tuck and roll. The bike, however, keeps on going, flipping end over end like a giant axe until it whacks against Sandy's skull and leaves a gash in her scalp.

I am somehow completely unscathed. All that goes through my head is a monologue expanding on the central theme of what an idiot I am. She's crying and crying, and I'm holding her head in my lap and rubbing where it hit her. Finally she quiets, and we just sit like that for a full 20 minutes.

"You never told me about your father," she says.

"What do you mean?"

"You never told me what happened with your dad."

"Well, he was an alcoholic and he's dead," I blurt with enough venom that it stops her.

She sits up, her face still completely soaked with tears. "Why do you say it that way?"

"Because he ruined my life. He ruined all of our lives!" I go into my litany of gripes. The baseball field happens to be just down the bank and across the road from the graveyard. She keeps pressing me for more details, and for some reason I suggest we go up there to his grave.

"He just ruined my life. That's all."

"Don't you love your dad?" she asks.

"I did, but I don't anymore. How can I? I hate the man." There we are, at the grave.

"Those are bad words," she says solemnly.

"Well, I don't know what else to say."

"If my dad died, I'd be sad."

"I was at his funeral, and I didn't cry a tear." Indeed, I was hating him through the whole funeral. "I never will shed a tear for him."

"Steven," she says. "That's very wrong." It is just short of an accusation.

"Well, it's the truth."

Silence falls between us as we stand looking at the stone with his name on it.

Shyly, in a small voice that is firm but also humble, she says to me, "I think you should cry."

What the hell. I assure her that I cannot shed a tear for him, that I hate him. There, by my side, she starts to get choked up, and I can hear her voice breaking a little bit.

"I want to cry. Please cry with me," she says. The tears start coming down. She just plain turns it on, and is weeping now.

Now, I don't know how it happened. I don't know if the sight of her tears touched some part of me that had been cold and covered up for so long that I didn't even know it was there, but sure enough, it hits me. The floodgates open, and I start weeping right there. Like a million pounds of pressure has been coursing through my veins and now it is finally being released. I go to my knees, holding her waist, just crying. Then somehow my fists are in the grass, pounding into the turf, yelling question after question. *You son of a bitch. Why did you have to drink? Why did you have to ruin my life?* And then my yelling slowly turns from accusing to confessing. *I miss you. I'm sorry. I loved you. Why did you have to die?* And there it was. The truth that I had tried so hard not to feel. I truly loved my dad.

I tell Sandy everything, everything from that awful day when I said the words that killed him. We are both on our knees at his grave, and she wriggles in closer to hug me.

I fell back then, in the grass, exhausted. The sun was overhead, still the same, the grass underneath felt still the same. But my chest felt like a full scoop had been lifted out of it. For a full minute, we didn't speak. The grass moved in the breeze. All was quiet. Finally, I could put all this stuff away.

I turned to look her in the eye.

"I think I love you," I said.

"I think I love you too," she said.

Later, I bust in through the screen door. Mom is in the kitchen doing a thousand things.

"Mom, you're never gonna guess what happened today. I have to get married," I blurted.

"That's nice," she said. Stirring, cleaning, folding, whatever she was doing.

"Did you hear what I said!"

She stopped, wiped her hands off and crossed them to face me.

"I said," I repeated calmly, "I have to get married."

Her face registered all the nine levels of hell in that one second.

"Because I met the girl I'm going to marry," I said. "I met the girl I'm going to marry."

"Oh," she said with a quick exhale. "Okay, well that's good."

Once I was a senior and Sandy was a sophomore, we had finally won over her parents, and we were allowed to date. One night I needed a part for my Ford Bronco, and we went out to the local junkyard called Karns' to get it. He had a bunch of German shepherds in pens out there, and one on a logging chain. These dogs were massive purebreds, greasy, ugly, and a sure way to keep intruders out of the junkyard. Karnsy must have paid a fortune for them. As Sandy and I rooted around, the one dog waited, calculating the length of his chain and our distance carefully. They are bred to do that, actually. Anyway, right when the beast figured we were close enough, it made its run for us. I literally threw Sandy behind me, and put up my arm to take the brunt of the attack. Luckily all I got was saliva and a good solid rush of adrenaline as the dog reared up just inches from my arm at the length of its chain. After we calmed down, Sandy gushed at how I had put myself in jeopardy to save her.

I had to do it again, too, against another German shepherd. One that belonged to a state cop was snarling and barking at the window of the cop's house as we rode by on our bikes, on the opposite side of the road. Before we knew it, the dog lunged through the plate glass window, shattering glass in a small explosion all over the yard. It tore out at us in a beeline with its teeth flashing. Instinctively, I pushed Sandy away on her bike, and put out my forearm to take the bite. This bite landed, but the cop had been home the whole time and yelled just quick enough to take the worst of the intention out of the dog's jaws. I have scars, but it could have been a lot worse.

I would absolutely have sacrificed my life to save hers, and she knew it. But there was one ravaging beast I couldn't save her from. Its name was cancer.

CHAPTER 11:

HURRICANE I

I don't know if Sandy would have approved of these marines. They hiked hard and drank hard. It's funny, you think you're going to remember everything. I thought I would remember all their names, and I figured I would be with them all the way to Maine. I couldn't shake them. I mean, they had Tracker, and he could figure me out every time. I never camped where the shelter was, but they always sent Tracker after me. Once I walked a mile past camp to find the only level place. I even took a dead right-hand turn because I wasn't supposed to be camping there, and I didn't want anyone to see me. But he found me there too.

"You cannot get away from us," Witch Doctor told me. "You're in our group now, and we like f----d up people," and he meant it. It was like being in that Eagles song, "Hotel California," where you can check out any time you want, but you can never leave.

We decided we would go into Franklin, North Carolina. It's a pretty nice town, and it has a store called Outdoor 76. I ended up getting a new sleeping pad to replace my beat-up one that finally leaked beyond patching. After shopping I met up with Witch Doctor and the guys in town. Veto was supposed to be there, and

I thought maybe I'd take her out for a beer. I must not have waited long enough because I didn't see Veto, but I did run into a guy called Mario. He had his own troubles too. I guess Witch Doctor was right—everybody on the trail is f----d up. I never met so many good people, truth be told, and it restored my faith in humanity. I mean it. We're all going to be okay.

I spent the night at Onward Hostel, and it was incredible. Good people, good bed, good food ... turns out Mario is at my hostel, too, but he tells me he's not going to keep on hiking after the next day because of predicted bad weather. I enjoyed visiting with Mario, and I can't say enough about Onward Hostel. Ashley was the sweet and ambitious driver who would take us around town, and she will one day make a difference in this world. Her dad said a prayer for me. I told him my story, and he was emotional during his prayer. I recommend you stay there if you are thru-hiking and need the encouragement. When you leave, the owner tells you, *Onward, friend.*

Now if I could go back and do this over again, I would have stayed with Mario for that next day. The day started fine, but I knew they were predicting a storm with hurricane-force winds. I mean, things happen on the trail, and you just have to hike through it. I had hiked in hurricane level winds before, right? So off I went.

For two days, I've been hiking with a guy named Butch, but we haven't seen anyone else all day. We are trying to make it out of the woods for the night, at 3,200 feet, give or take, at Stecoah Gap. The front moves in, and Butch decides he's going to hunker down and wait it out. I tell him I will go ahead and try to scout out a spot for us to stay, and then I will come back for him. Three hours later, the wind is picking up. In under an hour, it goes from no wind to 77 mph gusts. Trees are falling down all over. I begin to worry about Butch, who is an older fellow, and I think about turning around right then and there. But a trail runner comes along, overtaking me from behind.

"Man, you've got to get out of here right now," he tells me. "This is going to get worse."

"I'd better go back for my buddy back there."

"He's already set up camp," says the runner, "and I couldn't get him to leave. I suggest you get off; you can check on him in the morning. You won't make it back to where he is."

Trees are still coming down all over the place, but the runner assures me Butch is in a good spot. The runner takes off, and he has a small day pack on so he can run and keep warning people. He literally had set out just to warn people not to camp, and his athleticism impressed me. He encouraged me to run out of the woods. I only have a mile and 5/10ths to go, all downhill to Stecoah Gap. I decide he's right.

The hill is long. My pack isn't totally full, but it's probably about 22 pounds. Even as I run, I keep thinking how excited I am going to be to get to the Smoky Mountains. All I needed was to find a bridge or something to camp under and get out of the windstorm. The runner had told me that even the bottom of the hill would not be safe, and it sounded like he was right. I could hear the woods aroar with the falling of trees crashing down all around.

I look up and watch a tree go down right in front of me. As soon as my eye leaves the trail, my toe hits a low stump. I catapult forward, actually doing a flip. I land on both of my poles, snapping them. Everything not strapped directly onto my pack gets yard-saled everywhere. And sadly, I found later, that included my water filter, which I never recovered.

I'm on my hands and knees for about 15 minutes, collecting myself and my shit. My hand is bruised from where I tried to break my fall. At the same time, I'm keeping an eye out for falling trees, and the wind is still howling. When I finally stand, I fall right back down. I think, *Man, that hurt, I must have tweaked my foot.* I try it again. I have no poles to push up with so I crawl over to a tree, and use it to try to get up. I try putting a foot down. Pain.

I can't even hop. There's no place to camp here. The trees are coming down right and left. So, back to my hands and knees I go. I crawl.

I crawl for a mile and a quarter.

As I crawl, the storm ratchets up in intensity. My knee starts to hurt from crawling under the weight of the pack. I could feel my ankle swelling inside my shoe. I think, *I might actually be in trouble here.*

I unlace the boot to relieve the pressure, and it really starts throbbing then. I'm praying I didn't really hurt my foot here. I'm sure it can't be broken. It didn't really hurt when I fell. *I'm going to be okay. I'm going to be okay.*

Three excruciating hours later, I get to the bottom. I am exhausted and it's getting dark. My goal was to get under the bridge, but my pack won't fit. So I hide it by the road and drag my body under there. I try calling, with terrible reception, to get someone to pick me up. I decide to camp right on the spot, but just in case a car does come by, I make a sign, HURT HIKER, and put it by the road.

I get my tent set up, get everything out for the night, and take a few ibuprofen. Ice would be best for the ankle, but that's not happening, of course. I go over by the guardrail and put my foot up. I'm safe from falling trees there, and I'm trying to hitch a ride. I have food at least. I sure am not walking anywhere. I'll just take a break right here even though it's still windy as hell.

My phone rings. It's one of the hostels.

"Hey, sorry I was out of reception," a young guy says into the phone. "You need a ride or a place to stay?"

Oh, did I. I was so grateful. I gave him my location.

Lonnie shows up for me. Lonnie the angel. He did so much to help me. The hostel was the Stecoah Wolf Creek Hostel. The hostel people are there because they love the trail, love the hikers, and want to help.

Lonnie ended up taking me to Fontana Village, to a hospital.

The room glared white. The clinician was about 55 years old and looked like he was ex-military. He was very matter-of-fact and viewed the X-rays with a stiff frown.

"Your hike is over, son," said the clinician. I wanted to cry right in front of him. For 50 years I had looked forward to this hike, to making my dream—a dream I had once shared with Sandy—a reality. I had already come back from two major injuries to get this far. Now, my foot was broken.

I was numb. I sat in the X-ray room as long as they let me to just try to absorb it all.

"Man, we're so sorry," the nurses all told me. I couldn't respond. Not an *I know,* or *It's okay,* or even just a *F--k you.* Why did this happen? How did this happen? I should have never been running down that hill. I could have just stayed at the last hostel and none of this would have happened.

Four days passed, with my foot swelling bigger and bigger the whole time. I stayed off of it. I soaked it. I iced it. I stared at my phone. I did not want to pick it up and tell Jocelyn I was done, even though by now she probably knew something was up.

"It's over, honey," I finally told her. She was quiet, and she was crying.

"Dad, this is still early in the trail," my son Tristan encouraged me when I called him. "You can still come back from this. I promise."

In my heart, I didn't believe him. My foot hurt. But emotionally, I couldn't feel a damn thing.

CHAPTER 12:

THE HEART IS A BONE THAT HEALS

I got back home to Millville, Pennsylvania, around April 4. I couldn't hide how I felt from my family, but I hid myself from other people because I knew what they would say. I knew they would all tell me to rest and not go back too quickly, or even to put the hike off till the next year. But all I could think about was getting back on the trail. Jocelyn and her husband Tommy kind of tiptoed around the house with me, aware of how I was feeling. I couldn't understand how this could happen. I was sure that God wanted me to do this, and here I was, two months off the trail. I wrestled and wrestled.

It's a hike, I told myself. *It's not the end of the world.* I resolved to try to stay positive. And to avoid my friends and family.

But it was impossible. They called continuously. I would avoid having my cell phone with me so I wouldn't have to take the calls. When I would pick it up again, the messages were all there, 15-20 a day. Some people encouraged me, and some discouraged me from getting back on the trail. Some just prayed for me in their message. I knew I had to keep busy. So I had Jocelyn get me some pork bellies, and I smoked them over an open fire. My dog loved it, and the smell of smoke helped me think of the trail. But that only lasted two days.

Then I thought, *If I can't hike this damn trail, at least I can build it.* I couldn't walk, but I could sit, so I started remodeling a bathroom in my work barn to replicate aspects of the trail. It had a soaking tub, and I was able to turn that into something cool. I drilled a hole down through the outside rim of that acrylic soaking tub that I paid 50 bucks for. I figured, it was only 50 bucks, what the hell? I inserted a piece of mountain laurel and had it sticking right up through the top edge of the tub and up to the ceiling, where I guess some people would put the hand-held sprayer. I put the AT signs everywhere, some carved in wood, some burnt into wood, some in frames, some soldered decoratively. I am a licensed tinsmith, trained by my father, so I have a knack for this kind of work. I hammered a copper shelf and decorated it with a leaf pattern. All the walls were wooden, and I burned quotes and sayings from the trail on them. All these things were a way for my heart to still be there. While I also spent hours in therapy for my foot, this bathroom was therapy for my mind. Eventually I couldn't reach any higher than about five feet up the bathroom walls, and I was done.

What next? I still had to sit and keep my foot up. I decided to go see my son Tristan, who was in Arizona at the time. Tristan happens to be a physical therapist and he was able to connect with my physical therapist from my hometown. We worked together on my foot, and being with Tristan worked wonders on my heart too. I was still trying to figure out what God was doing with me. Never once did I wonder what I had been doing to cause my circumstances. Running down a mountain with a 22-pound pack on? C'mon. What the hell did I think was going to happen? In the end I figured, God just took His eye off of me for a couple of seconds, and I fell.

Now I don't believe God ever really takes His eye off of us. But obviously I was not convinced of that as a young boy, dealing with the hell that was Providence for our family, and still crushed by the guilt of what I had said to my dad. Sandy had helped me realize that I loved him, but that made what I had done even worse. I hadn't used a knife, but I had killed him with my words just the same. I hid all of this from my mom, of course.

My mom was a deeply religious woman who was trying to do her best to keep us all in line. She was big on Bible study. We would have dinner, and then without moving the dishes off the table or anything, we all reported to the living room to read the Bible out loud for 20 minutes. Then, we had a five-minute discussion about what we had read. I gave my mom a lot of attitude about it. I was fidgety and acted like I was bored out of my mind, but I had to take my turn like everybody else. It must have driven my mother crazy to think she was trying so hard to teach me about God while I appeared silent and oblivious. But I was listening the whole time! She knew I didn't believe. How could I believe? If there was a God, He could have saved us from all this bullshit in Rhode Island. He could have helped my dad quit drinking, right? He was either not very powerful, or else He couldn't be real. I decided He couldn't be real. I mean, if there was a God, He would surely listen to someone like my mom when she prayed.

But my mom's faith was incredible, and the Bible studies continued. We went chapter by chapter. It didn't matter if you had friends over. After dinner, into the Bible reading they went. Even if my mom had a friend over, into the Bible reading she went. And even when I started playing basketball, I had to miss games if they interfered with Bible study. That drove me crazy. I begged my coach to try to get me out of them. He finally called her.

"Mrs. Wright, I just can't believe you are keeping your son at home to have a Bible reading when he has a basketball game," barked my JV basketball coach into the phone.

My mom said, "I see. Now I want you to say that sentence back to yourself very slowly."

He paused. He hung up. The next day, he informed me he would not be making any more calls home for me. He told me I was lucky to have a mom like that.

I was actually convicted by these readings, if you can believe it. After five years we were finally in Revelation. I never said a word during the book of Revelation. I didn't know what was going on, but I did know that if there was a God, I was in trouble. I knew I was a sinner, and I knew there was no hope for me because I crossed every line that could have been crossed. I remember going to sleep, especially the summer after ninth grade, and dreaming about the seven-headed dragon. I would be scared to death, because I was very good at imagining things! Now, Revelation is a good book. I think it's well laid out, but it can be hard to understand all the symbolism. I tried to imagine what these things meant, and it scared me. I also thought, if this was inspired by God, it was so weird. How could John write this book and expect someone to believe it was inspired by God? Even John must not have known what it all meant either. But you know, God told him they would understand one day and that was good enough for him. He must have written it down even though he knew everyone would think he was crazy. So I had to consider that. I had to consider that it might be real. And if it even might be real, I was in big shit trouble. I let this go on until nearly the end of the book, maybe a month.

One Sunday when everyone was away at a retreat, I got a ride to the church where Tammy and George went. Both of them had accepted Christ into their lives. And I could see, wow, what a difference. Tammy especially had made a complete 180. I had always felt close to George, and when he came back from Vietnam, I could see the difference his faith made as he tried to deal with what he had seen there. I saw George, and I saw Tammy, and I knew that something inside of me was missing. I wanted to be like them, and not like me anymore. I went.

The next week I went back. For some reason, when the pastor made the altar call at the end, I went up front. Honestly I didn't know what was going on. But he was saying, *What if ... what if you are on your way home tonight and some guy crosses the line in his car, and it's a head-on crash. Boom, you're dead. Where are you going to go?* I was like Wow, that could happen, and if it does, I'm screwed.

So I go forward. Now there are two girls my age up there bawling, but I'm standing there just frozen. It is excruciatingly awkward. The girls are crying, and obviously they feel their need for Jesus, and I don't. After the pastor takes them through their salvation prayer, he turns to me.

"Son, you don't think this is real, do you?" he says. His voice is not overly kind, and he's a little bit curt to me.

"Yes, I do."

"No, you don't." He gestures to the girls. "These girls over here are crying their eyes out, and you're up here stone-faced. Well, those tears don't mean anything to God. What means something to God is the heart. You gotta want this."

I had to think about that.

"It's about what Jesus did and not about how you feel," he said, still kind of abruptly. "So," he says, looking me in the eye, "what's holding you up?"

What was holding me up? That was a very good question. "It just seems too easy."

"Okay, I'll grant you that. It is easy, for you. But it was hard for Him. Christ made it easy so everyone could come. And *that includes you.*"

Just for a second, I thought, *Maybe I am included.*

He continued, "Well, what do you think these girls had that you don't?"

I said, "I don't know, sir."

"Did you commit some sin?"

My face answered him, even though no words came out.

"Did you commit some sin?" He kept digging. "Did you kill someone?"

Now, I know he was exaggerating to try to make a point, but by sheer luck, he had struck pretty close to the mark. I had buried what I had done to my dad pretty far under, because I had to. There was a beat of silence before I spoke.

"Yes," I said.

"Oh." He dialed back on his approach. "Okay. Well, this is a whole different thing." He turned to the congregation and spoke to them. I had just admitted to this pastor something I had never told anyone before, something I would not even reveal to Sandy until that day in the cemetery a year later. My face was so hot. I felt like I probably would burst into flames and be cast into hell immediately. The congregation looked like maybe they could use the entertainment.

He says, "This gentleman thinks he committed a sin so bad that he can't be forgiven." He turns back to me. "Is that right?"

I nodded. I couldn't get any words to come out.

"So, you're looking at Jesus. Can you imagine saying to Him, 'Man, if You would have just stayed on that cross and bled just a little bit more of your precious blood, I'd be okay?' You don't think he suffered quite enough? For this big sin of yours?"

This hit me like a brick between the eyes. "No!" I said vehemently. "He suffered enough!" I knew this and believed it. God even had to watch His Son suffer. He told His only Son He had to do this to save these people. He let it happen to His own Son for me. The pastor asked if I understood him now.

The girls were really crying at this point. They had their hands on my shoulders and back, and I didn't know what that was all about, but I got what that pastor was saying. I got it now. I told him so.

"Could I ask Jesus into my heart?" I asked.

He said, "I think you're ready, I really do." And then he led me through the sinner's prayer, and I received Christ.

I left, buoyant for the first time since I had uttered those horrible words to my father. I was so grateful and relieved. I was so happy to know I would be going to heaven. But Satan is a roaring lion crouching at the door. As soon as I woke up the next day, I realized that I would have to tell my friends about God, and that I would have to live differently. I would have to quit stealing, quit drinking, and quit having all fun. I would be about as exciting as a prune. I decided I would have to be a quiet, secret Christian. I wanted Jesus in my heart, but I didn't want Him hanging out with my friends, ruining my popularity, and raising an eyebrow every time I stepped out of line.

Within a few weeks, nothing was different at all. I hid the life of drinking and stealing from Sandy. But at least I was convinced there was a God, and I was convinced He probably wouldn't like the way I was living. I sure hoped grace was for real.

Now, all these years later, I was hoping it still was. I was going to need all the grace in the Kingdom to get back on the trail and finish it. Now it also took a while for my knees to get better. I must have gotten a hundred little pebbles in my kneecaps when I fell and then crawled on them like that.

By the time I got back home from Tristan's, my spirits and my foot were on the mend. My foot wasn't so God-awful swollen and angry. I started to hope again. Maybe Tristan was right when he had told me on the phone that I could come back from this.

I was out of the boot in a few more days, and it really didn't hurt. I was wishing I was on the trail, even though I knew that was stupid.

It had only been five weeks, and the doctor had said a minimum of six.

With the boot off, I went to Brian, my physical therapist, and said, "What do you think?" I knew he cared about me and wanted to get me back out on the trail too. He fit my appointments in whenever he could, three times a week minimum. I was working hard, getting up in the morning to do the exercises, and sometimes I got up in the middle of the night just to get a few more reps in. I wanted to be back out on the trail so bad I could taste it. I wanted to be dirty and sweaty.

Brian said, "One more week. Everything looks great. But I don't want to take the chance. If you were a regular person, which you're not, I'd say it was okay. But you're going to end up breaking this again, and then we're both going to feel like shit. Then it will be even harder to come back."

I did what he said. I was completely out of my boot, but my ankle felt weak. I got back to the AT to try it out. I went for my first hike, with a hiking boot on, but it was so weak I couldn't hike. I was crushed. How was I going to do this? I tried to rewrap my ankle and support it in any way I could. Between Tristan and Brian we figured out how to support it, and I was able to do five miles a day on the AT right before the Smokies. On the fourth day I ended up having to go 12 miles. I didn't hurt my foot at all, but it was sore afterward, and I was afraid. I took zeros the next two days. I went to a physical therapist in North Carolina just to make sure everything looked good, and she said it did. She was a hiker, and had done the AT, so we immediately had a great conversation. I told her everything. When she heard my long list of injuries from even before the hike, she put her fist to her forehead and wagged her head back and forth.

"This is exactly what you have to do," she said, looking me dead in the eye so I would take her instructions to heart. "If you don't," she warned, "you won't finish. You'll be right back here." She didn't need to worry. She had my full attention.

She gave me tips for my back, my two shoulder issues, etc. She recommended I only do seven or eight miles the next day, and that's what I did for the next three days.

CHAPTER 13:

THE SMOKIES

I'm thinking the whole time, *I'm getting so far behind*. I'm never going to get to Maine in time. A full two months had passed since I had broken my foot, and I was only up to 10-12 miles a day. One day was 15. Everything felt good, though. I was trying to add a mile every other day, and now I was in the Smoky Mountains. It's rough hiking, but there aren't a lot of rocks or roots, just steep ups and downs. I was so careful going downhill. Tristan had told me to just slide downhill on my ass and not take the risk of getting a stress fracture. So I did that for about a week. I had a pad with me, and I'd put it on my ass so I didn't wear out my shorts. I hiked for another week.

    I made friends, but everybody was moving faster than me, and I had to take my zeros just to make sure I didn't hurt myself again. Another week passed, though, and I got caught up to the other hikers in the "bubble," a term on the AT that refers to the biggest bunch of hikers trying to make it north in one season. It was so nice to be hiking with other people again in a group. I was up to 20 miles a day.

I decide it's time to take a zero day even though my lungs and legs have all felt really good. I got into a hostel with several guys that I had been hiking with for pretty much a week, and I met a new guy. His name was Hunter McIntyre. I did not know it when I first met him, but he turned out to be a ten-time world champion at those HYROX competitions, where the athlete has to do these different physical challenges eight times, including push-ups, pull-ups, etc. In fact, he had just won a championship right before going out to hike three days before. He was taller than me, and had Nordic features with sharp blue eyes. After I got my shower, I didn't want to wait to get into town on the next shuttle since it wouldn't run until later. I decided to ask if I could borrow a bike to ride the three miles into town.

As I'm standing there admiring the bikes and considering, Hunter comes out and says, "Hey, you want to ride into town?"

"I was just going to ask them if we could use the bikes."

"I just asked," he tells me. "Do you want to go with me? I'm leaving right now. "

I said, "Sure," and off we went. Hunter needed to get some things. He really did not have experience hiking. He had just been training. But I could tell he could really ride a bike! I had to really push it to keep up with him. We went to dinner and the outdoor equipment store to get some things he hadn't known to pack. He had literally gone straight from the world championship to an REI store, and they had picked out everything for him. They had forgotten a few things, but I could help him out with that.

The two of us hit it off, and he asked if he could hike along with me. He wanted to do 40 miles a day. I told him I could only do half of that because of my foot. He decided to just stay with me for a day or two and then jump ahead when he wanted to go farther.

We headed back out on the trail the next day. I enjoyed talking to Hunter, and we stayed just ahead of a larger group of hikers coming along behind us. We went about 20 miles. We were both tired at the same time so when we got to a shelter, Hunter camped there, and I went on. I always camped a little distance away for privacy. Soon after, the rest of the crew caught up with us, and we had a nice on-trail dinner together. I warned Hunter that I liked to get up before daylight and get going. He thought he was going to get up early with me, but he didn't, so I just left a note to tell him where I was headed. He caught me around lunchtime. He didn't have a water purifier, so we shared my SteriPEN. The infrared light makes it easy to share between two people, but I should have thought of it when we were at the store together so he could get one.

We put in just under 20 miles together that day. Again, there is another shelter. He takes the shelter, I camp outside of it, and the other guys struggle in later. Next morning, same thing. I get a head start, he catches up, and we hike the rest of the day together. But today it rains, all day and all night, and I decide to stay in the shelter this time and let the mice run all over me. That's the thing about the shelters, the mice. At one point that night, one ran right across my lips. I instinctively reached up and smacked him into the wall. It didn't kill him. Same mouse got Hunter too, and then *he* smacked him. Tough little mouse. Later in town Hunter actually bought a mask to wear to bed so he didn't have to worry about that anymore. As a habit, though, I just avoided the shelters.

We did this routine for several days, until we took a zero on the fifth day. I asked him if he was going all the way, and he said no. The weight of the pack was maxing him out as it was. He said he wished it was lighter. He told me he was thinking about ditching his tent to make it lighter and just use the shelters every night. I knew people who did that, but it wouldn't be for me. Plus, I had been in some bad situations where I needed my tent. I talked him into keeping his tent. He never did stay in it, though, so maybe I steered him wrong. We hiked together maybe 14-16 more days, and we were averaging

22 miles a day. We had one 22.5-mile day. That was our best day. Our group was pretty much still intact. On our resupply days we would all meet in town.

Hunter was talking one night when we were alone in a shelter because we were ahead of everyone else. We really opened up to each other. He was younger, in amazing physical shape, and I enjoyed his stories. Here was a guy with abs like King Kong and a laundry list of physical achievements, but he was going through a lot personally. He said how tough it was to constantly maintain his image to everyone. He was a YouTube personality, and everyone expected him to be this perfect specimen of a human. I understood that. I told him that sometimes I felt like I had to put on a superhuman exterior too.

"Everybody fights with that in their own way, Hunter," I said. His chiseled jaw worked over his food as we chewed in companionable silence. The two of us would keep in touch long after the hike, and he still continues to call me to talk sometimes. People say that on the AT, the people are the hike, and they are. They really are.

CHAPTER 14:

PINK CROCS AND PONIES (HURRICANE II)

Before I tell you about how the norovirus decimated my body, let's talk hydration. Everybody on the trail uses some kind of hydration supplement. Hunter had given me Hydro which he invented. It's got sodium, potassium, and magnesium in it. I think the amounts are three times what you would get in a normal hydration drink like Gatorade. That's what I used, and it worked great for me. If I ran into anybody who asked about it, I would just tell them to look it up. I usually gave them some, because you don't want to be carrying all that around if you don't need to. I would carry enough for a week, maybe two, and have the next batch waiting for me at the next location—either shipped by my daughter or ordered by me. Anyone who plans to do a thru-hike really needs a support team to help you with supplies, to mail you the winter or summer clothes you need for the next season, etc.

My support system included some friends from Pennsylvania coming down to drop off some new Crocs for me and other supplies. They offered to take Hunter and me out for dinner. I needed the new pair of Crocs because I lost my original pair while I was fishing.

It was a beautiful spot, so I had to walk down just a little farther, then a little farther, and then somehow I was in too deep. The water was up under my armpits. My foot lost its traction on a rock, and I started moving on the current. I wasn't going to panic. There were high rocky banks on each side, so I decided to float down a bit to an easier exit spot. Now my backpack was supposed to be waterproof. It isn't completely (they never are), but it was holding air and acting like a life preserver behind my head. Zip, just like that, my Crocs were off my feet, and they bobbed to the surface. I tried to keep up with them, thinking I could grab them. I managed to get one, but the other was long gone. I got washed downstream about a half mile before I got stopped.

I tried to get a new pair at a hostel, but the only pair that remotely fit me were kind of a shitty knockoff with a tree growing out of them as a decoration. So my friends Randi Olshefski and his wife Mary Lou, and Greg and Cheryl Aukamp were going to bring a pair for me. We had a nice dinner, and Hunter enjoyed being with them too. He thought it was cool that people would come all the way from Pennsylvania just to see us. My son-in-law Tommy had picked out a nice hot pink pair of Crocs with sparkles for me. Funny guy. I was famous on the trail for these Crocs, so I decided to use them for a good purpose. I wrote on the right foot "Follow Me Steven C. Wright." On the left one I wrote, "Triple Negative Cancer Sucks." It worked. A lot of people noticed them.

Hunter and I have been hiking well, and we only have a few days left together. For Hunter's last night we went into Damascus and had a beer. There were a few other hikers there too, and we had a great time laughing and telling stories. Hunter and I ended up staying up in a hostel near Damascus. There Hunter and I parted, and I went on alone.

One of the guys at the bar in Damascus was named Avalanche, whom I ran into two or three more times. Avalanche had been sick with norovirus two days earlier. Now, I didn't know this until the end of our visit, and I thought nothing of it. But I would sure think it about it later.

It wasn't raining to start the day, but man, it turned into an absolute flood. This would be the second hurricane of my hike. I actually called Hunter and told him, "Thank God you aren't here, buddy, because it sucks!"

"Yeah, I know," he said. "We are having trouble driving, let alone hiking in this shit."

I saw a herd of wild ponies! They were soaked in the rain, just wandering around in the woods. Then they were following me on the trail. I can only guess I had something in my pack they liked.

There were also two youth events happening this weekend in this section of the trail. First, the Girl Scouts were having an event. They were everywhere with their counselors. There was also a group that sponsored hiking trips for inner-city youth, for teens and some younger kids. They were on the trail too. I thought, *What a sucky weekend to be on the trail with a pack of kids*. I had hoped when I came to the first shelter that I would be able to spread my tent out and dry it. But there were 25 little girls in there huddled in the back and still getting wet, so I had to move on. Next shelter, same thing, but with a bunch of the inner-city kids. *That's a pack of very unhappy little campers*. But I kept passing the kids, and everyone wanted to know about the ponies. I had 20 horses walking single file down the trail behind me at one point, but nobody else saw a horse! As soon as they would see another person, the horses would scatter. And then when I was alone, they would be back again. I had big ponies, small ponies, fat ponies, old ponies! It was like I was in a movie, but the downpour prevented me from getting many pictures of them. Though they sound like a hallucination, I swear they were real.

CHAPTER 15:

NOROVIRUS

I finally get to a good spot to camp, and I decide I may as well, since all the shelters are taken by the kids. I had hiked all day in the rain, and it continues to rain all night. When I wake up, it is still raining. The GPS says that thunderstorms are going to keep on throughout the day. Looks like there won't be any drying out any time soon. Not surprisingly, I don't feel 100 percent this morning, but what can I expect? I eat my regular oatmeal and peanut butter, a cup of the Mudwater mushroom drink, and I drink a full liter of Hunter's hydration powder.

In about an hour, I throw it all up. Once it starts, the nausea just does not quit. It is like clockwork. Every 10 minutes I throw up again. *Oh my God, what the hell happened to me?* Was my water filter not working? My guts were churning. After an hour and a half of throwing up, I have the first attack of diarrhea. Four more later, after another hour, I am in a bad spot. This kind of diarrhea is uncontrollable. You have no warning and no time to make arrangements, you might say. The truth was that I had shit my pants, all my pants, and had nothing left to wear.

This is how norovirus works, I learn later. I will not realize I have it until a few more hours pass. I start putting two and two together, remembering Avalanche, the guy I'd met who had had norovirus.

I am alone. The Girl Scouts and youth hiking groups are far behind me. After another hour, I'm feeling very weak and I'm not walking well at all. After another two hours, I'm out of toilet paper. I'm out of everything. I have used up my soap trying to clean out my underwear from the first three times it happened. I consider cutting up my shirt for toilet paper, but it's the only shirt I have.

So, I strip down naked. In the rain.

It is the only solution. I can't keep cleaning everything and there is nobody for miles. I try to keep going, but I am so weak. *I need to get some help.* I had passed a shelter earlier, and used it to look at how far it was to the nearest road, but I should have stayed there. The nearest road is six miles ahead, and the shelter is seven miles behind. Here I am in the middle, naked and sick as a dog on the trail.

I ain't doing this trail twice, I think, and decide to try to go forward. That's when the shivering starts, and my whole body quivers like Jell-O on a spoon. I'm freezing. I'm dehydrated, obviously, but fluid—clear fluid—is still coming out both ends from somewhere in my body. *Perfect time for a colonoscopy,* I think. Got to keep your sense of humor, even when you are dying. I keep staggering another two miles, and there's a big uphill. I'm dizzy. I lie down on the trail. I pull out the alpaca hoodie and try to cover up with it. I'm so cold. I know I can't stay here. I have to keep walking.

I make it about three more miles and check my phone for service. Spotty. Pretty bad, actually. I don't even have the little plug that covers the charging port, so it could very well get water in there and short out. My hands are so cold, and shaking, that when I try to dial something, I actually can't. I try to call Jocelyn with a voice command but it won't go through. I try speaking a text into the phone to her, but it won't go either.

I decide to put in my earbuds and hope somebody calls me. Would the call even come through? I keep going. There's a logging road ahead, not a real road, but maybe with the extra elevation I can get service. The downpour continues. When I get to the logging road, I'm shivering so badly I can't use my hands at all. I am just like the old trapper in the Jack London story who can't light his fire. And I think for the first time in my life, it's possible, it's really possible, I could die here. Right here. I'm weak, dizzy, and starting to see things that aren't there. I thought I saw a town, and I knew it wasn't there. On my Far Out app, which I always just leave open, I can see the road is gated, and I'd have another mile to get to that gate. I know there's no way I can get there. I can't take another step. I take another one-minute break, just lying right there on the ground. I'm going to have to use my GPS to call 911.

If you do that, they charge the shit out of you. Somebody told me five grand. I'm not going to push that button if I don't have to. But I'm even hearing voices that I know aren't there. I have to go on or push the button. I can't go on, so I put my hand on the button.

But my earbuds ring in my ear, and I can tap the earbud to answer.

"How's it going, Dad?" It's Jocelyn.

Relief floods me. My jaw is quivering, but I finally get the story out and tell her she's got to get me some help. I can't even push the button on my GPS that gives my exact location, but I know enough to describe where I am. She promises to get someone.

She is able to contact the Long Neck Lair Hostel. I get a call from a guy named Ken there, and I can answer by tapping the earbud. Ken knows already from Jocelyn that I'm sick. He tells me I've got to go one more mile, because there's no way for him to get through the gate to get me. I assure him that I cannot move, let alone go a mile.

Ken says, "Okay, let me try one more thing." Finally, he calls me back. He's able to get someone to unlock the gate. It's going to take him an hour, but he can get there. Somehow Jocelyn had gotten him the GPS coordinates, and he was familiar with the trail so he knew right where I was.

Over the next hour, I thank God and pray. I don't want to lie in the mud, but I don't have the strength to even lean against a tree. All I can do is lie naked in the mud in the middle of this logging road. The shivering feels more like convulsions, so I pull my alpaca hoodie over me like a blanket. It helps a little. When this guy gets here, I'm hoping he's not too grossed out. I plan to cover the seat with my raincoat in case I shit myself in his truck.

Ken's gray truck finally appears, slowly bumping over the rocks. He has to lift me into his truck. I can do nothing. At first he isn't going to take me to the hospital, because with norovirus you just have to let it run its course. But I look so bad that he decides I need the fluids.

Ken tells me it will take 12 – 24 hours for the virus to pass through my system, but consoles me by saying, *"You're going to be okay, buddy."* This is hard to believe, but I'm praying he is right.

I spent a few hours at the hospital, getting fluids and more fluids. Norovirus is highly contagious, and I was dumfounded my rescuer even let me in his truck. I mean, this guy took "Trail Angel" to a whole new level. He let me stay in his house and gave me my own personal room with a bathroom so I didn't infect anyone else. Every day he made me breakfast and slid it in under the door, through a space about two inches, just high enough for a plate of scrambled eggs. I was waiting to get better … and it just didn't happen. I ended up throwing up and having diarrhea for three and a half days. I was so weak, and I couldn't eat the second day. Finally on the third day, I ate the scrambled eggs for supper and then the next day it started to ease up. I decided to spend another day recuperating.

And all the while, I know I'm getting farther and farther behind on the trail. But I also know I can't hike in my condition. From the time I had started hiking in February, to the time they weighed me after having norovirus in the hospital, I had lost 28 pounds total, 22 of them just because of the virus.

CHAPTER 16:

COVID AND CONVALESCENCE

Finally, I started hiking again. I got about five miles done that first day, but I would come to a hill, and that was the end of me. I only did one "up" the whole day, and it wasn't even a big one, maybe just 1,000 feet, and I was still wasted. I couldn't figure out what the problem was. I was just so weak. I thought, *Maybe the virus did something to my heart.* Second day, no better. Just five miles again. After cruising along for 22 miles a day, five feels like a failure. My attitude started to suffer. On the third day I had another uphill section, maybe 2,000 feet, and it was rough. I got to the first shelter and had to stay. It took me seven hours to go three miles. My feet felt like they were full of lead, my lungs had no air, and each step required so much effort. The pack felt like it had a school bus in it. I started to worry I would never get back to my original strength. I ate every bite of my dinner, hoping to put on more muscle. At the end of the fourth day, things were going a little better. I was cruising along the top of a ridge and made it six and a half miles. I entered the triple crown area in Virginia, which has a pretty strong hill. I had to take a bunch of breaks, but I made it up there. At the first shelter, at like

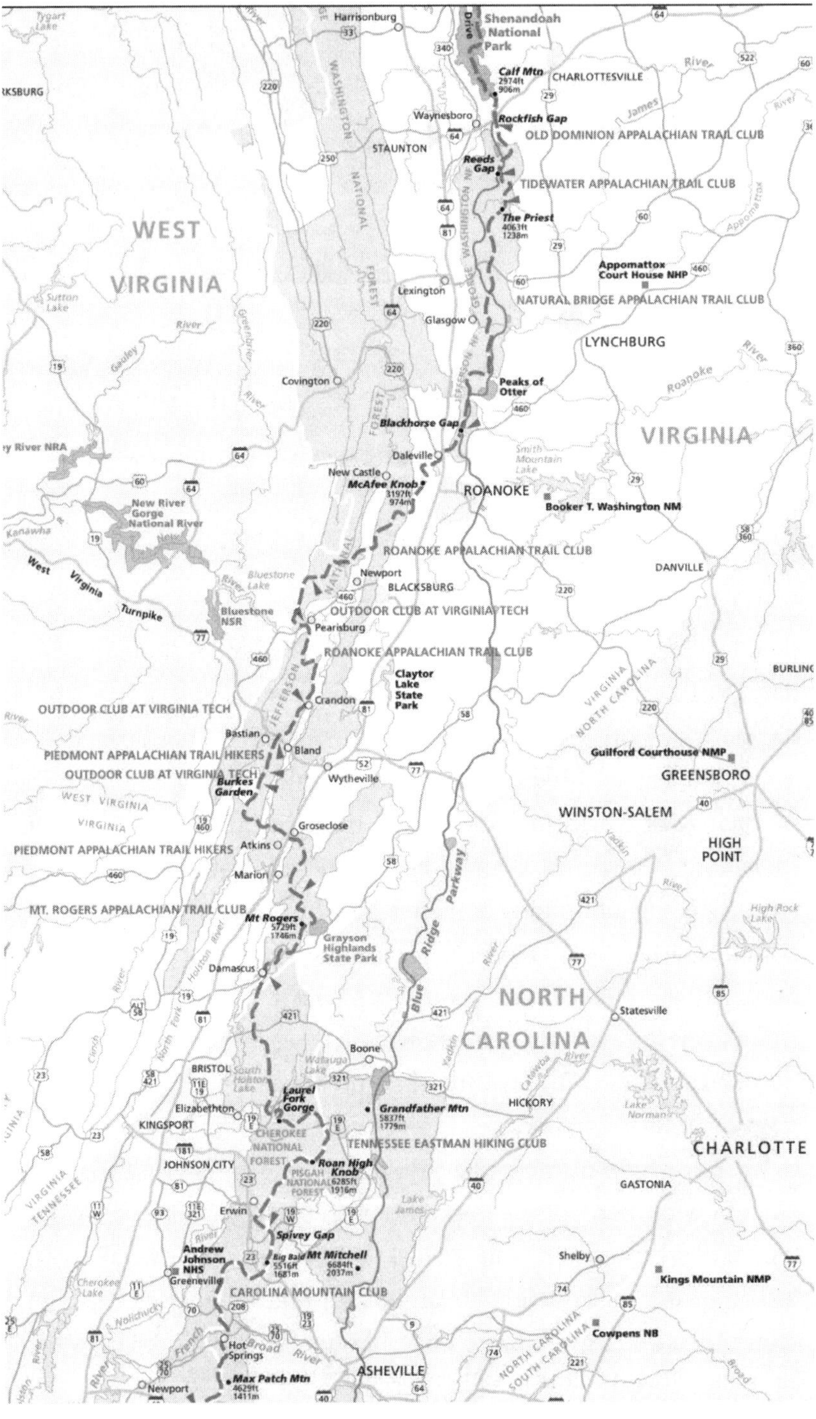

Shenandoah National Park
Harrisonburg
Calf Mtn 2974ft 906m
CHARLOTTESVILLE
Rockfish Gap
Waynesboro
OLD DOMINION APPALACHIAN TRAIL CLUB
STAUNTON
Reeds Gap
TIDEWATER APPALACHIAN TRAIL CLUB
The Priest 4063ft 1238m
WEST VIRGINIA
Appomattox Court House NHP
Lexington
NATURAL BRIDGE APPALACHIAN TRAIL CLUB
Glasgow
LYNCHBURG
Covington
Peaks of Otter
Blackhorse Gap
VIRGINIA
Daleville
Smith Mountain Lake
New Castle
McAfee Knob 3197ft 974m
ROANOKE
Booker T. Washington NM
New River Gorge National River
West Virginia Turnpike
ROANOKE APPALACHIAN TRAIL CLUB
DANVILLE
Newport
BLACKSBURG
Bluestone NSR
OUTDOOR CLUB AT VIRGINIA TECH
Pearisburg
ROANOKE APPALACHIAN TRAIL CLUB
Claytor Lake State Park
Crandon
OUTDOOR CLUB AT VIRGINIA TECH
Bastian
Bland
PIEDMONT APPALACHIAN TRAIL HIKERS
Guilford Courthouse NMP
OUTDOOR CLUB AT VIRGINIA TECH
Burkes Garden
Wytheville
GREENSBORO
WINSTON-SALEM
Groseclose
HIGH POINT
PIEDMONT APPALACHIAN TRAIL HIKERS
Atkins
Marion
MT. ROGERS APPALACHIAN TRAIL CLUB
Mt Rogers 5729ft 1746m
Grayson Highlands State Park
Damascus
Blue Ridge Parkway
NORTH CAROLINA
Statesville
Boone
BRISTOL
Laurel Fork Gorge
Grandfather Mtn 5837ft 1779m
HICKORY
Elizabethton
KINGSPORT
CHEROKEE NATIONAL FOREST
TENNESSEE EASTMAN HIKING CLUB
CHARLOTTE
JOHNSON CITY
Roan High Knob 6285ft 1916m
PISGAH NATIONAL FOREST
GASTONIA
Erwin
Spivey Gap
Andrew Johnson NHS
Big Bald 5516ft 1681m
Mt Mitchell 6684ft 2037m
Shelby
Kings Mountain NMP
Greeneville
CAROLINA MOUNTAIN CLUB
Hot Springs
Cowpens NB
ASHEVILLE
Max Patch Mtn 4629ft 1411m
Newport

five miles, I stopped. I needed to resupply and had to get to town. I decided to take another zero to do that.

I got into town, bought my supplies, ate a nice little lunch, and came back to hang out in the shelter. The next day I didn't get out of bed until 9:30. Me. At 9:30. I told myself to be smart about this, and I took another zero. I am proud of myself for this. My daughter was even proud of me. I guess after a lifetime of stubbornness, she saw it as a win too. I went out to eat both evenings.

Turns out that somehow, somehow I had contracted COVID. That explained so much. But I seriously thought something was wrong with my heart, because it kept beating so crazily. I couldn't believe I might have to go off-trail again.

This is when I met Homer. He is another amazing trail angel. He did the AT back in the '80s, and he is still in love with it. I couldn't understand a word he said because his southern accent was so thick. He and his family serve the hikers and work on the trail every weekend. They gave me a ride to the BeeCh Hill Bed and Breakfast right on the trail. The BeeCh Hill people again let me have a single room. This time I had to pay for my room, but it was not expensive, and I had to make sure I only used the bathroom upstairs. They fed me, but I didn't eat with anyone. After I finished the trail, and came back down to Trail Days, I made sure I looked up Homer and thanked him.

The Appalachian Trail Days Festival is an annual event where people who have hiked the AT, or just love the AT, show up to celebrate their experience on the trail. It is held in Damascus, Virginia, and the town population balloons to about 25,000 people. It's a blast, and it's a chance to reconnect with all the hiking friends you bonded with on the trail.

I still held out hope that I would get better and get back out on the trail. But I took four zero days at the BeeCh Hill, and I really didn't feel any better. I had a headache which subsided, but I was still too weak to hike. I bought a ticket to fly out for home the next day. I woke up so dizzy, I cancelled it and rescheduled for the next day. Same thing. I rescheduled again, and finally I could stand up and make the flight back to Millville, Pennsylvania.

Now, I had noticed when I had norovirus that my ears started ringing like crazy. And, when I was dizzy with COVID, I think it was worse because of my ear problems. My right ear always rang since my concussion in Rhode Island, but the ringing in the left ear was a new development. After I finished my entire hike, I would have another hearing test and learn that the norovirus had wiped out 25 percent of my hearing in my left ear. So now I *really* can't hear. All high pitches are completely lost to me. The doctor suspects the norovirus settled into my inner ear and created permanent damage.

When I get off the plane, Jocelyn meets me, and I look pretty awful. I'm depressed, I've lost 28 pounds, and my face and eyes show the exhaustion that COVID brings. I look like a prisoner of war or something. I have lost all my muscle. It will take another three weeks to rebound and be able to get back on the trail again. I try after two weeks, but I still am not strong enough. I still could not even walk up my steps at home.

Other than Jocelyn, I did not tell my family anything. I knew they would take one look at my decimated body and demand I get off the trail for good. They would say (and they wouldn't have been wrong) that it was killing me. When I finally couldn't hide anymore, guess what? They said exactly that. Argument after argument came from everyone: "Don't go back, don't go back until you're ready." No one seemed to understand that the clock was ticking, and every day I spent off the trail jeopardized my chances of finishing the trail as a thru-hike. Every day off the trail was like a Jenga block being pulled out of the tower that would make me whole again. I probably couldn't have explained it that well at the time, but I knew I had to do this trail. Everyone told me I "didn't have to" finish in one year. I "didn't have to" do this and that. I have never been argumentative with my family, but we sure had a few over this. They knew I was doing it for Sandy. They knew I was all f----d up in my head. But I had never told them that I knew, beyond a doubt, that for some reason God wanted me to do this … as a thru-hike, not in sections. So in all fairness, they didn't have the complete story. But conflict with them upset me greatly, even though I could see their point. My kids were the exception. They truly understood that I really did have to. Their support made all the difference.

When I broke my foot, I lost three-quarters of my followers on social media, which also meant less donations for Sloan Kettering. Once I got back on the trail, not all of them started following me again. Was I off trail? On trail? People really didn't know. For almost two months there were no donations. Their contributions were important to me, and they helped fuel my desire to get this trail done. When there were no donations, and something would happen to me (like the norovirus) I would question, *Why the f--k am I even out here? Nobody cares.*

I was arguing with my family and arguing with God. It depressed the shit out of me. I didn't want to see anyone. My family wanted to have a party for me, but I really didn't want to go. I agreed that I would if they all promised to not bring up the hike. That's what happened, until one of them couldn't help himself and brought it up. They all ganged up on me then, like a bunch of chickens that gang up on the weak one to peck the shit out of it. Finally, when I couldn't take it anymore, I told them to f--k off.

With their long history of faith, that had to be hard for my family to hear. Many of them had donated and supported me, and I instantly felt horrible. I grabbed Jocelyn and we left, so I could stew in peace.

I just wanted to be alone and wrestle this out with God. I got no answer from Him. But I did come to the conclusion that it was Satan trying to discourage and depress me. I had the promise from God, and of that I was certain. So it didn't make sense for God to try to stop me. It had to be Satan. Satan loves to mess up someone who's about to do something great or to get closer to God in some way. Even though I didn't know it (I hoped it!) at the time, that was exactly what was going to happen.

CHAPTER 17:

THE EPHESIANS EFFECT

Are you wondering how I went from being a ninth-grade boy who kept his salvation a secret, to a man who bases his life decisions on what he thinks God wants him to do? I have the church of Ephesus to thank for that, and my mom, of course … and a guy named Nick Kindt.

After Sandy and I were married for about a year, everybody started coming up to me and telling me we had to go to church. Sandy didn't go without me, and I didn't go. I mean, we were both doing fine. But my mother had other plans for us, and she constantly asked me if I was going to church. She even convinced a dozen or more of the adults whom I knew in our little town to start in on me about going to church. They all had the same instructions: Tell him you're praying for him, and that I'm worried about him. Tell him he needs to go to church. Well, it worked.

"Hey, let's go to church tomorrow," I blurted out one Saturday night. Sandy agreed and the next day we headed into Millville Methodist Church. Everybody was glad to see me, and we had a good time. As soon as I went once, they all started in on me about going to Sunday school. These people were relentless! Two months later, there we were, in a class taught by Nick Kindt. Now, Nick was a high school math teacher, and he was organized. He had the seven of us each study one of the churches in Revelation. Then we would all present our findings. I thought, *Here we go again, in Revelation.* Well, mine was Ephesus. Nick also tells me I'm going to go first. So all week Sandy and I study our churches, and the more I read, the more I feel the grip of conviction, again! The church of Ephesus is the one that has lost its first love. They were just going through the motions, but they had lost their fire. The prophecy for them is that if they do not repent, God will come to them and remove their lampstand from its place (Revelation 2:4-6). My commitment that night as a 14-year-old kid had only lasted about 12 hours. I sure had lost my first love.

"I feel guilty about what happened when I was young," I said to Sandy. I had never told her about that night with the preacher. All I could think about was that I had to repent. I was 25 at the time, and I finally made a real commitment to Christ.

This time it was for real. I got involved in the youth program and led a Sunday school class. I felt like I was forgiven for everything, and I took it very seriously. I literally could not get enough of Jesus. I read the Bible, all by myself this time, all the way through. I studied as much as I could. All my blind siblings used to listen to the Bible on cassette, so that's what I did too. I had a job that allowed me to listen to the Bible two hours each way to work. I came home fired up. Every. Single. Night. I was always in a great mood, because I was just loving on Jesus. And He was loving on me through His Word. I was feeling all kinds of healing. I got involved with prison ministry, mission trips, and more. This was an amazing time of growth for me. I felt like my life was complete.

Sandy had not yet made a commitment. She was sort of unfazed.

"I know you needed to do this," she told me once. "But I don't have to." She had lived a lot cleaner than I had, and her need was not as great as mine perhaps. She did eventually have her own moment after listening to an evangelist who came to our church. He was very convicting and had a great sermon that seemed perfect for Sandy. In short, he emphasized that even people who haven't done horrible things need Jesus just as much as a murderer does. This hit home for her. This was night one of a five-night crusade at our church, and by the end of the week she went forward.

I don't know. She may have done it for me. But it was real for her, and it became a turning point in our marriage. Now we were both on the same floor, and the elevator was headed straight up to heaven.

She was not as outgoing in her faith as I was. She never was as fiery as I was, but she did her own huge amount of good in her own quiet way. I was on an emotional high for a long time after that.

The church of Ephesus would come back to help me even now. While I waited for the virus to clear my body, I also started to read Paul's letter to the Ephesians, especially chapter 6, verses 10-20. Paul talks about how our battles here are not against flesh and blood, but against the spiritual power of darkness. Also Daniel 10 came back to me. I already had memorized both of them maybe 35 years earlier, because the idea of spiritual warfare had always intrigued me. Well now, with a decimated body, a battered heart, and a darkened mind, I was literally living it. I thought, *You suck, Satan. You tried to discourage me. But I'm not quitting. You can kill me, but I'm still going to keep going until I have nothing left. Bring it on, asshole.*

That change in attitude made all the difference. Now I had the blame where it belonged—on Satan the liar, the discourager, the murderer, the asshole. I mentioned this before, but *Attitude* by Chuck Swindall made the difference in my life again on this day. I had read it for the first time six years earlier. It had helped before, but this day it swung the pendulum in a crucial way. Today I was in the middle of spiritual warfare. If God was allowing Satan to hurt me, it was only for my good, or His glory, and I could take it. Again, Tristan and Jocelyn understood and agreed with me.

"It sure does seem like somebody's after you, Dad," agreed Tristan.

I wish I could say this was the end of my battle with depression. It wasn't, and I know now that it doesn't work quite like that. I would periodically have some really dark periods, and I would have many more broken bones coming! But I would look at them so differently now, and I would refuse to dwell on them. I would see them as Satan's attacks, trying to get me to cower down and slink off the mountain and away from my promise from God. Satan could be defeated with a good attitude and a whole lot of faith in my Savior. And really, even if he killed me, and maybe he would, I was okay with it. It would only be for my own good. I was going to trust God completely on this, come what may.

"Here's to you, Satan, f--k yourself. Go f--k yourself. You're an asshole." I must have cussed at Satan with every kind of cussword I could invent for about an hour when I finally came to this conclusion. It doesn't sound too Christian, does it? I think it was. I think every cussword that came out of my mouth that day was appropriate because I finally had identified my enemy. It was no longer like fighting in Vietnam as my brothers had told me, never knowing whom you should shoot, never knowing your enemy. I could see Satan's hand distinctly, and it was on me. I could fight against him now, because I had identified him. He was wearing a bright red coat called depression.

I got up each morning and dressed myself for spiritual warfare, just like it says in Ephesians 6:10-20: armor, boots, sword, helmet, breastplate. But even more, I thought of the passage in Daniel 10:6-14. In this passage, Daniel is in a time of great distress. He's been praying for 21 days with no answer, nothing, just fasting and praying. His patience and faith would stick with me. Three weeks later, out on the trail, I would have a full understanding of it as well.

I was home for only a little longer after this. I'm telling you, this change in my attitude started the true healing in my body. I couldn't walk up my own steps without being winded and dizzy, and I was scared to death that my heart was ruined from these viruses. I had my heart checked twice during this time, and the results were always good. But they reported I was still too weak to hike, and I had to let my body recover. I didn't fight it this time. I let it come. I thought, *If God still wants this to be a thru-hike, He's really going to have to change something, because I'm running out of time.*

Already I knew I would have to do a flip-flop. That's where a hiker stops, and goes to the opposite end, and starts hiking toward the middle again. It's still considered a thru-hike, because all the miles are getting covered in one season. I decided I would go back to the BeeCh Hill Bed and Breakfast, and hike north at least to Harpers Ferry to get this more rugged part over with. That area would be better now than in cold weather. Then, I could drive north and head south through Maine before winter came.

CHAPTER 18:

BERRIES AND SHROOMS

After being off the trail for five weeks, it is already August 4. It is, in fact, Sandy's birthday. The whole day, a part of me thinks of this.

Three of those five weeks were spent recovering at home, but I'm back and ready to roll.

I stop back into the BeeCh Hill B&B to thank them for being such awesome trail angels. They are actually having a family reunion, and they have shut the hostel down to accommodate their own family guests. They let me stay there anyway, because they really just want to see me make it on my journey. I'll say it again, people on this trail will convince you that humans are shockingly good and kind. At BeeCh Hill, I get to meet every single person in that family, and I truly feel like I am in the family myself. They are wearing funky tie-dye shirts, and we take a bunch of funny pictures, clowning for the camera and featuring my backpack, which they loved. By now my nickname was "The 'Shrooming Camel," and my buddy Chris had painted a cool camel logo on it for me when I was at home.

I can't believe how good I feel! The extra week I took off has made all the difference. I am not even winded going uphill on the first day. I have to force myself to stop after 10 miles. The miles are flowing. Everything is green and beautiful, and even the ripe blackberries are this gorgeous reminder of how blessed I am to be doing this. I stop and pick some for an hour. I hate to lose the time, but I'm in this moment, and I have to have some! All the regular hikers have cleaned the easy ones off the edges, but not me. I head right into the middle through the briars and get my belly full. I'm bleeding everywhere, but those berries taste so good!

After seven more miles, I put my pack down, and I notice my GPS device is missing. Oh no, what did I do? I think. I call Jocelyn.

"Where am I at?" I ask her.

"What do you mean?" she replies, because I should know where I am. I tell her the situation, and she checks the GPS. "You're heading south," she says. "I thought you were heading north today."

That's not good. Somebody had to have picked it up, and is heading south with it. She decides to try to contact the GPS, and maybe the carrier will hear it buzz. At the same time, I decide to drop my pack and run back through the blackberries toward the BeeCh Hill B&B, hoping to overtake whoever has it. I make it almost back to the BeeCh Hill before I find the guy. That's 14 miles out of my way! Oh well, another screwed up day, but I'm still just so happy to be back on the trail that I don't dwell on it.

I want the record to show that I did not lose the GPS out of my own carelessness during my wild berry-picking moment. The screw actually came loose, which then allowed the device to come free from its carabiner clip. Not my fault! From then on, I carry it in the mesh pocket on the outside of my pack. It can still receive a signal that way.

The forecast for the next week shows no rain. I think, *Man, if I was in shape I could be flying*. But I don't let it get me down. I thought my lungs would be at square one, but they are so much better than I expect. I couldn't be more grateful. I also stumble into one of the best mushroom patches I would see on the whole trail. I find chicken of the woods, and lobster varieties, and chantarelles. I have the prettiest looking lunch that day!

I learned all about mushrooms because they might be able to cure cancer. Did you know that?

CHAPTER 19:

CANCER IS A FORBIDDEN WORD

When Sandy and I drove home from Geisinger Medical Center, the words "triple negative breast cancer" loomed over our heads like a steel I-beam. My world, our world, was in chaos. I would fight like Karns's junkyard dog against anything, or anyone, that tried to take her away from me. And that's what we did. When conventional chemotherapy didn't work, as it typically doesn't for triple negative breast cancer, we emptied our savings to pay for experimental treatments without hesitation.

But in the end, there was nothing I could do. I just had to stand there and watch while the mysterious chemicals tried to break down the tumors in her body. I drove the car. I shopped for groceries. I ran errands. But I couldn't do anything. There was no way to throw my body in front of her and take the hit. I literally didn't know how to handle it.

That's when I started researching all I could on the internet. The kids did too. Ironically, my daughter's fiancé was a cancer research scientist. Do you think that's just a coincidence? Me either.

We learned that a lot of people had great results using mushrooms to bolster their health during and after treatments. Some mushrooms, some really poisonous ones, are being used to destroy tumors in mice. I had always been into foraging, because that was important for hiking and being in nature. Now I threw all of my hyperactive energy into learning about mushrooms. Luckily, we were in an area where I could find many varieties, and we picked them and learned to cook them. As a bonus, they were delicious.

For a while it seemed like we were winning. Sandy was feeling pretty good. But after a brief remission, the cancer returned with a vengeance. Jocelyn moved up her wedding date, knowing that Sandy's timeline was short. We decided that "cancer" would be a forbidden word at the wedding. We had high hopes that we could just celebrate our daughter's marriage and not worry about anything else, even if just for a day. The whole week leading up to the wedding, it didn't look good for our walk down the aisle. Sandy was throwing up every day, sometimes passing out afterward. Sandy threatened me that no matter what happened, I was not to carry her.

"If I fall down," she said, "just wait."

She made me promise her.

The morning of the wedding she was dizzy, but then seemed to rebound. Right as we are standing there ready to go down the aisle though, she turns to me.

"I'm not okay." Her pale face flickered with panic.

"Hey, just take 30 seconds here," I said. "C'mon, you can make them wait and build up the anticipation."

Sandy cracked half a shitty smile and closed her eyes to gather her strength. Thirty long seconds passed.

"Okay," she said, "I'm gonna try."

I got my hands around her on both sides, holding her up, and we started down. She didn't know but I had planted helpers on her side of the aisle. They had all agreed to put out a hand if Sandy went down. But they were smiling. We were all smiling, because she made it.

We had promised it wouldn't be a sad day. But as I danced with my wife, I cried and cried. I thanked God that she was in my arms and that my daughter was so happy and marrying a man that we loved.

"I think this is even better than when we got married," I told her. She wasn't happy about that comment until I explained. "You're with me, and I have the best marriage in the whole world. I am the happiest man on earth." And I was, just in that moment. I was trying hard not to look too far into the future.

Shortly after Jocelyn's wedding came the night we talked about picking out my next wife. Why do women feel the need to do that? She had picked out three, but I really didn't want to talk about it. Even as I hiked the trail north, trying to make up for lost time, her words drifted around in the back of my mind.

You know, Steve, I think you should still do the AT. I think maybe you could meet your next wife there.

And then she was gone.

CHAPTER 20:

BEES

By August 8, I'm at 800 total miles. I keep averaging 17 miles a day, with no problems. It's been a tough section, and there aren't any northbound thru-hikers any more. Just some folks doing their day hikes or sectional hikes.

One day two guys come sprinting down the trail with no shirts on. They are completely exhausted. They are swelled up and have welts all over their faces. They are young, one about 25 and the other in his mid-thirties.

The older guy pants, "Hey man, don't go any farther. There's an underground hornet's nest up there. I got stung 15 times, and my buddy here got stung seven. He's in bad shape." They had literally ripped off their shirts to free the bees trapped inside.

I look at his younger friend. His sweaty face is blotchy, and he's got a wild look in his eye.

"Do you need help getting him out of the woods?" I ask.

"No," the younger guy says, "I can still walk." He looks at his feet and then back at me. "But I am starting to swell up." They estimate they have another mile before they can get to a road. I can confirm this from having just passed it.

They decline my second offer of help, but I worry about the guy. I offer a prayer for him as I keep going. *This is stupid,* I finally say. *I just need to go see if I can help them.* Sandy had a bee allergy, and I know how scary it is to have trouble breathing after a sting. I put my pack down and turn to run after them. Again, they decline my help, but I figure I'll stay with them at least to the road.

I had done all I could. I turned around to go back uphill to where I had left my pack. Oh man, can you fly without a pack! Then the problem of the bees comes to me, and I figure I have to find a way to kill them or every hiker is going to have the same problem. Just then, another guy comes down the trail nursing a bunch of stings.

That's it, I think. I put on all the clothes I have. Now, I don't have rain pants, as I mentioned, but I did have these Patagonia leggings that I wear so I don't stink up the sleeping bag. I put those on my legs, my only socks, and a lightweight long-sleeve shirt I was carrying. I put my coat on over that. It's August in Virginia, so it's hot. I don't know where I'm going to run into these bees, but I also don't want to hike forever in this hot coat. I know it must be in a couple hundred yards. I walk and walk. Pretty soon I know I've covered at least a half a mile. Could I have passed it somehow? I turn around and go back.

When I was in Rhode Island in 1969, my buddy Raymond, some other guys, and I were messing around in a deserted woods. We found an old mountain stone foundation and started poking around there. As we were nosing around, the dirt we were standing on just caved in, right under our feet. To our left and right, all around us, was the biggest bees' nest I had ever seen in my life. It went a full three or four feet in a circle, and we were in the middle. The swarm started. The hum of their wings rose in pitch as they started flying up in little gray storms. Then they started attacking. These were underground hornets, and their stings were vicious. All of us were yelling as we each got stung again and again. We fled.

Well, I decided I was going to go back that day in Rhode Island too. I approached quietly and got a good look at the nest. By its size alone, I knew that none of my usual bee nest-killing tactics were going to work. But then I had a good idea. I could burn them out.

I thought a little gas bomb would do the trick, and I could launch it from a distance away. I had a glass bottle and filled it with gas. (I know, it's a miracle I'm still alive, literally. Do not try this at home.) I put a rag in the top for a stopper, with a just a touch of gas on the tip so I could light it. As soon as I touched it to a match, I hurled it.

It exploded into an inferno. Now, I got the bees. But there was a second problem quickly developing. The hot flames immediately went beyond the bees and found dry leaves and pine needles. The end of the story is that I burned the whole woods down. Now, this little woods is right in the center of the city of Providence. After the woods were aflame, the houses were going to be next. Luckily, the houses were all saved, but justice would still need to be served, and I was the one who deserved it. When my dad found out that I had been responsible for the entire conflagration, he turned me in to the cops. This is what got me on probation right before I went to stay at Jack and Connie's.

As I tiptoe back on the Appalachian Trail to where I hope this nest might be, I try to come up with a strategy. I won't be torching these guys. It would be just my luck I'd be the guy who burns down the AT. What else can I do? If I can find the hole, I can plug it with my little 18-inch hiking towel, and then cover it with a rock. If I add a little signage to give hikers a warning *BEES AHEAD*, that might do it.

Still, no bees.

I spend another hour or so looking, but nothing. I guess I won't be killing any bees today. I have to give up and get going down the trail. After all my extra curriculars on this day, I only make about 12 miles. They aren't calling for rain, so I decide to cowboy camp. If you cowboy camp, you don't use your tent or any covering. You just stretch out your pad and bag and enjoy the stars like the cowboys do in the movies. And I did enjoy them. The night was beautiful and clear. But in the night, *kerbang*, a thunderstorm pops up. Now most of the time when I cowboy camp, I unravel my tent at least, so it's handy. On this night I did not. The rain comes immediately, pretty heavy. I have my ground cloth under my sleeping pad to protect it, and I'm able to crawl into my tent without it being fully set up. Then the real downpour starts, and I'm able to finish setting it up from the inside. I'm wet in my sleeping bag, but I'm out of the storm at least. And I didn't have to sacrifice my towel for the bees, so I'm able to use it to dry off. My clothes are wet, but I'm out of the storm, out on the trail, right where I belong. It's a good night.

CHAPTER 21:

HITTING 900

I'm 30 miles away from Rockfish Gap, where I'm meeting Jocelyn and my friend Bob Burns, who's driving all the way down from Pennsylvania. They are going to join me for a few miles. I figure I can just hike until I'm too tired, and have an easy day into town the next day. I'll get my laundry done, get a good meal, get supplies, and then get back on the trail to meet them.

I feel fantastic. I know that my buddy Bob has not hiked much though, and we might be having some shorter, 10-mile days. I hike my first 25-mile day, and I end up five miles from Rockfish Gap. You just couldn't stop my feet. It was the best I had felt so far on the entire trip. I was super proud of myself because that's a marathon with a 20-or-so-pound pack. All my food was gone except for the peanut butter, or it would have been heavier. I had also managed to empty my fuel cannister (so I could just replace it and not have to carry two) by cooking a whole bunch of mushrooms for my supper the night before, beautiful ones in a lot of varieties. I had found some black trumpet mushrooms for the first time on the trail, and they were delicious. The chantarelles weren't ripe yet, but I also had a good amount of chicken of the woods and a lobster mushroom. They don't make much of a meal, but they taste completely different than most other mushrooms.

This is what thru-hikers do, not section hikers. You are always strategizing about how to make your pack lighter and trying to plan your stops to minimize the weight. I bet I had 20 or 30 shakedowns, which means I would re-evaluate everything because you really just have to get rid of a couple of ounces. A couple of ounces makes all the difference. You feel like you can really fly. It's summertime, so this is as light as the pack is ever going to be without heavy clothes and warm sleeping gear. My base weight, without food, fuel, or water, was 15-15 ½ pounds. I figure I can even send some more things home with Bob. After they join me, our plan is to get to Harpers Ferry, minimum. I was really hoping to get up to the border of Pennsylvania. Either of these would be a good spot for anyone else who wanted to join me, being just two or three hours from our hometown in the middle of Pennsylvania.

I wake up around 4:00 a.m. The only thing in my pack now is my oatmeal and peanut butter, and I wolf it down. Now my pack is totally empty, but that's okay because I'm headed into town. I'm in the Virginia Tech area, in some high weeds, blowing through them like I'm on fire. Normally the VT people would maintain the trail here. Of course I'm out of the hiking bubble now, so no one is maintaining it till next year again. I'm loping through without a care.

I only saw him as he moved to strike me, a yellow diamond-patterned body with a wedge-shaped head. Rattlesnake. I had almost stepped right on his head. He lunged, and actually it was the weeds that saved me. His fangs got tangled up in the weeds, so he did not make contact. I leaped away, and we went our separate ways. The snake didn't go far. I wanted to warn my friend coming behind me and looked for something to make a sign with. I found a nearby shelter and used a page from the registration book to make the sign.

I put it right on a tree where everyone could see it, warning them of the snake in the high weeds.

I get to Rockfish Gap and try to phone for a trail angel to come and shuttle me into town. Some are still running, but some aren't. At least in this area, day hiking and section hiking is still pretty common, so I was able to get my ride. I would have plenty of time to hang out in town a bit, get my laundry done, re-supply, and eat. First I had a steak, but I was still hungry. So I ate a hamburger too.

I enjoyed visiting with some of the hikers I met there. They all wanted to hear my stories, and I had a brand-new rattlesnake story too. I was happy to share. Then I got back to the trailhead.

Bob and Jocelyn are a few minutes late. I'm at the trailhead waiting, well fed, clean, and ready to rock and roll. As soon as they arrive, we are ready to go. When we are a couple miles in, I check with Bob. He's feeling good, so I tell him he can lead, and he can decide how far we go. Really, I don't want to push it, and it is more important to me to spend time with them than to stress about racking up miles. It is so good to see them both, especially my daughter. She has a bounce in her step and a big smile that just lights up my whole world. She has always been such a tough little thing, and she's at home here in the mountains.

Pretty soon we are at 10 miles, but there isn't really a place to camp. The next shelter area is at about 12 miles. Bob is still feeling good at 12, so we decide to go three more, to the next shelter. We probably should have stopped at 12, because when we wake up the next day, Bob is hurting. He's always so honest and funny, and he takes his limitations in stride. I know though, he'd do anything to stay out here on the trail with me. He decides to just go exploring in the area while Jocelyn and I continue on.

Bob wanted to stick around so that he could be there to give Jocelyn and me a ride back to Pennsylvania after we had made the 900-mile mark. He's too humble to admit it, but Bob was truly a trail angel for us. His faith is so deeply steadfast and reverent that he's inspiring to be around. In the end, Bob did have to hike just to get back to the main road on Skyline Drive. He easily found a ride back to the town where he stayed in his tent on the trail and checked out the local interests.

Jocelyn and I went on the next day. That night got extremely cold, nearly in the 30s. The realization hit that I was not going to be able to finish this trail if I didn't get to Maine sooner rather than later. They usually shut down Mt. Katahdin after the first week in October, and I knew I wasn't going to get there if I tried to get all the way to Harpers Ferry. We all talked it over. Bob took some of our heavier stuff so I kept my pack at 15 ½ pounds. Jocelyn and I would just try to get to the 900 mark, which was in the Shenandoah area of the AT. Then, we would know exactly where to start when I came back south to finish up.

In general, the rule is you are doing great if you can get 10 miles in before 10 in the morning. So we decided that by 10:00 a.m. we would get to the 900-mile mark, and then get in the car to head to Pennsylvania. That would mean 12 miles in the morning for Jocelyn and me, but we planned to get up a little bit earlier and get it done. And that's exactly what we did. Bob used an app to find our trailhead, and he had no trouble meeting us.

Then we drove home to Pennsylvania, with plenty of time to organize and get what we would need for Maine. As Bob drove, and even a little the night before while we camped, Jocelyn and I strategized about how to best approach Mt. Katahdin. We decide the best way is to go to Monson, Maine, instead, take a zero and collect equipment and supplies, and then start at the 100-Mile Wilderness and hike north toward Mt. Katahdin. At the base of Mt. Katahdin, a shuttle comes and picks you up and takes you to the northern tip, where you then hike Mt. Katahdin going south again. It's a little confusing, but it's the best way to do it. I'm excited to have this landmark of the trail finally in my sights!

SECTION III
MAINE

---

*You therefore must endure hardship
as a good soldier of Jesus Christ.*
2 Timothy 2:3 (NKJV)

CHAPTER 22:

STORIES FROM SHAW'S

Before we can go south, we have to go north, through the 100-Mile Wilderness and Mt. Katahdin. We have to get that done before they close it in the fall, this year on October 10. Then we can go south again.

We leave our house in Pennsylvania at 5:00 a.m. and drive to the northern end of Massachusetts. I know that's not very far, but that's as much driving as I can manage since I broke my back at 26, falling off a roof while working. We had to take another rest, too, just so I could get out and walk around for about a mile and limber back up. We arrive in Maine the next morning at a respectable hour at Shaw's Hiker Hostel in Monson, an incredible hostel on the trail. I've said it before, and I'm going say it at least a couple more times. It's amazing. It is a central meeting place. Everybody there is in the mood to celebrate because they only have about 100 more miles that lie between them and the end of their first thru-hike. There had to be 100 hikers there, and the place owns about three properties. Shaw's is run by Kimberly and Jarrod Hester, known as Hippy Chick and

Poet, whom I got to know well. I would run into them several times over the next month.

Jocelyn and I had planned to take a zero and recuperate from the long drive.

Immediately when we pull into Shaw's, I see a guy I had started the hike with. He was pretty excited to be on the last leg, and truly, I was happy for him. In all, I saw 11 people I had met on the trail and met still more who are friends for life. I knew I should have been right there with them, celebrating and anticipating the sweet finish. I'm not going lie. It stung a little bit.

"You know," I said to Jocelyn in the car, "this is when I should be finishing my hike."

"I know, Dad," she said. Her brown eyes were sad for me, but she kept them on the road. She sighed a little sigh, which I knew was to say, *Keep positive*. So I did. I had to remind myself again as all these hikers bounced around the campfires, high on being so close to the finish, and high on the satisfaction that they had made it. I wanted that satisfaction too, but I could remind myself to be patient. I just had to persist.

Our breakfast in the morning was one of the best breakfasts on the trail. You could tell Poet loved to cook. He was up at 6:00 a.m., putting on bacon and cooking it slowly. I was up with Poet, drinking coffee and talking with him. I also met two other people who had hiked the AT before, but were not hiking it this season—Hambone and Mountain Cat. They were working a summer at Shaw's because they loved it so much. Hambone found out about my encounter with norovirus, and that I couldn't eat gluten because of it. He had helped me out with a gluten-free beer the night before.

Here are the names of some of the others who were there: Smokin' Burrito (guess how he got that name ...), Greensmoke, Happy Feet, Moonshine, Blue-Haired Hiker, Hutch, and Sexy Legs. Happy Feet was from Japan and didn't speak a word of English. I hiked with him

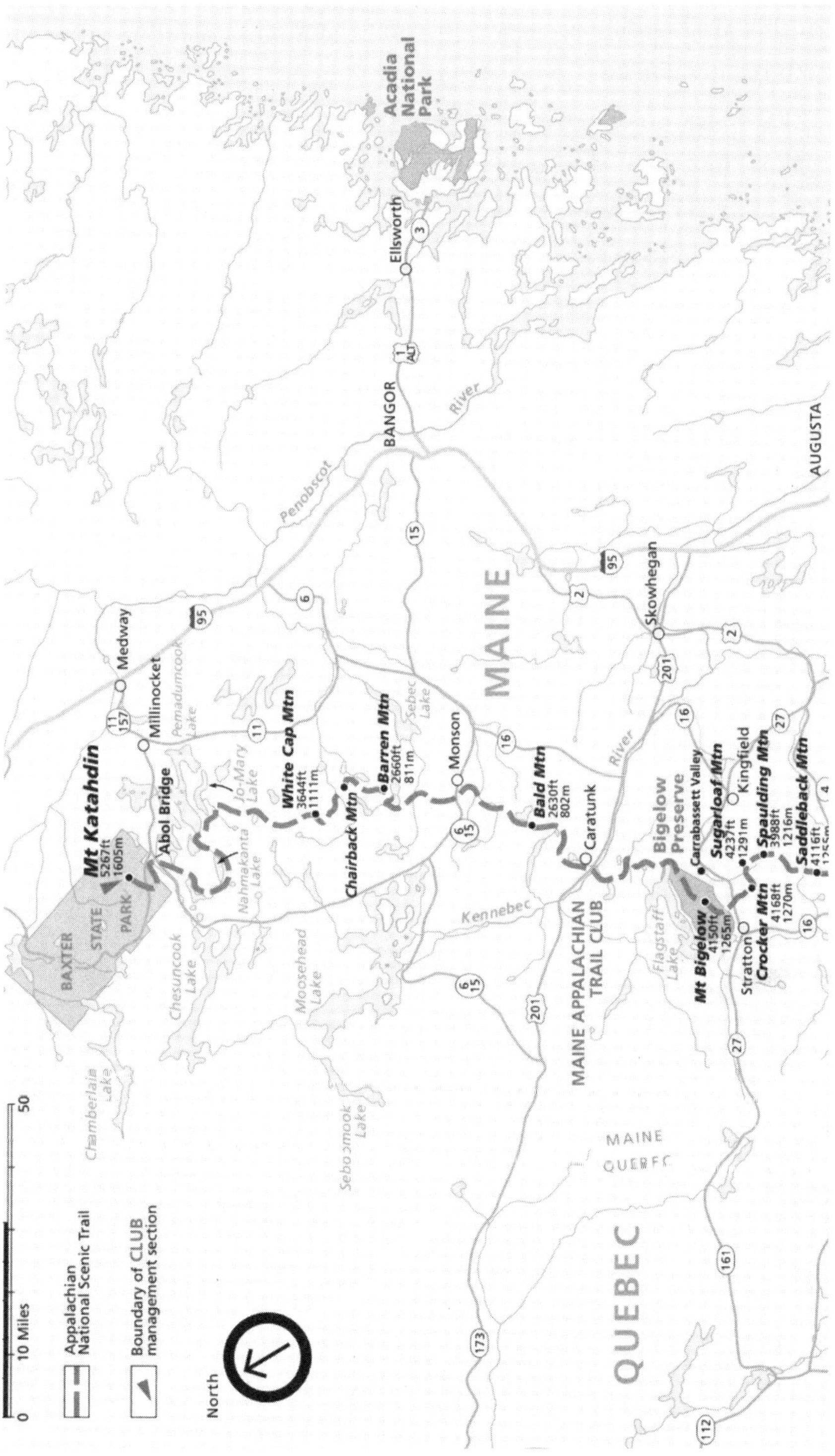

0
10 Miles
50
Appalachian National Scenic Trail
Boundary of CLUB management section
North
BAXTER STATE PARK
Mt Katahdin
5267ft
1605m
Abol Bridge
Millinocket
Medway
Pemadumcook Lake
Nahmakanta Lake
Jo-Mary Lake
White Cap Mtn
3644ft
1111m
Chairback Mtn
Barren Mtn
2660ft
811m
Sebec Lake
Monson
Bald Mtn
2630ft
802m
Caratunk
Chesuncook Lake
Chamberlain Lake
Moosehead Lake
Seboomook Lake
Kennebec
River
MAINE APPALACHIAN TRAIL CLUB
Bigelow Preserve
Carrabassett Valley
Flagstaff Lake
Mt Bigelow
4150ft
1265m
Stratton
Crocker Mtn
4168ft
1270m
Sugarloaf Mtn
4237ft
1291m
Kingfield
Spaulding Mtn
3988ft
1216m
Saddleback Mtn
4116ft
MAINE
QUEBEC
Skowhegan
Penobscot
BANGOR
River
Ellsworth
Acadia National Park
AUGUSTA
1
ALT
3
6
11
15
16
27
95
157
201
2
4
161
173
112

for four days back when I was in good shape, around when I was with Hunter. He was doing around 20-22 miles a day and so was I. I tried to learn a few words in Japanese, but by the time he got to Maine, Happy Feet did know some English expressions. Moonshine was about the same age as Jocelyn, with blonde hair, petite features, and a pert little nose. Jocelyn had an Appalachian Gear Company sweater similar to mine. Moonshine liked it, and Jocelyn talked her into buying one of her own. The two hit it off. There were other people from around the world there too, because Shaw's is so famous. It is an extraordinary place, and everyone there has amazing stories that are told around a campfire at six in the morning. Some people are already smoking their first joint of the day. I've tried having a couple of conversations with hikers about putting smoke in their lungs, but people will do what they do. Others are drinking coffee, like me. All of them are thinking about the food they are about to eat! The stories come out one by one, and you are blessed to be hearing each and every one of them. Here you are with people you've sweated with and been soaking wet with. You've encouraged each other to keep going. Maybe you've prayed with somebody, or are falling in love with someone. Maybe you plan to propose at the top of Mt. Katahdin. I actually watched a guy do that!

Some can't wait for the trail to be over, while others declare it's the best experience of their lives. Someone complains there's too much water on the trail (they aren't wrong; the mud is unbelievable), and then the next comment is how they can't believe it's almost over. Some of those people are thinking that they have to go back to work next week, and a profound sense of loss will overtake them. Everyone is filled with emotion, and so am I.

One person says, "In a sick way, I'm going to miss this trail."

Another, "Yeah I'm gonna miss these bleeding blisters, the starving for six months, the never-ending sore muscles."

Everyone wonders, *When in the hell is my body going to get used to this?* The truth is, your body never really does. Something is always aching. There is always a nagging injury.

Personally, I must have stubbed my toe a hundred times on this trip on top of everything else. Then I would hike 25 miles on it—not a good combo. First thing next morning, I'd hit that same toe. Every time.

Everybody agrees—it's the best and it's the worst. Charles Dickens wrote, *It was the best of times, it was the worst of times.* And he would be exactly right when it comes to the AT.

The stories circulated around the fire, some about norovirus, some about broken bones, and still more about lost or damaged equipment. But one girl named Castaway was quiet. Her short hair was still wet from the shower, and she wore all new leggings and a sweater, too nice for a hiker. Someone finally asked her, "What's your story?" What she told us blew us all away.

Castaway was from Florida. She had never hiked before and bought all new equipment to head out to the AT. On the first day, she headed out for water, got turned around, and couldn't get back to her tent. All she had was her water and water filter. She went one direction, no tent. Reversed to the other direction, no tent.

Completely inexperienced in the woods, she was completely lost, and had no way to figure out where to go. Darkness was coming. The thought of facing it without the protection of her tent was paralyzing. And then suddenly it was dark, pitch dark, and she couldn't see her hand in front of her face. No headlamp, no phone, nothing in the thick darkness. Extremely grateful for her water and filter at least, she found a pine tree and crawled under it to sleep. It was cold, and it rained. It feels like it never stops raining in Maine. The whole night she thought surely, in the light of the new day, she would be able to find her tent. Daylight came, and she started walking. Very,

very lost, she realized she was making circles and tried at least to find a hill to climb. She had no earthly idea where she was.

People had told her she would never be able to do this hike. At this point it seemed they might have been right. She knew she had to find something, somebody, and make it out of the woods. The day passed, her stomach growled, and night was coming with every hour that ticked by. The only thing she could think of was to get something, anything, to eat. She found blueberries and raspberries. Then it was pitch black again.

Another full day came and went as Castaway ate berries and wandered, wandered. Surely, a wild animal would end this by ending her. But it didn't. And another day came and went, and another. She could feel herself getting weaker, lightheaded, and very tired. After a week, all hope of finding the tent, finding anything, had expired. She just walked and her limbs felt like they were full of sand. Sooner or later, sooner or later, she had to run into someone. It was all that was left to hope for.

There's a reason why it's called the 100-Mile Wilderness. It goes on forever and forever. You can't see out, because you can't get above the trees which fold in around the trail like thick velvet. The beaver dams create a labyrinth of sticks and endless marshes, with water crossing after water crossing. She hasn't even come across any sign of a trail at all. What's certain is that the berries aren't going to last forever, and she can't go on forever. It is entirely possible to die out here, in this forest.

Ten days pass. Her stomach cramps. She thinks, *If the bears, or even wolves (are there wolves?) get me, all they will get is bones. There won't be a body left to identify.*

After 17 days of walking and starving, in the gray hours of the early morning, she sees something that doesn't look like a tree or rock or water. Is it a tent? The possibility of finding another human strikes like a match on her brain and the tears of relief begin immediately. Then reason prevails. No one is expecting her, and she probably looks pretty alarming. Some people shoot first and ask questions later. She keeps her approach quiet and gently scratches on the outside of the tent. "Excuse me?"

Inside is a young family. There are some initial tense moments while the family figures out why she is at their tent at this early hour, and why she looks so bedraggled. Once her story is out, the family feeds her immediately, covers her with blankets, and gets her back to their parked car. They take her straight to an emergency room, where she gets fluids, a shower, and spends the night. The next day, she goes back to Shaw's.

We are all dumbfounded and can't believe what we've just heard. Can it be real? Or is it just another bullshit campfire tale? Each of us imagines her out there lost, or imagines how easily it could have been any one of us. Jocelyn in particular fully registers the potential for exactly this kind of disaster and vows never to let me out of her sight. I assure her that I had just made the same vow about her.

It's a fact. The trail becomes something different for everyone, and yet, it always leaves its impact on you. Even though some of the comments and stories make you want to quit right on the spot, there is something strange that compels you to go anyway. Not to quit. And I felt it then, just like I always had. I was going to finish the first thing in maybe my whole life. It was like I heard that hostel owner telling me, *Onward, friend.*

Now, I personally did not share my story. I wasn't at the point yet where I fully understood how the hike would end, physically or mentally. I still had a lot of hiking to do— 1,300 miles, in fact.

Finally, breakfast was ready. The stories continued while we ate. Shaw's has a tradition of giving away a stack of pancakes, decreasing in size from the diameter of the plate all the way down to a tablespoon size one. I won this prize! I had my picture taken with it, and then ate as much of it as I possibly could.

I'm so excited for the flip-flop. Maine has always seemed like a mystical place to me, a place of extreme wilderness. In the whole world, I feel I was meant to be in Maine. I mean, where else do they call a place *The Hundred Mile Wilderness*? Where else is there a giant mountain at the end and a place called *Knife Edge* with steep drop offs of up to 2,000 feet on either side where you climb hand over hand over rocks in howling wind? Maine is like a meat grinder—you put hikers in and just pieces come out on the other side. I'm so excited I can hardly contain myself. Jocelyn and I pump other hikers who have just done Katahdin for information. Which way should we approach? What can we expect? How was the weather? Normally the weather is pretty terrible up there. We also discovered that the indigenous people, who hold Katahdin as a sacred area, would be gathered there at the top for their annual ceremony just at the time we would be there.

Truthfully, I was also especially excited since Jocelyn would be with me for a whole month. When else in our lives would we be able to have such an experience together? I wouldn't have to describe the sunrise or the sunset, because she would be there to see it with her own eyes. It would be precious beyond words.

CHAPTER 23:

100-MILE WILDERNESS

We went to bed that night with great expectations. We woke up so early that we had to go for a little walk to kill time before breakfast. Because they are so beat up, some guys are taking additional zero days before heading for Katahdin. The way it works at Shaw's is, if you are starting out into the 100-Mile Wilderness, you go into the shop first and get what you need. Then the other guys can go in. I just needed one more thing from the shop, and then we were off. We are each carrying 10 days of food, because that's what you need for this section. That's a lot of weight.

But Jocelyn and I are ready. We pile into the bus for the trail, and we are in the first group. Before you unload, and the whole way there, Poet gives a history of the 100-Mile Wilderness and Katahdin. As he talks, we begin to understand how he got his name. The cadence of his voice, his beautiful imagery, and his way of bestowing perspective on the listener are all evidence of his namesake.

After the history lesson is over, Poet calls all of us to caution. "Look, you've come this far. Don't do anything that would jeopardize your finishing this trail," he says. We all wholeheartedly agree.

It's one of the toughest hikes on the trail, and we will be careful indeed. He talks about mud, knee-deep mud. And downpours. There are no bridges on the creeks and rivers in Maine, so you have to watch every crossing, especially after a downpour, and make sure it's safe. His precautions were gentle but firm, like a benediction over us all. It seemed all off-the-cuff, but it could have been memorized, I guess. It was beautiful.

The sign *100 Mile Wilderness* is at the trailhead. Somehow, I'm even more excited than when I started the hike.

The woods here are totally different. While Shenandoah had been groomed, and the trails were pretty "easy," this trail was not. The first step in was a muddy quagmire, and we knew we were in it, crawling up boulders and then sliding down the other side into mud. The farther we go, the more spread out the hikers get. We only had about seven miles in at the first break because it's so slow going, muddy from the rain the night before. One of the guys, Turtle, had been at Shaw's with us. He was a monster of a man, but a great guy, and he hiked with us. We had talked at Shaw's, and I had met his dog, named Pup. That's right, this mature golden retriever has its own trail name. Turtle and Pup were different from other hikers. They had done the trail before several years ago. Pup is the only dog that has completed the Appalachian Trail twice. He was never off a leash the entire time.

We enjoy our lunch with Turtle, and he notices I have already found some mushrooms and am carrying them. He mentions he has always wanted to try foraging for mushrooms.

"Can you teach me how to do it?" he asks.

"Yeah," I said. "If you want to tag along with me, I'll show you all the different varieties that you can eat." That was the start of a great friendship for us.

At this point, our packs are heavy with the 10 days of food. I admit to Turtle that I don't want to collect too much because of the weight. On a normal day, I don't collect mushrooms until after lunch so I'm only toting them for half a day.

Turtle says, "I'll make you a deal. You just show me which ones to get, and I'll pick us a whole bag and carry them. We'll eat them tonight."

"It's a deal." The three of us, plus Pup, stuck together, picking mushrooms all the way to Katahdin like a trio of grungy Little Red Riding Hoods.

Turtle had Pup well trained. To keep the dog safe, Turtle would actually put Pup up on his shoulders and carry him during a water crossing. One time, on slippery rocks in a deeper creek, Turtle lost his footing. He went underwater, but managed to keep Pup high and dry like a golden-haired Lord Krishna. Jocelyn and I love dogs, and this calm, obedient companion was a heartwarming addition to our group.

At dusk we had another mile to go before we were at a shelter or a designated camping area. Turtle had our giant bag of mushrooms. All day he wondered out loud, "What will they taste like? I can't wait!" Our total take included chicken of the woods and trumpet mushrooms, which I was surprised to see all the way up in Maine. We also found chantarelles, because by now it was later in the summer, and they were just exploding everywhere. We also got coral mushrooms, which had just started blooming, and bear's tooth. Turtle's pack was completely full of mushrooms, at least six to seven pounds worth. I didn't want to use up all my fuel for this feast, so we looked for a place where we could have a campfire, and I could cook them that way.

Turtle loved mushrooms! He did ask me if he was going to die from eating these, but I assured him I had been eating them the whole hike. He might be one of the only hikers who just trusted me on this issue. He was like a little kid waiting for the Christmas cookies to come out of the oven. Jocelyn loves them too, and the smell as they cook is divine. I discovered I could make a version of crabcake out of coral mushrooms, bear's tooth, and lion's mane. We would just char the top and bottom of the mushroom cake using the olive oil, salt, pepper, and garlic. Olive oil, even just a tablespoon, has protein and promotes enzymes that help digestion. I carry quite a bit of olive oil, but I could see there was no way we were going to have enough if we kept doing these mushroom cakes.

I considered having to kill a possum for the grease if we were going to keep this up.

For the next few meals, I rationed the oil more strictly, and it turned out Turtle and Jocelyn had some olive oil too. I had researched mushrooms in Maine, so I knew I would have them to cook, and that let me pack a little less food. With the ton of rain they had, there were mushrooms everywhere to pick. It didn't even look like anyone was picking any either. They were all there, just waiting for us. I made sure to school Turtle on mushroom etiquette. You can't pick all of them; you have to leave some for the next guy. Again, keeping the pack as light as possible is the name of the game, and my mushroom habit usually helps.

Jocelyn and I are adamant about taking a bath every single day on the trail. This is not the norm for hikers, and your nose will inform you of this if you are ever around them. Even if it's just a wipe down, I can't go to bed dirty. I'm the best-smelling hiker out there, I'm pretty sure. Truly, there's water everywhere, and it's not terribly cold. Okay, it's cold, but you can get clean without freezing to death, so why wouldn't you do that? On our first night after the mushroom feast with Turtle, we swam in a little lake. It had been made by beavers and had a grassy floor. When you surfaced, you came up like a sea monster with grass on your head. Jocey didn't appreciate the grass wrapping around her legs, but we lingered in there, sitting in about a foot of water just talking. It was at the base of a hill with another hill in the distance. Everything else was so flat.

The 100-Mile Wilderness is so desolate and beautiful, but Castaway was on our minds. We were probably somewhere near where she had become separated from her tent and gotten lost. Thinking about her 17-day ordeal was sobering. Near our tent was a hemlock, and I imagined her curling up underneath it, desperate and hungry, clutching the water bottle.

We started the second day early, beating Turtle out of camp, and we put in 12 miles this day. It was the same as the first day with mud and river crossings. This was new for us. All the other states had bridges, but Maine does not. Most crossings are knee to hip-deep, but it's fast water. It's flat, so it doesn't seem like it should be a strong current, but it is. In some places, the beavers have things dammed up, and you have to walk around the ponds that they make. Then, you're basically bushwhacking through pure mud. You can't see the white blazes, and you have to make sure you get back on track. It sounds rough, but it's fine. You get used to being muddy. In fact, the stream crossings become a good way to get the mud out of your shoes. Of course, as soon as you get out and go a hundred yards, they are all muddy again.

The mud creates other complications too. I strained a groin muscle by slipping several times on logs that had the bark on top shaved off or were moss covered and slimy. Just a regular step that kicks out awkwardly can do the damage too.

But I am content here, in Maine, in this vast wilderness. The massive mountains don't start right away, but I was soon to discover them. They aren't thousands of feet high like the Rockies. They are only a couple of a hundred feet above sea level. When I think of this desolate area, so far from any civilization or any help, I am humbled. When I was a kid, all I wanted to be was a mountain man, and here I am. The humility is restorative, and I can feel the change in me, a healing. I feel at peace with myself, and a calmness. I don't know if they make the words that I would need to describe exactly what this feels like, a homecoming, a centering. A profound serenity overtakes me in this place.

We come to a stunning lake. The sun glitters off the tiny waves. The velvety trees come right up to its edge down a steep bank. The woods are clear here, not like the rest of the trail. You can see through the trees. A small stream runs right into the lake where I stand. The verse in Romans says, and it's true: *For since the creation of the world, God's invisible qualities—his eternal power and divine nature—have been clearly seen, being understood from what has been made, so that people are without excuse* (1:20 NIV). In this absolutely perfect and picturesque place, I can feel the presence of God, so close, so real. The sun sets right over the lake, fiery colors blend and shift, touching the edges of clouds and igniting them. All of those colors then swim together over the glassy surface of the water, and I am a witness to it all. My photo of this lake trumps all the beautiful pictures I have ever taken. Usually, photos leave me a little disappointed, so small and contained compared to what it felt like to be there, seeing God in the mountains and the trees. This photo stands alone as a pure, captured moment that is actually accurate.

I think, *Sam is going to love this one.*

Sam Harding is my father-in-law. He had gritted his teeth behind his fossilized jowls, lying on the sofa without a shirt on the first time I came to pick up Sandy for an "official" date. Which is to say, we didn't have to sneak around anymore. I knew I was supposed to look him in the eye and shake hands, so I did that. It took a while but finally he put out his hand. I awkwardly waited for Sandy to appear so we could go out to the movies, trying not to collapse with my weak legs. Years later, he became less scary, and possibly less formidable, though my respect for him has endured. Truly, we have become friends. Man, can he tell a story! My son and I would go hunting with him. So often I really didn't care if we got anything. The pleasure was all in hearing his stories, the details, the suspense, and always the satisfying ending. My kids loved him, and I loved him. Sam also loved me like I was his own son and was terrified of the dangers the trail would present for me.

"I'll be dead before you get back," he told me. Now, Sam's been telling us he's going to die for the last fifty years. All of his uncles died at 52, and he figured he'd go too. But he didn't. It became a running joke in the family: *Yup, it's over. I'm gonna die*, we would say, mimicking his deadpan delivery. We were all sure this guy was going to cheat death forever. But sadly, even this gem of a man could not. I was safely back and off the trail before he passed just at the beginning of 2024. Before I left for the trail though, I promised Sam some great pictures. He loved hunting, but he loved the woods even more, and I wanted him to be able to feel like he was in the wilderness with me. So for him, and for a woman named Diane Derr, I did all I could to get the best photos of all the sights.

Diane Derr had sent me a message on Facebook saying *I have always wanted to do the trail, but I'm too old and buggered up to do it. So I am living it through you Steven Wright!* How many others were there like her? I thought of all the people who would not be able to do what I was about to, and the weight of being able to gift them with my experience brought tears to my eyes.

These two people, Diane and Sam, are the reason I climbed over 75 trees, just like I had climbed the one with James in Providence all those years ago, to get the very best shots. I got pictures that nobody has ever taken before, and that's a fact. Other people were able to capture the same view maybe, but I got a totally new perspective from 20 or 30 feet off the ground. I was never just taking a picture, I was on a mission to deliver the trail and all its beauty to Sam and Diane, and anyone who could not do this trail. I wanted them to see God in the trail, the Creator at His finest, like I did. These things moved me, and made me who I am. I wanted to share that. That photo of the lake was so vivid it made me cry. I'm a passionate man, I guess.

Sam had my photos on a digital player that displayed them in a shuffled pattern. But, the family edited them, so that none of the ones which might alarm him were included. Now, I had one picture with five bears that I had seen all together, and Sam told everybody that I killed the bears and ate them to survive!

If I could be even one one-hundredth of the man he thought I was, I'd be Superman.

Sam's mind failed him a bit at the end, but I enjoyed his inventive retelling. Even when people tried to correct him about my encounter with the bears, he would stubbornly ignore them. In fact, he would augment the story. By the time he was done I had killed the bears with my bare hands.

Well, I didn't kill any bears with my bare hands, but maybe next time, Sam.

I believe everything that did happen, though, was for a reason. I believe that on and off the trail, nothing is an accident or trivial. Even that sunset at the lake was maybe a gift to me from God for a good reason. I treasured it accordingly. Instead of worrying about getting on with my hike, I sat there for a long time just contemplating my life. Jocelyn and I both became quiet and let our thoughts run.

Now at this point on the trail, I am not convinced that God is good, entirely. I thought He had been cruel to allow Sandy's torment at her death. When our family fell apart in Rhode Island and we all endured life-scarring experiences in Providence, I was convinced God could not be real, as you read before. At least I had grown past that denial. And, as I had battled back from the norovirus and COVID, I had been able to clearly identify my enemy. But Sandy's death nagged and nagged at my faith, fueling my anger toward God back into flame again. The mind amazes me. Just when you think you have things figured out, when you think you have God figured out, something happens to put you right back on the seesaw of faith and doubt. My mind kept toying with the old doubts again. How could God have allowed such a death for my beautiful, loving wife? He certainly could not be a personal God. He couldn't care about us, at all. Maybe He was masterminding the overall picture, but there was apparently zero concern for us peons down here.

I looked at the dramatic display of His power and might in this sunset and was suddenly so sorry that I had ever lost faith. I was so sorry for all the times I indulged myself in anger and hated Him. In this sunset, I could only see love, love pure and simple. Forgiveness. Healing for our shredded hearts. The tears came again, and I thought Sandy would have loved seeing this. Without a word, Jocelyn hugged me, and cried with me.

Some moments shared with your children are immortal, capturing the poignant emotions and encapsulating them in memory to be revisited later again and again.

I was a lucky man, a lucky man to have adored a woman who adored me in return. Together we had built a life and built a family, and the beauty of it rang like a bell. That bell was called gratitude. That bell can ring for all of us, can't it? When the right moment inspires it?

When the colors faded, and there was nothing left but the dark water of the lake, we headed back to our sleeping bags, physically and emotionally emptied out. A blessed man, tucked into the hand of God, I slept.

We woke early to a beautiful sunrise. Instead of leaping out of bed in the dark, I just rested, soaking in all that I had seen and felt, before seeing the sun come up in its own splendor. Jocelyn and I ate and discussed the sunset together, processing what we had felt. Jocelyn had her grief as well to work through, and the sunset had made her think about how she missed her mother. She missed her brother. One of her happiest times was when we had all hiked Fraconia Notch in New Hampshire together as a family.

We are still hiking with Turtle and Pup, but they beat us out of camp this morning because Turtle just eats his usual 39g protein bar. He joins us to wolf down a cup of coffee and then takes off, but Jocelyn and I aren't far behind. We catch up at lunchtime. At this point Turtle announces that we are going to stick together for the rest of the day and pick mushrooms for supper. As per usual, I make it clear that he is going to be carrying them. He is happy to oblige. Again, he ends up with a sack full, and I think *Oh man, this is going to be another blow out mushroom night.*

Turtle is a man who gets very excited about eating supper, probably because aside from some jerky, it's the only "real" food that he eats. He is on fire. We made the "crab" cakes that I described before out of coral mushrooms. The crispy dark brown outer layer was the perfect counter-texture for the savory and tender mushrooms inside. Olive oil is the key! We made a full cake, the size of the whole pan and about three-quarters of an inch thick for each of us. It became one of my favorite meals on the whole trail. The forest just overflowed with mushrooms. The only down side to our mushroom feasts was that our packs weren't getting any lighter. If you don't eat it, you have to carry it, and my pack was pretty damn heavy. Just to make myself feel better, I ate a couple scoops of peanut butter.

After we ate, we jumped in a lake to clean up, then crawled into our sleeping bags to fall fast asleep. We expected an all-day downpour the next day, starting around 10:00. Turtle's plan was to get going early and try to get to a shelter before it got too bad. When Jocelyn and I got up at 5:00, Turtle was already out of there.

For now, there's no sign of storms, and we have a good start. By 9:30, however, it's a complete washout. Creeks are rising at an alarming rate, and the trail is a mud bath. It's raining so hard that these big ass drops of rain bounce back up, about four or five inches back into the air. After several hours of slow hiking in this, we finally get to the shelter, just praying there is room for us.

There really isn't. The shelter is pretty much standing room only. Setting the tent up is out of the question, and we are soaked through. Apparently, there is a spot for tents and hammocks about 300 yards away, and luckily most of the group is traveling with hammocks. I think for sure they will just abandon the hammocks, but they didn't really have all you would need for a shelter night. They have sleeping pads, but not ones that are really designed for ground sleeping. Also, lucky for Jocelyn and me, Turtle had got there first and saved us two spots. I'm not normally a fan of the shelters, because of the mice traipsing over your body all night. But on this night, I will be pretty glad to be dry. We hang out there for the rest of the day. After the hammock folks leave, I actually have room to string up three different clotheslines and hang out our wet gear. Some of the hikers in the shelter with us are just finishing up, so we have a nice afternoon hearing their stories. One of them, Possum, is actually someone I had hiked with way back when I had started the trail. He remembered me, because we met the day after everyone else had quit in the cold, about three days into the hike. Possum was as old as I was and had 100 percent gray hair. By now he is able to entertain me with his experience from the miles he had hiked to get here. He is flip-flopping, like me. He has been off the trail too, for three weeks, healing up shin splints. I do not know the percentage of people that get shin splints on the trail, but a lot of hikers complain about them. You aren't done completely if you get them, but they do take a while to heal.

"I didn't think I could do this," Possum said. "I thought I was too old, but here I am."

Here he was! That much closer to his goal.

Even though we were stuck in a shelter all day, the stories and conversations made it enjoyable. Turtle made sure Jocelyn got included in the conversations, introducing her as "Tag-Along," the trail name that I had coined for her. He loved telling everyone that she was a professional ballet dancer. "She's the first one I've ever met!" he bragged.

Then everyone wanted to know what it was like to be a professional ballerina. And Jocelyn got to be the hit of the show on this day. I thought, *Shut your mouth, Steven, she is having a good time! Let her be in the spotlight.*

Jocelyn, oddly enough considering her profession, doesn't like being the center of attention. I love it. I'm loud, but Jocelyn is quiet. She watches, listens, and takes it all in. I like to brag about everything. Her words are more carefully measured. She doesn't brag about anything, even though there is so much to brag about! That petite little frame has been up on roofs with me working, and we've done church steeples together. She's strong, agile, and has great balance, which is good for dance, but also great on a roof! I taught her how to do slate roofs, which not many roofers will tackle. The hikers are asking her what it was like to be a roofing ballerina, and I'm just beaming with pride. The little girl with the brown pony tail has grown up to be so capable, caring, and wise beyond her years.

Our children have the best parts of Sandy and me. Watching them become who they are, as any parent knows, is the greatest joy. I'm so lucky they both love hiking! Hiking has become a glue in our relationship, a center touchstone that we all can come back to. We did some beach vacations of course, and the oceans are lovely, but the mountains will always draw me.

Jocelyn has rescued her body from ballet now. She was having ankle issues, and she came home to be with Sandy and me at the end. I wondered whether she would be ready to tackle the 100-Mile Wilderness, but she has just been at an instructional retreat for yoga, and it prepared her well for the hike. I love seeing her full of new inspiration and physically strong. She knows how to breathe, and her expertise has helped me over and over again. She helped me breathe in pain, and to breathe when I couldn't sleep. It's more of a secret weapon than you can imagine. She was a huge part in getting me through my hike, in both practical and emotional ways. My son Tristan was too, as you'll see a little farther down the trail. His knowledge as a physical therapist will again make it possible for me to adapt my hiking to accommodate an injury. The three of us were a team on this trail, and I could not have done it without them.

CHAPTER 24:

JOUSTER DOWN (THE SHOULDER INCIDENT)

It's September 3. Jocelyn, Turtle and Pup, and I decide to take our lunch by this beautiful stream that is full of salmon and trout. A fisherman is at work, and he catches several just as we are sitting there watching him. The water rushes by, in a big hurry after yesterday's rain, running fast and deep. The sky is blue, and the whole world seems crisp and clean again. There is a rock that slants into the stream, and I slide down it just for the thrill of splashing into the ice-cold water. Then I slide down a small waterfall on a rock that is polished smooth like glass, just like a waterslide. When my head ducks under, I lose my breath in the cold and come up sputtering happily.

With a good lunch and a little bit of mischief under my belt, it's time to get going again. We have to leapfrog from stone to stone to get across the stream and regain the trail. Wearing a pack makes this trickier, because your balance is off. With my cap on low to deflect the bright sun, I'm leading the way. I'm two hops away from the shore when I don't see the log.

Sticking out from the shore, just out of view above the brim of my hat, is the butt of a log about six feet up. I'm putting some umph into my final leap, going airborne with full confidence, when the log end pummels my left shoulder, knocking me into the water like a losing jouster. This is the same side where I had torn my rotator cuff back in February, and that injury has plagued me the whole trip. But I've never had an actual dislocation before, and the feeling is strange and deeply painful.

I land in deep water, which is again moving fast. It takes me immediately downstream for several yards. I'm taking on water, coughing and yelling in pain at the same time. I can't get my footing, twisting and turning with the eddies and trying to stay vertical. My shoulder is in agony.

Finally I do get a foot down, and another, and I'm up against a rock but I can't haul myself out. Turtle grabs me like a rag doll, pulls me out by my pack.

I lie on the rock. We are both panting, and my shoulder screams again that it isn't right.

"Turtle," I say in between breaths, "you gotta put it back in." His mouth moves, but he doesn't respond. Jocelyn looks on with dread. I can see she thinks this must be the end. But I know how to put it back in. I've seen it done to my buddy in the hospital once. "Just pull on my hand, and it will go back in," I tell Jocelyn. With my eyes, I try to seem confident. My daughter doesn't want to hurt me, and it can't be a timid pull. "Turtle," I turn back to him, "you gotta pull on my arm."

"Man, I'm afraid I'm gonna hurt you." This mountain of a man is suddenly shy and awkward. Admittedly disappointed in both of them, and desperate to end the pain, I bend over and pin my hand under my foot. Jocelyn and Turtle look on in horror. What choice do I have? I jerk my torso up in one forceful motion.

It fails. Stabs of pain ripple through me from the shoulder outward like electric shock waves. Bright lights stab into my eyeballs and somehow I stay conscious. My fingers slipped out when I pulled, and they are bleeding all over the place. I don't even notice them. This pain in my shoulder must end. I will do anything. I step on my hand again and jerk back even harder.

No luck. As before, the blinding pain shoots through me, and I am essentially delirious. Again, the fingers slipped out. Somehow, I heave myself back up and bend over to try again, so absolutely desperate to make it stop. I pin my hand deep under my foot, making sure my fingers won't slip out no matter what. I grit my teeth and make sure the fingers are absolutely crushed under my wet boot. I growl and give it all I've got.

With a watery pop, the ball is back in its socket, and instantly relief floods my system. The pain is gone. Jocelyn's huge eyes are staring in a mix of fear and disbelief, and the tears make streaks down her face. Turtle's mouth hangs open, and he's completely frozen in place. Even Pup gives me his whole attention. We all look at each other.

"I got it," I tell them, and then immediately vomit over the rock and into the stream. They come closer to check me out. But to tell you the truth, that was really the end of it. I literally felt fine, except for my bloodied knuckles. Now obviously, we are all worried that it could come back out again. I'm assuring Jocelyn that I'm okay, but her brain is having trouble accepting what she has just seen. We decide to just rest a little bit, and I keep telling her I'm okay, and I breathe just like Jocelyn has taught me. I'm actually in a good mood, thinking, *Wow, that really hurt like nothing before, but it's over, thank God!* Jocelyn's mood does not match mine.

"Jocey," I chuckle, "you gotta breathe." She chuckles weakly in return but rolls her eyes and then punches me in my good arm.

"Don't do it again," she advises. "You scared me to death." God, she looks like Sandy sometimes.

"You just hit a hurt man!" While it's nothing compared to the initial agony, the shoulder has started to throb, and it will continue to bother me to the end of the hike.

"DON'T do it again," she says and there is no chuckling. "I can't take it."

I assure her that I definitely have no desire to repeat any of it.

"If you do it again, I'm going to punch the shit out you," says Turtle.

"I didn't do it on purpose," I protest. We slowly settle ourselves down. But even as we rest there, a tiny thought sneaks in, *Geeze, what else can happen?*

Turns out, plenty is the answer to that question. It's better not to ask.

Off we go. The pack is uncomfortable, but bearable. It's not too long before we catch up to the people we were hiking with. We are on a timeline here, and I'm buzzing with relief that I can still hike after the shoulder incident. That's what I'm calling it now, *the shoulder incident*. Even Jocelyn seems to have recovered, and we are all tripping along. I do not hike with my stick in my left hand for a few days, just really trying to baby my shoulder. When I get to a spot with reception (even this is a miracle; it's the first place I've had any at all during this leg of the trail, and I won't have it again for several more days), I call Tristan to get some advice on how to hike with my newest injury. Thank God he answers his phone. He actually recommends using both sticks again, so I don't create an imbalance and screw up my back in the process. He advises me not to put any weight on the stick, and to make sure I don't put it out in front of my body as I move. He assures me that it will heal. But when we get to our resting spot tonight, I need to take a few of the pain meds, and then use the medical CBD cream on the shoulder. I typically use it on my shoulder anyway, because of the rotator cuff, but now I really need to lather it on. And he was right, my back hurts. I could have tweaked it during the fall as well. Talking to Tristan is so comforting, and he promises that I can't have done any more damage than was already done in the rotator cuff.

I am a lucky man to have these two kids who know what the hell is going on, because I would be completely lost without them!

"Please try to be careful and not hurt yourself again," says Tristan. I cannot imagine why everyone feels the need to say this to me. "You'll be fine," he says. "But you've got to just listen to me and just do what I say."

So, now the roles are reversed, eh? I am the child and they are the parents. Tell me when the hell that happened?

I'm not at all disheartened by *the shoulder incident*. I figure, it's that asshole Satan trying to discourage me any way he can. I'm trusting God now, and we are moving *onward, friend*. I might not be the greatest Christian, but at least I know who the enemy is. I can see his dirty bloody hand in every obstacle that comes my way.

The three of us (plus Pup) are pretty much hiking together all day. I'm mostly silent, watching the trail unwind under my feet, and just thanking God that I'm still okay to keep hiking, and cursing the enemy.

"What the hell are you saying back there?" asks Turtle. Apparently, the thoughts running in my head were audible. "It sounds like you're having one hell of a conversation with yourself."

"Yeah, I'm giving Satan hell," I say. "This guy's a real asshole."

"Yeah, he's been after me too," says Turtle.

Turtle continues by telling me some stories about his own life. "Sometimes," he says, "you get so discouraged you can't see up."

I think, *That's pretty accurate.* You can't see anything but darkness, and the darkness encompasses you. You wonder how you can even get into a state of depression like this, but you know, it's not something that happens overnight. It takes a little time, a little beating down of a soul over and over until the defenses are worn away. Then the lies come. They get fed into the system bit by bit and you believe them. Then, when you finally do try to look around, everything is dark. You think, *How the hell did I get here?*

"I think I'm insane, Turtle," I tell him. My voice makes it clear I'm not joking. "I think I lost my mind a few years ago, when I got depressed." After Sandy's death, I had stopped taking a medication I was not supposed to stop, and it changed me. I was having real nightmares of Sandy dying again, and I knew it was the drug. I just stopped taking them. I didn't even take the lid off, I just flushed the whole bottle down the toilet. I don't think I'll ever be the same. The Steven Wright of the past is dead, spiritually and mentally. After that, I tried to act like I was a great Christian, trusting God, but I wasn't. I really wasn't at all. Blinded by grief, I couldn't see anything but a wall of self-pity. And I let myself get that way, I truly did. I didn't want God's comfort, just like a child who is too pissed off at his parent to accept the hug that would make it all better. In a way, I was content in my grief. I guess that's what happened. I describe all this to Turtle, and add the disclaimer, "But like I said, I'm insane."

He chuckles. "Yep. Camel, you are one f----d up dude. But I love ya, and so does Pup."

I look behind, and Jocelyn is shaking her head again. I guess sometimes, it's a guy thing. Turtle and I both know that his chuckle really means, *It's okay. I'm f----d up too.*

We get to the camping site. I cannot wait to take the ibuprofen, because my shoulder is letting me know it had a rough day. I jump in the creek to take a cold swim before heading to bed. I'll have to crouch down to let the cold water run over my shoulders. The cold takes my breath away and instantly numbs my limbs, but I know I have to stand it as long as I can because it will really help my recovery. I last about 30 seconds before leaping out with my teeth chattering. I know that isn't long enough. I force myself to get back in, quick before my body can protest on its own, and I duck my head under. Instantly my head cramps into a headache in the cold. I think, *C'mon Steve, every second you're in here the swelling is going down.* I make it to the five-minute mark before leaping out. Jocelyn jumps in for her nightly bath, and lets out a yell.

"Why didn't you warn me!" she accuses. She stays in there for about thirty seconds.

My shoulder pain is actually cut in half though, whether from the cold or from numbness, I don't know, but it feels so much better. I apply the salve all over both shoulders and my back. I also take a tincture of medical marijuana under my tongue to help me sleep, which I've done for a few years now. I don't actually even feel like eating tonight, because I'm just exhausted from hiking in pain. Pain takes it out of me more than hiking, and I am wiped.

Jocelyn cooks, and I go to lie down. I eat lying down and don't even finish my meal. Pain in general in my back and my shoulder would plague me pretty much for the whole rest of the trip. Surprisingly though, the yoga breathing really helped me cope, and again I have Jocelyn to thank for that. Without that control, I don't know if I could have continued the trail. But here I am. *Take that, Satan, you asshole, I ain't quittin'.*

I sleep like a champ. No interruptions. No midnight pee break. I wake up feeling amazing. Even Jocelyn now seems convinced I really am okay. All day she talks about how she had thought I was going to be out for the count.

"Yep," chimes in Turtle, "Camel, I thought I was gonna have to put you down."

"I would've let you do it too, if I couldn't have gotten my shoulder back in," I tell him.

CHAPTER 25:

KATAHDIN

On day seven, we got an early start. They only let a certain number of people up Katahdin at a time. There were 14 of us, but today was special. As we expected, on this day the indigenous people are there to perform their annual celebration of dancing and prayer at sunrise. We would see them during our ascent, in little groups together. They wore their traditional clothing, and they had been on the mountain long before we were to say their prayers. We would see them at the top too, which is more like a little plateau, instead of just one pointy peak. We always gave these clusters of worshipers a wide berth, trying to respect their space and their ownership of this beautiful mountain.

We register at the ranger station in the Katahdin campground, and the ranger gives us the whole spiel about the best way to summit the mountain. We decide to use Hunt Trail to go up, and then come back down using Abol Trail, into the campground there. After that, we will catch a lift to Monson, Maine, where we will regroup at Shaw's, and take another zero.

The day that everyone who does the Appalachian Trail dreams about is finally here for Jocelyn and me. The day is stunning, at least at the bottom. We've been warned that the weather can change instantly, violently. What might start as a sunny day can turn freezing cold with hurricane-force winds. You can't spend the night on Katahdin, so everyone in camp is up at 4:30 a.m. to get going. You have to be back down by 4:30 in the afternoon, because that's when the last shuttle will take you back to Monson. It takes us a little longer than we like to get out of camp. But we are excited, and the day seems perfect. We have a nice breakfast and a couple of cups of coffee with Turtle and Pup, and we're off.

Daylight is coming, and it isn't long before we get our first view of Katahdin, and the rocky but lush landscape all around with huge timber. You're in the trees for the first mile. They are tall, thick conifers that stand like wise old friends as you walk by. And then, you are suddenly above the tree line. The mountain is not as high as Mt. Washington in New Hampshire, probably nearly 1,000 feet less. But, it's east of Mt. Washington, which is the reason for the nasty weather. It juts up out of nowhere. You are literally on flat terrain, and then suddenly this rocky volcano pops up. Whether you're from the east coast or the west, this mountain will stun you with its raw beauty.

Once we officially clear the tree line, the views are everywhere we look. Gazing up, the trail is just littered with massive boulders the size of Volkswagens and even houses. They are stacked one on top of another. It's hard to control your speed, because you want to fly up this thing. The mountain humbles you, though, because there are treacherous places with steep drop offs. The trail is well marked. There are no trees and no path. You are just crawling on your hands and knees up and down and over these boulders. There are painted white blazes on the rocks which mark the trail.

Jocelyn and I reach our first plateau. We survey the view in awe. In a crazy way, I think, this is like a desert, only everything is green and flat, with the occasional lake dotting the plains in the distance.

We hike on for another half hour and come to another plateau. Again, the view is spectacular, and we can even see the descending side of the hill as we make a right turn.

We are hiking up on a ridge, like the tip of a rooftop, with the ground sweeping away on each side, up, up, becoming a mountain on our left and right. It's not terribly steep, and our footing is good, but it's still challenging. We probably go for a mile on this ridge. Finally, we start up again, and we can see the top of Katahdin.

We've caught up with Turtle and Pup, and it feels good for us to be doing this together, after all we've been through since our start in the 100-Mile Wilderness. Pup will make history with us today as the oldest and only dog to hike the Appalachian Trail twice. And yes, because the boulders are so high, Turtle is practically carrying Pup on his huge shoulders up this whole mountain. Turtle makes it look easy, even over the water crossings. But I can see the sacrifice in it, too, the way that a man will do whatever hard thing he has to for something he loves ... or someone.

We have maybe a quarter of a mile to go.

This whole day has been sunny and clear, but here comes the cloud. On the Appalachian Trail, it never fails. So much for the views. We are actually inside the cloud. As we get to the summit, Jocelyn tells me to walk ahead, so she can film me making it to the top. There is a wooden sign there, and everyone gets a shot of themselves at the sign. When I get there, I am just as emotional as if I am finishing the whole trail. I know in reality I am not even half way through the whole trail, but I still feel a tremendous joy at being here. Hikers, some that I had started with in Georgia, are celebrating, jumping up and down, and laughter rings out against the rock. I feel like I have completed the whole trail with them, even though I am only at about 1,000 miles. I climb the sign itself and strike a victory pose for Jocelyn to take my picture. This is one of the dreams I've had my whole life, to stand on this exact sign, on this mountain, and raise my sticks. I never dreamed I would be doing it at 64, but hey, better late than never.

Then she and I take some pictures together. We are finally here. Together. As we smile for pictures, I can only think of how proud I am of her, and how lucky we are to be here. Jocelyn truly wanted me to do this hike as much as I did for myself. I know her prayers for me were said often and in earnest. I think she knew there was healing on this trail, and our moment here together at the top of Katahdin is a waypoint, a benchmark, on this journey of healing. My sunglasses hide my happy tears.

"Well, Dad, you did it," she says, and she wraps her arms around me.

The complete cloud cover has not dissipated, though, and we have to leave. The next hikers are right behind us. Knife's Edge is our descent, and it can be sketchy. It has some sheer ridges, where the drop off on each side is steep, and most people crawl across on all fours. We have maybe a mile until we get to this part. I wanted to give Turtle a hand with Pup, but he declined. They had gone 2,200 miles together, and he wanted it just to be the two of them for the last mile as well. I think I might have made the same choice.

All the while we are hiking, the occasional cloud goes by, but we are so high up that we are in the cloud as it passes. The skies are clear and sunny, but then in the cloud it is practically drizzling.

After Knife's Edge, we pick up Abol, which is a new trail down the rest of the mountain. I'm not sure why, but this trail is new, and it doesn't count toward your 2,200 miles. Abol is steep, and I start to think that maybe our other choice might have been better. But, the ranger had advised us to go this way, and here we are. I felt bad for Turtle. He carried Pup down the entire way because it was so steep, taking Pup off his shoulders occasionally while they worked together to get down. We made it down in plenty of time for us to catch the shuttle back to Monson. In fact, we waited almost 40 minutes, still feeling pretty high from our hike. When the shuttle came, we piled in and headed back to Shaw's.

That night, back at Shaw's, I scrolled through the pictures. I had been in pain the whole time, but the victory had been worth it. The finish line seemed possible now. Picture after picture became a brick in the wall of my self-esteem. I could do this. I would do this. Yes, hiking with the pain would suck, but I was on a mission that was greater than just finishing the Appalachian Trail. My mission was to be healed, and I wanted it so badly. I wanted to feel like myself again, to feel happy. That day on Katahdin, I had a moment of happiness that I could draw on like a well to get me through the rest of it. Turned out, I would have to draw on it much sooner than I thought.

CHAPTER 26:

BIGELOWS AND BROKEN BONES

It's official now, I'm heading south. I had to go north through the 100-Mile Wilderness and Katahdin so that I could do those before they close in October, but now I'm ready to head south and close the gap to where I left the trail in Virginia. Poet drops Jocelyn and me off at the trailhead, wishing us well. We will miss Turtle and Pup. Turtle says he is done with the trail forever now.

"I'm gonna sell the goddamn tent," he told me, "so I never have to look at it again." He is completely over hiking, and he's done with mud.

We'll see about that. He probably said that the first time he finished the AT too.

As for me, I'm sky high and ready to go, and still so happy to have Jocelyn with me, my Tag-Along. We crank the miles off today. There's no getting out of the mud, though, no matter how long it's been since the last rain. It's so flat that the water just lies there. We cover about 17 miles. In Maine, I'll take 17 any day.

The whole time we pass more northbound hikers that I recognize from March. They have made it all the way up here and are headed for the 100-Mile Wilderness and their big finish at Katahdin. It's so much fun to check in with them. Every time I turned around there is a new person heading in to the last leg. You know how they compare pictures of the presidents taken before and after their terms in office, and you can see the wear and tear? The hikers look like this, all so different from when they started. They are all 20 pounds lighter, or even more (one guy lost 65 pounds), unshaven, and beat up like boxers at the end of a fight. I ran into Witch Doctor, in fact. Out of all the guys in his group, three had made it and were coming up behind him. I crossed paths with them that same day. I introduced them all to Jocelyn—she had heard all the stories. Each guy in that group had gotten some kind of injury that pulled them off the trail to heal for a bit: shin splints, pulled muscles, etc.

Mud-covered, Jocelyn and I end our day at a lake with a lovely sandy access way into the water, perfect for our nightly bath. We spend the next two days like every other day, talking and moving well under sunny skies. I've dialed back on the mushrooms. I think we are mushroomed-out after our feasts with Turtle, and I'm not sure I've ever said that in my whole life. But I did find six different varieties that make a pretty combination of colors in the pan, orange, white, black, and even a deep red, and some lobster mushrooms which add more orange. It almost looked more like a fruit salad than a bowl full of mushrooms.

We also did the Kennebec River crossing, which must be by canoe, and you have to time your arrival to match the canoe ferry times. This water crossing is actually a dam release, and authorities will fine you if you try to cross it on foot. It looks like a foot crossing would be possible, but because the water at Kennebec can instantly rise two feet all at once if they do a dam release, hikers can get caught. The water moves with great force then, and some hikers have been killed trying it on foot.

Jocelyn's time with me is almost over. She needs to go get her car, drop it off where we will end up, and then she will take an Uber to meet me at our destination for the night, Harrison's Pierce Pond Camp. There are no bridges, so it's really out of her way. I'm only hiking about six miles to get to Harrison's, but there's really no way around it for her. I have to get across another river in the meantime. I get a lovely ride across from a guy and his dog. The dog spends all day in the canoe with the owner, just ferrying hikers across. I jump out of the canoe, hug the guy, pet the dog, and I am back to the trail.

Tim, the guy who owns the cabins at Harrison's, is known to have really good breakfasts, and I am not going to miss a good breakfast. We had heard that this guy cooks for people on Thursday, Friday, and Saturday. He's been doing it for 38 years. It definitely is a hassle to get to his place, but it is a beautiful rustic home which is surrounded by rustic cabins that Tim built. All the buildings overlook a trout stream, are heated with a wood burner, and have no electricity or plumbing. You have to hike way back in, and you have to make a reservation months in advance for the gourmet dinner package. We are just going to try to stay in one of his cabins without the gourmet dinner.

I get there first, a good hour before Jocelyn does. There are four waterfalls on the way there, and I can clearly see the trout swimming in them. Everyone has said this is a sportsman's paradise, excellent for bear hunting, etc. Tim confirms he can feed us and has room for us. I grab a shower in the main building. Even if he doesn't have a room, a hiker can always stay at Pierce's Pond, which is a shelter about three-tenths of a mile from this place. Then you could just hike back for breakfast. Nobody did that when I was there, because the traffic on the trail is definitely slowing as the season ends.

That night, Tim did have a gourmet dinner planned for his guests who had reservations. But, if he has any left over, his policy is to offer it to the hikers who are staying. A free gourmet meal?

Sign me up! Jocelyn and I ate roast beef and salmon, a beautiful salad, roasted asparagus with sea salt, a hiker's dream. We found out that Tim had lost his son in the military. Normally he does not talk about it, but after hearing that I lost my wife, he did open up a little bit.

"I know how you feel, buddy," he said. And even as the first word left his mouth, the tears sprang out of his eyes. Some wounds never stop hurting.

"You don't have to talk about it," I told him. I took a breath. "Let's talk about something fun." And we did. We talked about the trophy trout he had up on the wall.

Jocelyn and I visited with the guests who were there with reservations and went to bed with our stomachs full, anticipating our 12-pancake breakfast the next day.

Tim gets up pre-dawn to cook, knowing that hikers want to get on the trail early. I didn't set my alarm and overslept. Maybe I was in a food coma. The pancakes were all that we were promised, and we ate our fill.

They are calling for some rain the next couple of days, and it might really put her down starting around three. Right now the sun is shining, our stomachs are full, and we are ready to go, trying to get in as many miles as we can before the rain starts. We get in 14 miles before we come to the shelter. The rain is just beginning, not as hard as what they predicted. We had one eye on a hurricane brewing, but with limited reception, we couldn't stay glued to watching its progress. We heard updates from other people, though, and it sounded like it might come up the coast at some point and impact us. We figure that's three days in the future, and we should be in Stratton, Maine, by then. As we spend the night in the shelter, a bad thunderstorm rumbles over us, dropping plenty of rain and whipping the trees around, but it passes.

The next day, with our gear packed and ready to go, Jocelyn and I look at each other and sigh. More mud. Well, here we go again.

We had had six dry days in a row, so maybe it won't be so bad?

It is bad. We wade through standing water continuously, with a quagmire beneath. We get into the lake area and are literally leap-frogging again in the rain, rock to rock over deep mud. Jocelyn is leading the way and makes a left-footed leap forward onto the next rock, which is slimed, just like all the rest.

Her foot doesn't stick. It slides forward while her back foot stays where it is. She goes off into a full split which tests the limits of her ballet training for sure, and then into mud that is at least hip deep. She keeps sinking more and more, looking up at me and trying to move her hips and legs to free herself. I was able to pull her out by the armpit.

"I've pulled a groin," she tells me. I can't tell if she's more mad or in pain. I look down at her one foot, which for some reason has no shoe on it. We look at each other with a silent, Oh no. The shoe is still in there somewhere. I fish around for it, poking and reaching with my hand while trying to stay out of the mushiest parts. Next, I actually wade around in the mud, and I feel the trail sneaker with my foot. I am up to my chin in mud, virtually swimming and pushing the shoe ahead until finally it breaks the surface and I can get it in my hand.

Now, how about the groin pull?

"I can do it," she says. I recognize the determination in her eyes. Even as a little girl, once Jocelyn set her mind to something, she would do it. They don't take wimps in ballerina school, you know.

"Okay," I say. "Let's see how it goes."

She's able to hike, but she's hurting, I can tell. Of course she does not complain, but I can see it in her gait and the occasional wince. She also has stopped chatting, and that's a sure sign she's pissed. We get around the lake, and we are in the area they call the Little

Bigelow. We are grouped with some young folks heading south on a two-week trip, not thru-hiking. They are all in great shape and headed for New Hampshire. I'm in the lead, and we aren't yet in any high elevation. We pick our way down a mud-covered rock slope. Behind me I hear Jocelyn yell.

I turn to see her sprawled at the bottom of the rock, cradling her elbow. She had landed on it with her full weight, and it was already bruising. Again, she will not say a word, but I can tell it's a painful bruise, and it bothers her as we continue on. She refuses to talk about it, brushing off my inquiries with an artificially light voice, so I start to wonder if it might be worse than I thought at first. She's keeping up, but now I've got her on my mind with every step.

Alone again, at a shelter for our lunch, I ask one more time. "Are you okay?"

"No," she finally confesses. There is a spring here, so we decide to take a couple of minutes and clean off and rest. She's able to lie down by the spring and get her elbow in the ice-cold water. We recuperate there for about an hour and a half. Finally, she downs an ibuprofen, and at her urging, we are off again.

In the rain. In the mud. We keep plugging away up the Little Bigelow and down the other side. The Big Bigelow will be tomorrow.

That night Jocelyn is still hurting and the injury is keeping her from sleeping on her back the way she normally does.

The next day is more rain. We put on our muddy wet socks, our muddy wet shoes, our wet raincoats, and start out, thinking we have two days to do this before the hurricane. But the rain is a torrential downpour. Maybe this *is* the hurricane? But there is no wind yet. The trail is just more miserable the farther we go, and we are not making any time at all in the mud. We just keep going.

But then the wind does pick up. I can't hear a thing with the wind and rain beating on my hoodie, so I'm not talking either. We get through the day with only about 12 miles in. We pull into a shelter and decide to spend the night there. There is a quick break in the rain, but the forecast is calling for more downpours, so we don't get our hopes up. We are both hoping for a fire, first to save our fuel cannisters, and second for the morale lift. A fire can make you feel so much better. We start gathering wood, and I drag some larger pieces back to camp where I can break them up smaller. My usual strategy is to plant one end between two trees growing parallel to each other and then push until I break it. Everybody knows this trick.

Just as one of my big branches is about to snap, in walks a hiker we had met before. His wife broke her leg on the trail. They were in their 50s, and she fell in the Smokies somewhere, not long after I fell. He was still hiking, though, without her. He sat with us at our shelter, and we complained together about the rain and mud, and the prospect of two more days of it, and a hurricane after that.

I went back to breaking firewood. One piece was about four to five inches in diameter, too large to snap in the pair of trees. I put it across the fire ring and was going to break it that way. There was a large rock in the middle, and I thought it would precipitate the break. So, I lifted the log like it was an axe and slammed it down on the fire ring. It did not break. Instead, it ricocheted back with equal force and caught me right between the eyes.

I did not completely go unconscious, but all time ceased. I was stunned with my head vibrating like they do in the cartoons. I knew my nose had been the target, and I also didn't want Jocelyn to see that I got hurt again. So I started moving slowly again, trying to maintain the fiction.

But our visitor rats me out. "I think your dad busted his nose," he says to Jocelyn. With her back to us, she just laughs at his joke.

I'm stumbling and dizzy, but am still trying to get more wood. *If I keep on moving, she'll never know,* I tell myself.

Finally she walks around to where she can see my face. I watch all the shades of shock, then panic, then worry cross her face. "Your nose is crooked!" she exclaims. And by now it is bleeding all over the place. Without a word, I keep pulling more wood, completely encompassed in my stupor. "DAD," she says. "Put that down! You're hurt bad."

By now my senses are returning. Indeed, I suspect my nose is broken. "Can you straighten it?" I ask her.

"I can't do that," she says with exasperation. "And there's a HOLE in your nose."

A hole? Apparently a splinter had impaled the skin above my nose and come out the other side. We finally sit, and she uses her phone in selfie mode, so I can see the damage as she runs the video. I can't breathe out of it like this, so I want to get it straight. I first pinched my nose like I was going underwater and tried to straighten it, but that didn't work. Next, I put a hand on both sides and try to sandwich the cartilage between my palms. I moved it too far and had to readjust it. I finally got it back to center.

It feels like it clicks back in place, but now it really starts to bleed. I have massive-sized bandages with me, so I put one on my face, under my nose.

I decide not to eat. The nausea is on its way. I lie down with my head back, take a couple of ibuprofens, and try to get the bleeding to stop. I am not a back sleeper because it hurts my shoulder. A few times during the night, I tried to roll over and put my cheek on my arm, but I couldn't do it. My whole face hurt.

With just a few hours of sleep, Jocelyn and I beat our friend out of camp. You guessed it. It's raining again. My head is still throbbing. The throbs begin at my nose and then come wave after wave over the rest of my face and my skull. After sleeping all night on my shoulder, it is acting up too, refusing to support my weight on the stick, and protesting against the weight of the pack. But we are in the Bigelow Mountain Range now, and we have to get out before the hurricane arrives. We need a big day today, 17 miles. That's a lot in the mud of Maine, with a face full of throbbing pain. Indeed, this turns out to be the hardest hiking day of my entire life.

The Bigelows are a huge granite outcropping with a steep slope on the right, and a huge drop off on the left side of where you walk. You have to watch yourself here. Because it's now practically monsoon conditions, I take one misaligned step and my foot slips off to the left.

I try to catch myself with my left arm. It can't catch anything, let alone my body weight. I tumble over, crashing against rocks and underbrush. I'm trying to protect my face, cradling my head in my arms, but my left shoulder hits a log and pops out of joint again.

"What the hell!" I am pissed. There are people hiking with us, my shit is everywhere, and now my shoulder is out again. *Why is this happening?* I get up, and move around to gather my stuff. I'm able to kind of twirl the shoulder, and like magic, it pops back in. Relief floods me. I won't have to crush my hand in order to put it back in this time. But the shoulder is pissed too, and starts throbbing with pain.

Jocelyn thought I smashed my face off of the rock. Luckily my face-shield had worked and I just bumped my chin. I also jammed a finger on my right hand, but I didn't think I broke it. I was right. After a month it was better, and that doesn't happen if you break them. If you break them, they stay screwed up forever. I don't actually break a finger until later on in the hike.

So there I am, with a buggered up left arm and no hand function on my right arm. Even better, I'm going to put in 17 miles today if we don't want to sleep in a hurricane.

When I put the backpack back on, I can tell there's something else going on in there— besides the obvious, of course. It feels like there's a big knob sticking up on top. *Oh God, I broke my collar-*

bone too? Jocelyn and the others are helping me get my pack on, and I feel terrible for taking their time. They are in the same boat we are, trying to get out of here before the hurricane. They get me going again, but the pain is just overtaking me with every step. My backpack is pulling on whatever bone is sticking up, and it is excruciating. I decided to put my sticks away and use my hands to hold my sternum strap away from my left shoulder as I walk. I'm more aggravated every hour that goes by.

At 11 miles, we come to a shelter.

"Dad," Jocelyn says, "we can just sit this hurricane out right here." Her eyes are wide with concern again. The drops of rain stick to the wisps of hair that peek out from around her hood. "I'm afraid you're going to hurt yourself."

I look at her face, and I look at the woods. The black trees are endless in all directions, jutting out of the quagmire of the trail and dripping with the godforsaken rain. "I just want to get out of the woods," I tell her. The two of us limp along then, her nursing her elbow and groin, and me with my bashed-in face and non-functioning shoulder. I feel like everyone in the group has some kind of injury by this point. Everyone has a slip-and-fall story and a limp to go with it.

I cannot control my attitude at this point. I'm being a pain in the ass to everyone, and my mind is roiling. *If my collarbone is broken, I'm done.* But I can't let Satan win. I don't know how, but I can't let him win. I start praying and that calms me down, a little. But it doesn't slow me down. I'm hiking way too fast for Jocelyn and her pulled muscle, mean as a polecat, and what's worse – I'm tempted not to care. But I don't want to hurt her, and that hitches in my gait a bit. I just want to get out of here. I'm so over it all.

Finally, around six at night, we get down off the mountain. We are close to Stratton, and the shuttle driver Jenn comes to get us. Jenn and her friend (another Jenn, two owners, same name) own the Maine Roadhouse Hostel. Relief and gratitude wash over us all when she pulls up in the small bus-type vehicle. Jenn takes one look at me and wants to take me to the hospital. Which, if I broke my collarbone, was probably a good idea. But she had other pick-ups, and didn't even know if she could get me there tomorrow.

I begged her just for a shower, and asked if we could stay at her hostel. She promised they would make room for us. I swear I would have cried like a baby if she had turned us away. The two lovely Jenns took good care of Jocelyn and me, and we stay for five days. The hurricane hits the day after we got off the trail, and dumps inches and inches of rain on the town and the trail. We spend the time sleeping through all of it in nice warm beds, eating hot food, taking hot showers, nursing our injuries, and trying to remember how fun hiking is supposed to be.

CHAPTER 27:

HURRICANE III

In the shower, I could see the big brush burn on the injured shoulder. Upon additional inspection, I found I tore my Arc'teryx rain jacket, which is worth more than I am. I patched it up pretty well; neither of us is giving up at this point. With my sanity returned, I apologize a dozen times to Jocelyn for hiking too fast to get out of the Bigelows. I'm deliriously happy to be at the hostel, and not in the woods for this hurricane. Three is way too many. How does anyone finish this trail in hurricanes? I came to find out later that this year did break records in terms of rainfall on the Appalachian Trail. And, it had the highest number of thru-hike failures. While we were at the Roadhouse Hostel, I ran into some of the hikers that had started in March, the Blue-Haired Hiker and some others, who were also waiting out the hurricane. One girl was hiking alone with her dog, and she had met a young man on the trail. They ended up hiking together the rest of the trip, and I remain in touch with them. As always, the trail bonds complete strangers for life. You understand exactly what the other person has accomplished, and you're cheering each other on, as well as mourning when someone cannot finish.

It occurs to me that this might be the end of hiking for a while for me if my collarbone is broken, and that means I might not be hiking with my daughter much more. She takes this in stride, because her groin and elbow injuries are not healing quickly either. It's actually fun to be sitting out this hurricane here in Stratton and not out in the mud. Jocelyn agrees. I won't get to the hospital to find out the facts until after the hurricane passes.

We are not staying in the main hostel here. Jenn and Jenn own two buildings, one hotel inside Stratton, and one hostel out of town. We are at the downtown hotel. Stratton has a nice restaurant and a lovely bar that overlooks a lake.

At this bar, I settle in to eat a nice burger and start a conversation with the waitress. Or rather, I looked like hell, and she asked me what happened. She was skinny with dark hair, and had librarian glasses on. I tell her the whole story, including my fundraising for my wife.

"How is your wife doing?" she asked.

"She died," I answered. "She had triple negative breast cancer."

The waitress steps back from the bar, her face like a stone wall as the seconds pass. "I have triple negative breast cancer," she says.

My heart ached for her, and I wished I'd never said a word. She was young, maybe 45. My story about Sandy certainly couldn't offer her any optimism. "My wife's story doesn't have to be your story," I told her. "I'm trying to raise money for research," I continued, grasping at the only straw I could find. "I hear they've made great progress fighting this disease."

She told me that she had been clean for five years, and I assured her that five years meant that she had made it.

"Well, that's what I'm praying," she said.

"I will pray for you," I told her. I prayed for her right there. And I still pray for her every day. I hoped I didn't scare her too much, but I was so glad God had decided we should meet.

I continue to pray for the other women fighting this cancer too. They are so scared. I look at this cancer as a demon instead of a mere disease. It's a pawn of Satan, f-----g with us and discouraging us, hurting us in any possible way it can. Every time I let myself think about this disease, my blood just boils. And I put the blame right on Satan, where it should be. He is a liar, a cheater, a deceiver of the brethren, a lion in sheep's clothing. He is the reason why everyone who has been born, except for three people, have had to face death. He is a cheating son of a bitch. Sorry I can't control my language thinking about him. He took away someone very precious, and he tortured her. I'm glad the Bible has been written, if for no other reason than I can see the end of this dickhead. He burns in hell forever.

Okay. Enough of that asshole.

As I leave the restaurant, I stop just outside the door. I put my left hand on the post by me, and speak aloud one more prayer for the waitress. *Dear God, help this young lady to live. She walks by this post every day, and every time she does, Lord, help her to feel this prayer. Be with her. Watch over her. Protect her. Grant her peace. Don't let her feel any anxiety about this f-----g cancer coming back. I lift her up to you. Please let her live. Please don't take her away from her children. Let her live. Don't let her think about my wife dying, just let her be glad she has made it this far. Please bind Satan's hands, tie them so he can't move in this woman's life.* I continue on, then finally end with *Amen*.

I open my eyes and a guy stands there, looking at me. Neither of us speak, but he gently and firmly moves me out of the way. The whole time I had been blocking the door. Nobody in, and nobody out, while I prayed. The guy was just holding people back, waiting till I was good and done to restart the traffic. Oops.

No one said anything as they passed me. Some patted me on the shoulder. They could see my tears and acted with respect. Finally one guy says, "Man, you were passionate in that prayer." He looks conspiratorially at me out of the corner of his eye. "But I've never heard anybody swear in a prayer before." He chuckles. "But I could see, whoever you were praying for, you had great passion." A beat of silence passes. "Were you praying for my friend? The bartender?"

"Yes, I was," I confess.

"How do you know her?"

"I don't," I admit. "But she has the same cancer that my wife had, and my wife died, and I just don't want her to die."

"I don't think she will," he assures me. "She's in remission."

I told him I knew that, and I was happy to hear it. "I just wanted to make sure I got my two cents in to God on the subject," I said. I also let him know I had wanted God to intervene so that the waitress wouldn't be anxious about hearing my wife had died. We talked for quite a while outside that door.

"Everybody loves her," he told me. He thanked me for praying for her. He patted me again on the shoulder and nodded. I nodded in return, and he walked away.

Back at the hotel Jocelyn was working for the owners, making beds or doing other tasks while we stayed. After my shoulder feels a little better, I am able to work there a day as well. At first I was going to work on a chicken coop for them, but the other guy with supplies never showed up. Instead, I hung blinds and put blankets over beds, etc. We ended up sharing our story with Jenn and Jenn, letting them know we are trying to raise funds for Sloan Kettering. They decided to comp our whole stay, including our meals, for the whole five days we were there. They were an incredible blessing.

The hurricane passed and the following day the Jenn who preferred bib overalls gave us a ride to the hospital a couple of hours away.

"Welp, you're all buggered up, buddy," was the doctor's professional conclusion. "Kind of like you were in a car wreck."

"That's what it feels like," I agreed.

"Your shoulder is in rough shape," he said. "Why don't you go home, rest up, and do this trail again next year."

"Can't do it, friend," I told him. "Just teach me how to get my pack on with it like it is." I had brought my pack, specifically anticipating this conversation. I knew people would not understand that I felt committed because God had told me I should do the trail. That was okay. From this guy, I just needed to know how to get my pack on. I had separated my clavicle, and that was the bone sticking up.

"Can't you fix it?" I asked.

"Well, no," he said. "I can push it down so it doesn't hurt as much." Then he reached over and shoved down on the bone with the thumbs of both his hands. Ow.

Then it popped back up again, but not as bad this time.

"What are you going to do about your torn rotator cuffs?" he asked. "And your shoulder being dislocated? You know it's just going to keep happening."

"Yeah," I agreed. "That's why I'm here."

Seeing I wasn't going to budge, he said, "Okay, but you aren't going to be able to do this without somebody to help you." He knew Jocelyn was about to head home, and he didn't know how to get around needing a second set of hands. He helped me put on my pack, and we stood there thinking about the situation.

"What if I cut my sternum strap?"

"Well, that could work." As they were, the shoulder straps were right on the bone. I needed them to be in closer.

I had my knife with me, and I sliced through the sternum strap, and then pinched the ends together. That avoided the clavicle bump. It felt better.

"Just look for a stump or something, so you can slide into it," he said. "Then once you get it on, try to keep it on. Don't keep taking it on and off, because that's what's going to hurt you." Made sense.

He could see I was dead set on finishing. "You hikers are a different breed, aren't you?" he concluded.

I agreed wholeheartedly.

He wished me luck, recommended a few more days off, and told me I had done a good job with my nose.

I thanked him, and we shook hands.

SECTION IV
SOBO (SOUTHBOUND) -ISH

For our light affliction, which is but for a moment, is working for us a far more exceeding and eternal weight of glory.
2 Corinthians 4:17 (NKJV)

CHAPTER 28:

BYE-BYE TAG-ALONG

Jocelyn had heard the whole exchange. The doctor's allowance for me to continue made her feel better about my finishing. I can't hike with my sticks for at least a couple of weeks, and that will be tough because I know I've got a lot of elevation coming up. Soon I will be entering the White Mountains, which actually start in Maine, and many people don't realize it. Western Maine is brutal. But if I could make it through the Bigelows, then I could handle the Whites too.

Jocelyn's departure is tomorrow, and I'm emotional thinking about the time we've had together. I'll be brokenhearted to see her go, but I'm deeply grateful to have spent this last month together on the trail. I'm so proud of her, proud of us. The poor thing is still sore in both places, and she definitely is done on the trail. She hates to leave, I know, but it turns out this injury would plague her for another month to come.

Jocelyn's husband, Tommy, was hiking the Pacific Crest at the same time—believe it or not. He had started his hike a month before I did and was also hiking to raise funds for breast cancer awareness. Jocelyn's plan was to go join him, but she could not. That broke my heart. I had prayed they could do this together, just as Sandy and

I had always wanted to. In the end, Tommy hiked over 1,000 miles and raised $500 for cancer through LinkedIn. He is a tremendous young man, and I couldn't be more proud and more grateful that my daughter has someone to treasure like him.

The next day, our last day, I try to do everything I can to help my body heal. I use Epsom salts in a tub for the fifth day straight. I figure, this is as good as I'm going to get. Jocelyn is going to give me a ride to the trailhead, a decent number of miles away. We say goodbye to Jenn and Jenn, who want a picture. I cringe and protest, knowing my face still looks like a pizza.

Jenn (bib overalls Jenn) says, "Nah, I want you just the way you are. You look tough as hell!" She gives me a big hug with a smooch on the end. That's it for me! I turn into a Steve puddle in her arms.

"You're in trouble now," says Jocelyn, beaming.

Joycelyn and I grin for the shot. They snap the shutter and tell me to put our Polaroid picture on their famous pole that features hikers from years before. The only open spot was down by the bottom, but Jenn's not having that. She moves it up to eye level so everyone can see it. "That's better," she says. "That's where you'll stay."

So Jocelyn and I made it onto the famous pole. We say goodbye.

"You can quit smiling now, Dad," says Jocelyn. But I can't wipe the shit-eatin' grin off my face because I just got a hug and a kiss from a pretty girl. Shoulder? Clavicle? Nose? I can't feel any pain at all. A hug and a kiss are good for 500 miles, I always say. It's time to start hiking!

It's tough to say goodbye.

Jocelyn and I have been through hell together, seen waterfalls and sunsets together, counted on each other, wept together, laughed together, and eaten great food together. These memories I'll keep for a lifetime. All day long I thank God for my incredible daughter, who now has her own taste of the Appalachian Trail. I watch her drive away. The fall leaves are just starting to sprinkle down and

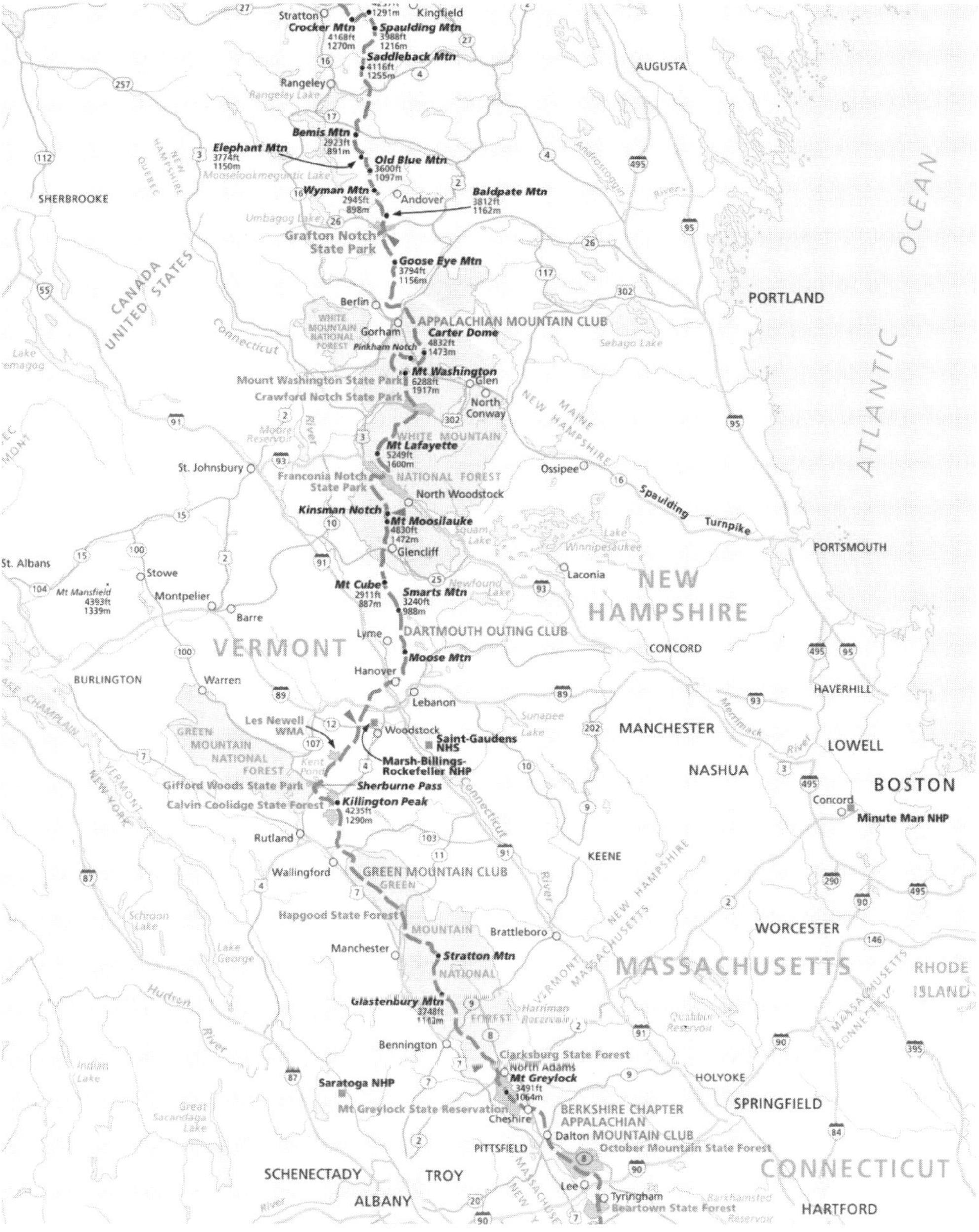
Stratton
Kingfield
1291m
Crocker Mtn
4168ft
1270m
Spaulding Mtn
3988ft
1216m
Saddleback Mtn
4116ft
1255m
AUGUSTA
Rangeley
Rangeley Lake
Bemis Mtn
2923ft
891m
Elephant Mtn
3774ft
1150m
Old Blue Mtn
3600ft
1097m
Mooselookmeguntic Lake
NEW HAMPSHIRE
QUEBEC
Androscoggin
River
Wyman Mtn
2945ft
898m
Andover
Baldpate Mtn
3812ft
1162m
SHERBROOKE
Umbagog Lake
Grafton Notch
State Park
Goose Eye Mtn
3794ft
1156m
OCEAN
CANADA
UNITED STATES
PORTLAND
Berlin
WHITE MOUNTAIN NATIONAL FOREST
Gorham
APPALACHIAN MOUNTAIN CLUB
Carter Dome
4832ft
1473m
Pinkham Notch
Connecticut
Sebago Lake
Lake Memphremagog
Mt Washington
6288ft
1917m
Mount Washington State Park
Glen
Crawford Notch State Park
North Conway
MAINE
NEW HAMPSHIRE
ATLANTIC
Moore Reservoir
River
WHITE MOUNTAIN
Mt Lafayette
5249ft
1600m
St. Johnsbury
Ossipee
Franconia Notch
State Park
NATIONAL FOREST
North Woodstock
Spaulding
Turnpike
Kinsman Notch
Mt Moosilauke
4830ft
1472m
Squam Lake
Lake Winnipesaukee
PORTSMOUTH
St. Albans
Glencliff
Stowe
Mt Mansfield
4393ft
1339m
Mt Cube
2911ft
887m
Newfound Lake
Laconia
NEW
Montpelier
Smarts Mtn
3240ft
988m
Barre
HAMPSHIRE
Lyme
DARTMOUTH OUTING CLUB
VERMONT
CONCORD
Moose Mtn
BURLINGTON
Warren
Hanover
LAKE CHAMPLAIN
Lebanon
HAVERHILL
Sunapee Lake
Les Newell
WMA
Woodstock
Saint-Gaudens
NHS
MANCHESTER
Merrimack
GREEN MOUNTAIN NATIONAL FOREST
Kent Pond
Marsh-Billings-
Rockefeller NHP
River
LOWELL
NASHUA
VERMONT
NEW YORK
Gifford Woods State Park
Sherburne Pass
Connecticut
BOSTON
Concord
Calvin Coolidge State Forest
Killington Peak
4235ft
1290m
Minute Man NHP
Rutland
River
KEENE
Wallingford
GREEN MOUNTAIN CLUB
GREEN
NEW HAMPSHIRE
Schroon Lake
MASSACHUSETTS
Hapgood State Forest
MOUNTAIN
Brattleboro
WORCESTER
Lake George
Manchester
Stratton Mtn
NATIONAL
VERMONT
MASSACHUSETTS
RHODE ISLAND
Hudson
Glastenbury Mtn
3748ft
1143m
FOREST
Harriman Reservoir
Quabbin Reservoir
River
MASSACHUSETTS
CONNECTICUT
Bennington
Indian Lake
Clarksburg State Forest
North Adams
HOLYOKE
Saratoga NHP
Mt Greylock
3491ft
1064m
Great Sacandaga Lake
Mt Greylock State Reservation
BERKSHIRE CHAPTER
APPALACHIAN
Cheshire
SPRINGFIELD
Dalton
MOUNTAIN CLUB
PITTSFIELD
October Mountain State Forest
SCHENECTADY
TROY
CONNECTICUT
Lee
Tyringham
Barkhamsted Reservoir
River
ALBANY
Beartown State Forest
HARTFORD

a bright orange one stands out. It is fragile but strong at the same time, drifting its way to the grass.

At the trailhead, some guys from the hostel are right behind me. I had become friends with them there, but I would never see them again after today. They go right, and I go left, southbound. I'm hoping I cross paths with more people from May when I busted my foot. I'll probably also run into people from June when I had norovirus and COVID.

I'm moving well. I'm feeling good actually, no pain still. I guess the hug and kiss are still working their magic. The skies are clear and sunny, and the White Mountains are before me. The rain is supposed to happen, but I think it will pass by. I'm taking on elevation all day, up and up. I end up with another 17-mile day. That feels like a huge win.

No falls. No broken nose. No diarrhea. What a day.

Except for putting my pack on and taking it off, there's been relatively no pain either. I keep forgetting about my busted nose, which is now running all day in the colder weather. Every time I go to wipe it, it takes about half a second to remember it doesn't want to be touched. I camp alone tonight, feeling the absence of Tag-Along like holes in Swiss cheese. I tell myself I'd better get used to it. The north bounders won't be around much longer.

I run into another young couple. The guy had been part of the group of marines. He broke away from the marines and bumped into another young lady who was about two days ahead of them. They stayed together then for the rest of the hike. They planned to summit Katahdin together. I love the romance stories! Every time I heard about a couple that the trail had brought together, I thought of Sandy's words about finding my next love. My book might be better if I had a romance story to put in it, but it must not be time yet for me to find love again.

CHAPTER 29:

SADDLEBACK AND MAHOOSUC NOTCH X3

It was a calm peaceful night, and I'm off again early the next morning. I pass some tents in the woods, and I have been hiking since five with hardly any pain. I pause at a vista, and the tent people arrive there too. Then the young couple arrives, and I passed them again back and forth because we were both putting in 18-mile days. A few days pass where I don't bump into them, but I'll get to them again into Vermont.

I'm now in at Saddleback Mountain. I camp a beautiful night about halfway up the mountain. When I get to the top of the mountain the next morning, the weather takes a turn. While it isn't precipitating, there is so much moisture in the air that everything is white with frost. It's still September, but it's a different world at 4,200 feet. I had been a little chilly the night before, but this frost convinces me it's time to exchange my summer sleeping bag for my warm winter one. I'm downright cold. I have no pants. I had long ago shed my rain paints, and I don't have any extra shorts. My pack will never be lighter than it is right now. It weighs in at just a few ounces below 15 pounds. This is a depressing thought since I'll be piling in the winter gear and it will just get heavier from here on out.

Luckily, I have some cell reception, and I can check in with Jocelyn and make arrangements to get my warmer gear sent to me through Tristan. With his new job in Boston, he can join me for some of these sections in New England. I can't wait. Just as I treasured the time with Jocelyn, I know the time with Tristan will be irreplaceable too.

On the top of these high mountains, the swampy lowlands and torrential downpours of the 100-Mile Wilderness seem far behind me. The weather warms up too, so I put a hold on sending my warmer gear to Tristan. I won't carry the extra weight until I'm desperate. I'm even sick of carrying around my sticks in my pack. It seems so stupid to be carrying them around on damaged shoulders, even as light as they are.

But when I try using them the next day, it's no good. I've been wearing my clean pair of socks on my hands so they can function, but if the weather stays cold, my old frostbit hands won't be able to grip my sticks anyway. I have to pack them back up. The altered sternum strap seems to be working, though, and with the clear weather I'm able to do close to 20 miles a day. Mahoosuc Notch and New Hampshire are coming up.

The hiking isn't easy here; I'm in the White Mountains. About 15 miles of them are in Maine, and I can tell the terrain is changing. Like Katahdin and the Bigelows, these are massive mountains. This terrain is fun. I didn't miss my sticks too much, and I'm hoping I don't really need them at Mahoosuc.

Looking back, they would have been a pain in the ass.

Mahoosuc requires climbing over boulders and through spaces too small for you to wear your pack through. You're taking your pack on and off as you go. I'd heard as many as six times, just to get through rock crevices. With my shoulder messed up, and having to be careful about putting the pack on and off, it might be quite the adventure.

I get to Mahoosuc with about an hour till darkness. I know I can do it, even with my shoulders, and I am up for the challenge. As I take my first step into the boulders, I see an older guy coming toward me. Of course I want to chat with him. It turned out he had done the AT three times in his life, and he's closing in on 80 years old. His last thru-hike was in the 1980s. Now, this guy had actually hiked with Earl Shaffer, the author of the book *Walking with Spring* which had inspired me in high school, as well as the second guy to do the trail. It was like I had met someone who had hiked with royalty! I could hardly believe it. He told me he does the White Mountains every year, and it's his very favorite in the whole United States. Beyond that, this mile right here, in Mahoosuc Notch, is his favorite mile of all. It takes him a whole day to get through it, and he camps on both ends. He has done it every year since 1989. He is fascinating. I talk a long time with him, even though I know I am burning up valuable daylight. He actually is the one who cuts our conversation short.

"I didn't even look at the time!" he exclaims. "I'm sorry, young man!" He's calling me a young man. He has a little way to go before he can set up camp for himself. "You gotta go," he tells me. "You're gonna be finishing in the dark."

I fly up this rock scramble. Seven. It turned out to be seven times I had to get the pack off, over the clavicle, and then prop it up somewhere to get it back on. Then, I scaled boulders, again, the size of Volkswagens and houses, clambering and straining. It was all I had dreamed it would be. You're not really hiking, you're boulder scrambling.

Luckily, there are lots of places where I could rest my pack to get it back on, just like the doctor ordered. I really don't think anyone can do this stretch with their pack on, even a super light one. You have to just stuff it through ahead of you in some places. After 45 minutes, the boulders were behind me, and I had conquered Mahoosuc Notch like a pro. It takes some people all day! I go to fill up my water bottles and hydrate and discover that one is missing. *Oh my God, I think, now where did I manage to lose it?* Then I remembered taking it out while talking to the older gentleman, and I knew right where I had set it. While I was talking to him, I had taken a drink. I found out later I had accidently kicked my one water bottle off the rock. I only carry two now because, after all, my name is Camel.

No way was I going to be the first hiker on this trail to leave litter behind. I had to go get it. This section of the trail, and the trails in Maine, were some of the most pristine trails I hiked on. Everyone respects the wilderness. There is no graffiti, not one speck of litter. I couldn't ruin it.

Sigh.

I take my pack off and head back to get that bottle. It's almost dark now, and I am practically running through these boulders and slithering down the sides of them. Without my pack, I'm fast and light, with hardly a nod to my shoulder. Down is still slower, so that takes me about 50 minutes. I grab the dang bottle. Headlight on, I go right back the way I came.

In the darkness, it was a totally different scramble. I met some critters—a bear and some raccoons looking for crayfish in the stream. I also came across some permafrost down in the one stream. I had heard about it, but was shocked to actually see it, just a layer of frozen river underneath the stream. Apparently, the mountains on both sides of this stream caved in during an earthquake years and years ago during the Ice Age. So if you want some ice-cold water, headache water I call it, you can reach down and get some. When I had originally gotten to the top, there had been no water. I had both bottles with me, so I filled them now. When I finally got back to the top, it had taken me an hour and 15 minutes in the dark.

I was a little sweaty and wished I had dunked myself in that cold water. Now I probably wouldn't sleep well all stinky and dirty. I've already explained my feelings about this.

Well, I had dreamed about Mahoosuc Notch, and now I had hiked it three times. I might just be the luckiest guy on the trail. It was time for food and sleep.

CHAPTER 30:

SOUNDTRACK FOR FRACONIA NOTCH

I wake up after Mahoosuc Notch and feel great. My shoulder and clavicle don't hurt as badly as they did. I can't believe it's already been a few days since Jocelyn left, nearly 150 miles ago. I miss my Tag-Along.

My goal today is to get into New Hampshire. I'm walking a ridge trail, admiring the scenery on both sides. It made me feel like I shouldn't be there. I guess an earthquake hit this area at the turn of the century, and boulders were left perched precariously above the trail. Occasionally one does fall and takes out a bunch of trees. It was incredibly rugged. I kept wondering where I would run if one let loose.

I pass a guy, who stops me and asks, "Didn't I run into you in March?"

My face is still bruised and my eyes are both purple. I'm sure I look weathered and aged, just like every other hiker does. I don't recognize the guy.

"Look into my eyes," he tells me. "I've grown a hell of a beard."

Well, wouldn't you know it. "Is that Possum?" We had hiked together for three days in Georgia, and then met up again in the 100-Mile Wilderness. He was trying to finish up his flip-flop and still had to get through the Presidentials up in New Hampshire.

"Yup!" he says with a grin through the beard. "Camel, you look like shit. What the hell happened?"

I tell him the whole story, the short version. I tell him the worst injuries are ones he can't see.

He says, "It looks like your nose is still busted." I know what he means. It's taking a long time to heal. I ran out of bandages so I just quit putting them on it.

We sat down and decided to have lunch together. It was too early, 10:00 a.m., and not the greatest spot, but we wanted to catch up.

We finished lunch. I told him to stop by the Maine Roadhouse Hostel and say hi to Jenn and Jenn. Then we said goodbye. I don't know if Possum ever finished, but I heard that they did have a hard snow. I did not see his name in the books where they record the finishers. Anybody heading north at this time is going to run into a tough time. Now, I can't remember how Possum got his name. He was a hell of a good guy. And to tell the truth, he did look like a Possum with that beard.

As I expected, I'm running into fewer and fewer hikers. Even the number of south bounders is thinning out. Instead, I am running into people who are hiking the "48's in the 40's." Those are the 48 peaks over 4,000 feet, which is just in New Hampshire. People try to do this in one year, and I can imagine how tough it is. New Hampshire itself is tough. Some hikers rate New Hampshire as the toughest state on the trail. There isn't one easy mile in New Hampshire. The "Whites" are indeed white. They have snow on them early on, and they stay white long into spring. The Presidentials are nasty too, Mt. Washington and Fraconia Notch. The views are spectacularly rewarding though. Even if your view one day might be obscured by clouds, the next day you will get a good one.

As I was about to enter New Hampshire, I checked out the face of another hiker coming up the trail, and I saw something familiar. It was Moonshine! She was doing a flip-flop too. I first met Moonshine down in the Smoky Mountains and then had visited with her again at Shaw's. She had hit it off with Jocelyn over the sweater, as I mentioned.

"Hey," I yelled. "Where's your sweater at?"

She looked up and her face broke into a smile. "The 'Shrooming Camel!" she proclaimed. We chatted, and she seemed to be doing well. "I remember you like hugs," she said, and gave me one. Another hug to fuel my hike! We sat down and ate our lunch together.

I wished her luck as we parted.

"I think I might finish!" she called out, stepping brightly away with her poles clicking.

That girl did the whole trail alone. I saw several women alone on the trail, but 90 percent of them had dogs. Moonshine had assured me she had not had any incidents to report, and I was so glad of that.

When I entered New Hampshire, it was a good thing I had a trail angel waiting for me. His name was Blue. I had met Blue in May after my broken foot, but before I came down with the norovirus. I saw him again in the 100-Mile Wilderness. He told me that when I got to New Hampshire, I should give him a call. He promised me some trail magic and a nice steak dinner. Now that I am here, I am going to take him up on that, for sure.

I give Blue a call. He is in Buffalo, headed back to his home in Michigan, but puts a hold on that so he can provide a little trail magic for me. He literally turns the car around and drives back to New Hampshire, and we figure out where I can intersect with him on a road. Now, stay with me, because this gets confusing. There are three sections to come: the miles between Mahoosuc and Route 2; the section south of that which is called "The Presidentials" because it has mountains named for the presidents; and then another section south of that called Fraconia Notch. Right in the middle of all that is a town called Gorham, which has a campground.

Blue wants to do the top section with me, I am saving the Presidentials to do with Tristan, and I'm going to do Fraconia Notch by myself. I'm going to have Blue drive me all the way south to just below Fraconia Notch, and then I'm going to hike north. After that, Blue is going to give me a ride back to the campground at Gorham where we will spend the night. Then the two of us will go south again, from right below Mahoosuc where I left off. We will hike together all the way down to the start of the Presidentials, where I'm going to meet Tristan, and finish up the middle section.

That's the plan. I thought it was incredible that he would do that kind of running around for me.

He meets me at a road crossing and takes me all the way down to just below Fraconia Notch. From there I'm going to head north. Fraconia Notch means a lot to me, and to everyone in our family. I had been there twice before. It was one of the first spectacular views in my early hiking experiences, even though I had traveled widely out West and even in Alaska. It still remains a favorite to me today.

Making good on his offer, Blue bought me the steak dinner and two beers, and I'm looking forward to spending more time with him on the trail in a few days. When he drops me off at Fraconia, I go on to do the three big peaks by myself. It is just stunning. The whole time I'm hiking, I'm getting a lump in my throat. Sandy was here with me in July of 2014, and the kids were with us. It was the same year that her cancer appeared, though she was not diagnosed until September. We did the whole hike together that day, starting early in the morning and finishing after dark in the evening. It was a hell of a hike for anyone, let alone a woman with a hidden tumor festering inside her. I will just always remember being above the tree line and seeing all the trees and shrubs just ripped to shreds. We all kept remarking on each little beat-up tree and asking it, *What is your story?* Pretty soon even the little knarly trees disappear, and there's just bleak wilderness. You feel so small on a big, big mountain. The trip became one of the best memories of my whole life with her.

But today it is just me. I summit the first hill, then the second. The air is clear and sunny, and I can see for miles. It's October now, so the sun is warm. There is a cool edge to the air, and the leaves are awash with fiery colors from horizon to horizon. We do have spectacular fall colors where I am from in Pennsylvania, but they can't compare to the show that the leaves put on in New Hampshire. They stretch out like an orange-and-red sea, with the bald tops of the mountains poking through at intervals. I think, *Most thru-hikers don't get to see it like this,* and I feel lucky and blessed to be here.

In general, when you break through the tree line of a mountain, you're going to get one of two kinds of weather: sunny and hot, or cloudy and rainy. And, just because you get one, doesn't mean that a few seconds later you won't get its polar opposite. It can go from 80 degrees to 60 degrees in a second. Then you'll get a wind out of nowhere in that cloud.

I'm hiking out along the ridge with some music blasting in my earbuds. I'm listening to Crowder, a gritty Christian musician who looks like a mountain man even if he isn't really a hiker. He may be, I don't know. But his music gets me going, and his talent for hijacking all kinds of styles of music into his genre is unmistakable. His music, more than the music of any other artist, really spoke to me during my grief over losing Sandy. His lyrics are raw, and he's not afraid to use a little rap, a little overdrive, or even a little banjo, or a little foot stomping to get just the right sound.

I listen to "The Eye of the Storm" by Ryan Stevenson, a song all about knowing God is in control when we face tragedy. I also had some Lauren Daigle in my playlist. Her first and second albums were favorites for me. Her song "Rescue" spoke to me with authority. Katy Nichole's "In Jesus' Name" helped me so much. When I felt all alone, when I was scared, when I didn't think I would make it, when I got hurt, I would sing along with Katy, and imagine all the people praying for me. Even Zach Williams's "Rescue Story" is a powerful song that moves me. I've listened to Jenn Johnson's "The Goodness of God" on repeat on some days, and felt comfort, even when I could not accept the comfort of God. I mention them now, but they played on my earbuds often, and each song gave me its own little measure of solace. I imagined my family with me, and it strengthened me.

But Crowder? He can bring it.

Everybody in his band can bring it. They are as good and tight as any rock band I've listened to.

On the top of the mountain, Kari Jobe's "Revelation Song" came on. I took out my earbuds and let the song play as I videoed in a slow circle, looking at the panoramic view. Alone on the mountain, thinking of the wonder and power and mystery of Christ, I was humbled and in awe of it all. I was awed by the beauty of His creation, awed by how He loved me through all the shit I had been through, and all the shit I did against Him, and still somehow He loved me. Incredible. As the song played, and I turned in my circle, I saw people off in the distance making their way to me. The first guy had long hair with dreadlocks, and he was listening as he approached. I was still videoing, and the music was still playing:

> *Holy, holy, holy, is the Lord God Almighty, who was and is and is to come.*
>
> *With all creation I sing praise to the King of Kings,*
> *You are my everything, and I will adore you.*

The guy stops and stares. I keep making my slow circle. I think he wants to talk to me, but I'm not sure. Behind him is an older fellow and his wife. They stop too.

"Well," says the older guy, "I guess you're a Christian. That's just about the most perfect song I ever heard for on the top of this mountain." He and his wife both smile. "Keep playing it, buddy."

So I did. I didn't respond, just kept turning. Now the guy with dreadlocks is filming me.

After I finish, we talk, and he keeps filming.

He wants to be a professional photographer, and we have a great conversation. I still don't know if he was a Christian. I was nearly out of sight when he finally quit taping me.

I have three days to get to the Presidentials, and they are about 60 – 70 miles away, which means I need to put in 20-mile days. The forecast looks great, so I'm not too worried about that. The trails are clear. The hardest part will be descending the mountains, because that's just tough on my old knees. At least I was able to use my sticks at this point, thank God.

On the first day, I make 24 miles. I have hiked for an hour in the dark, and the night is clear, with stars peppering the night sky in abundance. I get to an abandoned, blown-down fire tower. Only the rocky nubs of the foundation poke up out of the mountain in a chest-high square. I decide to cowboy camp inside that foundation, and what a show the heavens have for me this night. A brilliant meteor shower lights up the sky. I see a bear up on top too, and I don't know why he isn't down by the water. Usually that's where you see them. This bear is poking around the foundation, and I finally yell to scare him off. After dinner, I look around for a tree to hang my pack on, and there just aren't any. It's okay. I have a scent-free bag. I put the pack inside it, wrapped it in about three more things, and then put it away. It might not work in grizzly country, but in the black bear area it will be fine.

My view of the sky is tremendous. With the foundation all around me, all the light which might get in from the side is blocked. With no competing light at all, the stars are all the more brilliant. The meteors leave their glowing streaks for seconds when they pass by. Have you ever done this? You can look up a chimney, and because it blocks out all side light, you can see the stars so brilliantly. Try it. I didn't want to miss a single shooting star, so I resisted sleep that night, just gazing at my own private show. I played music here too. I also kept filming video, trying to capture the star streaks, and I actually let the video run all night. In the morning, the phone was dead, and none of the images turned out anyway. At least it's clear in my memory.

A couple of raccoons visit me in the night, jumping down over the edge of the foundation in their masks like little cat burglars. I actually enjoyed the company. If the bear came back, he didn't wake me up. In the morning, I concluded that I should be in a great spot to get a spectacular sunrise picture. So, I take my time, eating and packing up, and keep watching the horizon. It does not disappoint. The soft peach colors wash over the wall until the whole place is bathed in warm yellows. I get my photo and begin to walk into it.

I can be there in two days no problem if I average 22 miles a day. Got it. The day will start with a long descent, and then a long upgrade will follow. The weather is still cooperating, and I make my 22 with no problem.

CHAPTER 31:

THE INTERVIEW

As I take off early the next morning from where I camped near a hostel, I spot a young girl wearing Lycra shorts and a nice backpack and coming toward me in a little hurry. Her face told me she was trying to catch me, so I paused. I thought maybe I had hiked with her or something. She seemed in good shape, like a hiker.

"Hey, can I talk to you a sec?" she yells to cover the 75 yards between us. She catches up closer. She had curly hair like Joanie on *Happy Days*. "Are you a thru-hiker?"

"Yeah, how'd you know?"

"Well, you handle yourself like one. I saw you leaving early, and"—she bit her lip before laying this on me—"I want to interview a thru-hiker." She continued, "I've always dreamed of doing this trail one day. Right now I'm doing the 48's at 40, and I'm three-quarters of the way done. Would you mind if I hike with you?"

"Not at all," I told her. The people are the trail, and the trail is the people. I love the people!

We take off together, up a steep incline, and she pumps me for information the entire time. Her name was Jill. Jill was a good hiker, and worked as a school teacher on the border between Vermont and

New Hampshire. She kept her pace up to mine with no trouble. She might have been the same age as Jocelyn, in her early 30s. I had to explain all my flip-flopping, ending with my plan to meet Tristan at the Presidentials and head back south again. Finally, we got around to Sandy, and my efforts to raise money for Sloan Kettering and triple negative breast cancer research. Jill had even more questions then, but let me know I didn't have to answer if it was too personal.

"It does me good to talk about it," I assured her, "so ask away."

She was very thorough in her quest for the details. She asked me about my trail name, and the camel and mushroom illustration on my bag. She didn't take any notes that I saw, but she certainly had my info. If Jill ever writes about it in her diary, or writes a book, I'll be in there as the crazy old hiker. We have a nice conversation the whole way and decide to have lunch together on an overlook. It had been a cold start, but by now the sun is warm on our rocky outcropping, and we dangle our feet over the edge. It is part of a ski slope. Like a couple of lizards, we soak up the sun. For the better part of an hour, we fill our stomachs, hydrate, and bullshit.

On our way down, my hiking shoe blows completely out. My foot is entirely out of the shoe. While most hikers carry duct tape, I don't. I use Zip tape. I also carry Shoe Goo, but you can't use that while you're wearing the shoe. That has to be for a repair that you're making on a day off so it has 24 hours to cure. I wrapped the Zip tape around and around the shoe, till it was secure again. But, because the bottom is covered in tape, there goes your tread. It's not bad on flat rocks, but if you need traction, you're in trouble. At this point in the hike, I have Zip tape on pretty much everything.

I have Jill hiking behind me, because I can't hear her questions the other way. Sometimes, I turn around to hear her better, and wind up stumbling over something I don't see. But it's worth it to have the company, and I love how young people are so enthusiastic and energetic. I'd be all alone soon enough. The longer we walk, the louder she speaks, because by now I've mentioned my hearing issues to her. The farther we go, the more it starts to feel like we are in a *Saturday Night Live* skit, but she is being really respectful, so I can't begrudge her the narrative.

She's peppering me with questions about Sandy. How long had we been married? How am I doing with it? What was her death like? I knew she wasn't trying to be nosey or unkind, so I answered. I wondered if she was trying to write an article.

Before we know it, it is dark. We find a spot to camp not too much farther down the trail. I had gotten all the miles I needed and then some. The next day would only be an 18-mile day to get to the rendezvous with Blue.

In the pre-dawn hours the next morning, the interview continues. "When did you first dream of doing the AT?" she asks. My response takes way too long, and we don't get out of camp as fast as I'm used to, not till around seven. That was okay. She offered to get me a ride to anywhere I needed to go, but I had Blue coming for me. We had flown over the trail that day and had not stopped for lunch. I was hoping Blue could get me into a town early enough so I could get a pair of replacement shoes. I also had Jocelyn send me my hiking boots, and I had made a call to her in hopes that they'd get to Gorham when I did.

Blue is there at the road, right on time, and I bid goodbye to Jill and wish her well. I got another hug from her then, and we went our separate ways. We did not keep in touch, actually, the way I did with so many others. I guess she got all her questions answered when we were together.

"A hug, huh?" Blue busted my ass the whole afternoon about that girl. "I leave you alone for one second and look what you do."

Blue was a marine and can put down the miles with no problem. He is also a diehard Michigan fan. Thus, every item in his wardrobe is blue (or yellow), and you guessed it, that's how he got his trail name.

Blue drives us back to Gorham where we spend the night and then get going right away in the morning. Blue is faster than I am, but he's been resting for a month. He's also been partying with some of the other finished hikers for the last few days while I was hiking. I think this is why he didn't want to join me right away down at Fraconia. We are joking and moving fast, having a great time.

At the end of the day, there was a place where we could stay, so we did. Our plan was to get up the next day and hike through to Gorham, where I was meeting Tristan. But when we woke up, Blue didn't seem quite right.

The month of complete rest had not prepared him for our hike yesterday, and Blue was hurting. He had a pulled groin that really constricted his mobility, and he was sore all over.

"Man, I hate to do it," he said, wagging his blue hat from side to side, "but I'm going to have to let you go on today. But when you get to Gorham, I'll give you a lift from the trail to the camping area." This is where Tristan would be meeting me to do the Presidentials.

I wished him and his groin muscle some good rest, then headed out alone. It was only 12 miles to the camping area, so I was there by one o'clock and done. I know that makes it sound "easy," but it isn't. You're still going up and down the "Whites" carrying a pack, but in the way of comparison, it wasn't so bad.

My taped-up shoe was looking a little worse for wear, and I started to think about replacing it. I got to my rendezvous spot with Blue really early, and was able to get a ride with a lady who was a lawyer in Boston. She gave me a ride for about 15 miles into town to get new shoes. I ended up getting a pair of Hoka high tops, knowing that the snow was coming. I loved them, but they did not last. I only got under 190 miles out of them. That means they cost over a dollar a day, and I just can't afford that. Jocelyn's husband Tommy loves them, and a lot of hikers wear them. They were very comfortable, I'll admit.

That lady from Boston hung around then, just to see if I needed anything else. On the trail, they say, "The trail provides." Well, it does, because the people do. She was ready to take me to Boston if need be, and we had a nice time visiting. She gave me a quick hug as she left, and wouldn't you know it, Blue was just pulling in to pick me up.

I had to hear another round of ribbing about me getting hugs from ladies on the trail. But in between wisecracks, we did get to eat another hearty dinner together as I waited for Tristan to arrive. For all his teasing, Blue just couldn't do enough trail magic for me. I was so grateful. A year and a half later, I got to do some trail magic for Blue in return. I met Blue and his cousin when they hiked from Harpers Ferry up to Pennsylvania. I just had to get them back to their car in Harpers Ferry. I was planning on buying them a good meal, but that rascal Blue ended up paying for my meal again. My trail magic is slightly less magical than his, I guess.

CHAPTER 32:

SUFFERING

Tristan is held up in traffic as I wait for him at the campground. It's a Friday, so the traffic can be nasty. He brings the boots from Jocelyn, but I had already bought the Hokas. And it was a good thing I did because – here's a fun fact – my feet started off as size eight in March but now, in October, I'm officially wearing a size ten. Some of that is extra toe-room for going downhill, but my feet definitely got bigger and stronger as I hiked. When Tristan showed up, the pair of boots Jocelyn sent with him were just too small.

They are forecasting bad weather for tomorrow, but not tonight, so instead of staying at the campground, we decide to just get going and get up the mountain a little way and camp there. So as soon as he gets there, he changes his clothes and organizes his pack, and we take off. He's brought some gear for me besides the boots, so I reorganize too. It's a little late in the day, and we plan on hiking an hour after it gets dark. That will put us a bit of the way up Mt. Washington before dark.

Tristan is 27 now, younger than Jocelyn. He started out as an angelic-looking little blond, but now he is a sturdy young man with the same boyish bright stare and close-lipped smile. He's a combination of Sandy and me, and his face doesn't show his emotions like Jocelyn's does. But he's loyal and fierce like she is, willing to stand up for what is right. One time he was up on a roof doing a job, and the client was in the yard, just screaming at his kids. I wasn't there, but a friend told me that Tristan climbed down off the roof, and went over to the guy to calm him down a bit. He was 18 at the time, and that father was a full-grown man. Tristan is quiet, but he will say what has to be said.

I've had both my kids up on roofs as soon as they were old enough to be safe. I think they both appreciate having those skills. One time Sandy, Tristan, and I (Jocelyn was away with dance) went on a mission trip where the goal was to do some construction. I was assigned to be a foreman, but not for Tristan's group. Turned out the guy who was Tristan's foreman didn't know as much as Tristan did about putting up scaffolding, and he literally turned that job (as well as some others) over to Tristan. His counselors were amazed at how capable he was for being so young and couldn't wait to share with me at the end of each day. I was so proud, and a little surprised too. Apparently, he had been paying closer attention than I thought. And that kid can handle a skid steer even better than I can. He can load it right up on the truck, and if it tips a little, he doesn't panic.

We take off up the mountain. Several hikers are ahead of us, all of them weekend hikers. Our plan is to cowboy camp under the clear skies at Osgood Tentsite and get an early start the next day. We want to bank some miles before the predicted rain in the afternoon. There are several tents around us already, maybe eight, and we chat with the other campers off and on. We eat, and then we lay our bags on the flattened tents, which we could spread out over a little wooden platform they had built at the site. These platforms were maybe 150 yards apart, so we still felt like we had some privacy. With no moon, the stars were out again, brilliant in the velvet black sky. A lot of the hikers were out of their tents gazing at the constellations. And again, the occasional shooting star would whoosh past, resulting in a gasp of delight from the two of us.

Tristan had an extra bounce in his step in the morning. I could tell he was happy to be out on the trail. He can't be more excited than me, though. I'm chattering away with him, so happy to get caught up and to be climbing these amazing mountains with him.

We blow through another camping area that has some hikers in it too. Looks like the mountain will be crowded today. But still, no one is stirring. We hike for an hour and a half and take a small break with a protein bar as a snack. As a college and high school athlete, Tristan has remained in excellent shape, and he's setting a blistering pace. We are pushing our speed as much as we can. There are antennas on this mountain, so it's easy to get reception and we keep checking the weather. Tristan is way more conscientious than I am. That kid will calculate each risk and weigh it against the reward before putting a plan together. Me, I'm more of a ready-fire-aim kind of guy, so I appreciate his careful and calculated approach. The stars are still out with just a sliver of moon as we start along the trail together. They would soon disappear into bright sunshine though, with zero humidity and warm temperatures. One by one the stars blink out, and day is upon us.

People are finally stirring as we pass through more camping areas, but they will be quite a while getting packed up and out of there. It's 6:15 a.m. and lovely to hike in a flannel shirt and a T-shirt underneath. I'm wearing my alpaca hoodie that I've mentioned a zillion times, and my smart wool T-shirt underneath that I've decorated with a sharpie marker. It says CANCER SUCKS. I wore these two things on the trail every day without exception. Even on the hottest, sweatiest days, these shirts don't smell, and that's a winning trait for me.

Hiking up, and fast, for another hour, we break the tree line. After another hour, we summit Mt. Madison. The view is incredible, with crystal clear skies. Obviously, the weather man had it wrong, and I couldn't be more glad. I really didn't want it to be shitty weather for him like it had been for his sister. I bet we've taken 50 pictures already of this awesome view.

Now we have a descent, and find ourselves at a water source. We again chug a good liter of water and stow about 16 ounces each on our packs. We stuff in another protein bar, some cashews, and a little beef jerky, and then we begin the climb to Mt. Adams, the second Presidential. We are dreaming of the hot dogs promised in the visitor's center at the top of Mt. Washington, which we should reach by late afternoon. Who knew hot dogs could be so motivating? We are still crushing it with our pace. There's always a special kind of magic when both hikers can go at the same pace, and no one feels like he is slowing the other guy down. Tristan and I are perfectly matched this way.

Mt. Adams delivers another stunning vista with panoramic views. I thought they would be so similar, but they weren't. This mountain is a little higher, so the views are all different and even more breathtaking. You're looking down on Madison, but up at the Presidentials to come. Would it be like this for each new mountain? I couldn't wait to find out. We take another 10-minute break for, you guessed it, a protein bar, cashews, and beef jerky. As a treat, we also house a Snickers bar. I love them, and they do give you calories and energy.

As we happily chew on the chocolate and caramel, we notice a tiny cloud up on the top of Mt. Washington. It's really just a puff of a thing on the very tip of the mountain. We are in great shape!

Well, that's what we thought.

The closer we get to Mt. Washington, the bigger the cloud seems to get. Maybe the Presidentials should post the same warnings as rearview mirrors: *Objects on the next mountain are larger than they appear.* The cloud still appeared to focus solely on the tip of the mountain, though, and we were not deterred. A little fog for us would be no big deal. We've already seen such beautiful views. Plus, there will be hot dogs. Can't forget the hot dogs. We start talking about how many we are each going to eat. The answer is three. Three hot juicy dogs for each of us. Maybe an order of fries and an apple. I'll add the apple to make it healthy.

When the sign says we have one more mile to go, we enter the cloud. It was like someone flipped the rain switch. And the wind switch. Rain pummels us at 40 miles per hour, and we scramble into our rain pants and raincoats. The farther we go, the harder it rains, and the harder the wind blows. We have to yell to hear each other, trudging bent-over like the letter C and dripping wet. By now the wind is at 55 mph and we are walking sideways up rocks. I can no longer see blazes. I'm trying to navigate by my trail map on my phone and hoping it doesn't short out from the constant onslaught of rain. If it does, we are screwed, because you can't make out where the trail is at all on the rocks.

"Three hot dogs are waiting on us, Bud," I yell back to encourage Tristan. I might have said something similar to him as a toddler, but things are desperate enough that I hope he won't blame me too much for regressing.

"That's all that's keeping me going," he laughs. "I'm starving."

My stomach confirms that I am too.

We are also soaked, even with the rain gear. This is no ordinary rain. This is sideways-blowing-up-in-your-face rain at 55 mph. It ricochets off the rocks, off the mountain, and back into our faces. Again, we are walking bent way over trying to make headway.

We had been to Mt. Washington on family trips before, but always in a car or on the Cog Railway. Both times there had been rain and fog up top, but not this. We had expected some rain, but not this. I could not wait to eat those hot dogs and hike down out of this for another mile to the shelter. We are still making good time, and I'm still checking my phone to make sure we are not too far off the trail. I hadn't seen a blaze for three or four hundred yards.

Then we come to the railroad tracks. Apparently we had drifted off the side of the trail a bit. We knew the railroad went up the mountain, so I put my phone away, and we just followed it.

The train itself rounded the bend toward us. The tourists inside stared from their warm, dry perches and pressed their faces up to the glass to get a better view of us. I felt like we were native animals in a safari. The conductor could have been saying, *Behold, the native rain-soaked, pack-wearing Nutjob in his natural habitat.*

Probably, the tourists were just thinking *What the hell is wrong with these guys?*

Hmmm. What indeed.

But Tristan and I plugged on, and the wind blew harder.

Then the train came back down again. We were still going up!

This is one hell of a long mile, I thought. We are not really making good time anymore. We have done away with our sticks, fastening them to our packs, so that we can walk with our arms up in front of our faces to block the rain from hitting us in the face.

We keep screaming back and forth to each other: "Hot dogs! Waiting! Three apiece! Hot dogs!" like vendors at a ball game. I believe we had both officially lost our grip on our sanity at this point.

At last, the building at the summit comes into view. As we explode through the door in a burst of water and exhalations, everyone turns to look at us. We slowly adjust to being inside and start peeling off our hoods. We head to the counter.

It is here, at the ranger station, that we learn the gusts have crested at 65 mph and were blowing steady at 55 mph.

At the counter, the clerk announces, "Sorry fellas, the kitchen is closed."

Six more devastating words have never been spoken.

They had Doritos, which we grimly ate, and a couple of apples. This was our official "lunch" for the day, although it was probably 3:00.

We decided we had better get to the shelter, which is called Lake of the Clouds Hut. We did not check the weather, and maybe I can blame this oversight on the trauma we suffered over the lack of hot dogs. Maybe. We would come to learn later that the tiny cloud we had seen was not the problem. A front was moving in. We did ask the guide if we could camp up top here, but he informed us it was not permitted. The weather is just too unstable, plus we could freeze to death.

"It happens all the time, so don't try it," he orders us. He tells us the Lake of the Clouds Hut is about a mile away. "I think it's open. If it's closed, there is a room underneath, called the dungeon. But I have to warn you, it's rat infested."

A mile to the hut doesn't seem too bad, and we can make do with whatever we find there. We really have no choice. We put on all our wet gear again and head back out into the weather. By this time the rain and wind are even worse, and I can't see the trail again. No railroad either. We work our way around the mountain, and now the rain is not in our faces, so I can see the trail.

It only takes us about 20 minutes to go the mile and get to the shelter. It does appear to be locked. I circle around it and find the door to the basement area, and it seems to be locked too. But, when I hit the door with my knee, it opens. Hallelujah. As the door swings aside, a rat bolts across the opening.

But here comes Turbo. He was a thru-hiker trying to get all the way to Springer Mountain in Georgia. He lived up to his name, moving fast and steady, and averaging 25 miles a day in these White Mountains. We had left the ranger station just in front him, bumbling around trying to find the trail, and he had no trouble overtaking us.

I look at Tristan. "I don't really know if we want to sleep with rats." They've stored furniture in there, and we can tell it's really not meant for sleeping. I can see a pair of old wooden cots, with a pile of stuff on each of them. The floor is buckled up a foot. We couldn't even stretch out on it if we wanted to. As we are inspecting the situation, Turbo pops his head in. He agrees, it's pretty bad.

Tristan and I agree we just can't do it. We are going to move on to the Mizpah Spring Hut just a few more miles away. Turbo decides he will stay in the dungeon. We wish him well.

"Be safe, brother," he tells me as we leave.

The wind kicks up another notch. The rain stops, but the wind is picking up tiny granules from the mountain and whipping them at our faces. We feel like we're walking in a sandblaster. Eventually there is so much debris in my eyes that I have to put my sunglasses on and Tristan does too. It's way too dark to be wearing sunglasses.

We take a quick break in a lean-to to get out of the rain and sandblasting. We are already soaked through. The temperature is dropping, and the cold goes right to your bones. *A typical day on the Appalachian Trail*, I think. *Poor Tristan getting indoctrinated right off the bat. At least there's no mud.*

But he's not complaining. He's enduring and trying to be tough, just like me. Overall, we are descending, with some little ups as we go. We go about five more miles, with a half mile more to go till Mizpah Spring Hut and Nauman Tentsite.

The last half mile is treacherous, and the sandblasting continues. We are supposed to be scrambling down boulders, but we end up sliding on our butts. The rain and the wind make it slippery and cold. Both of us take spills but have no injuries, thank God. We see a sign that says just three tenths of a mile to go, and I'm praying that God will help us get there in one piece. By now, we are in scrub trees, and the sandblasting ceases. We will descend another 500 feet here during this last little leg.

From behind, we hear grunting and the sounds of pebbles displaced by feet. It's Turbo, and he passes us. Apparently, he draws the line at rats as well. But this means that when we get to Mizpah, one of us will not be able to stay. And it won't be Turbo, because he's going to get there first. In general, all these places save a spot for thru-hikers, but only for two at a time.

We keep going. What is our other choice? My kids are tough as nails, both of them. These conditions are definitely testing Tristan and me. At one point we both slide simultaneously side by side down a boulder. It might have been fun, under completely different circumstances, I guess. But this is not fun. Tristan's rain pants are chaffing him now, after all these miles soaking wet, and pretty soon we are going to be too beat up to continue. He can hardly walk, and I'm not much better. I really didn't know what we would do if we couldn't stay in this next shelter.

The clerks at Mizpah aren't really happy to see us come through the door, dripping water all over the place. Mizpah Spring Hut is a more high-end hostel, with expensive rooms, as well as expensive food. Tristan, because he is not a thru-hiker, will have to pay whatever it costs to have the room. He is more than willing to do this. Turbo is there, so he's got one of the thru-hiker spots, and I can have the other. Relief floods through me in waves.

I do a "work for stay," but I am still frozen from the weather. I don't know how well my hands are going to function because of my old frostbitten fingers. All the clothes I have are on my body, so they are wet, and I don't have anything dry to wear. We manage to get our wet raincoats hung up. Tristan goes up to his room, and I'll be sleeping in what they call "the library/game room" with Turbo on our pads and sleeping bags. It was warm and dry under a ping pong table in there, and that was fine with me. I didn't really have anything to dry off with either, but while I scrubbed pots and pans for a half hour, it didn't bother me. In fact, it warmed my hands up. By bedtime, I was kind of dry, at least, so that was fine.

The dinner was incredible. We had waited all day for some real food, so that made it taste even better. Tristan was served his meal, because he was a paying client, and Turbo and I waited for leftovers. They were excellent! The manager even gave me some extra. Apparently my hand-warming strategy led to very clean pots and pans, which impressed him.

We didn't stay long in the morning, forgoing breakfast. We just wanted to get out of there and get down the mountain. We said goodbye and thanked everybody, then headed out the door.

I did continue to run into Turbo several more times, as far as Stratton, Vermont, in the mid part of the state. He ended up quitting at Harpers Ferry, and so did Castaway.

It stops raining just as we hit the trail, but everything is still soaked. The mountain is so steep that there isn't much mud. The trail isn't too challenging, so we get to the bottom in one piece. We have to walk a few extra miles to our car, because somehow we didn't have it in the right spot. We trucked along the road, and actually tried thumbing a ride. Eventually someone pulled over, but by then we only had a quarter of a mile to go. Hey, anything is better than nothing. When we got to the car we jumped in, pretty grateful to be in a nice dry vehicle, and pretty grateful to be together through it all.

Maybe this hike had not turned out to be the recreational bliss that Tristan or I had imagined, but there's something to be said for suffering alongside someone else. It bonds you like fun never can. The two of us had seen amazing sunsets, shooting stars, and we had also endured, conquered, and pushed our physical limits together. What an amazing 46 or so hours we had spent together. Just like the time I had been able to spend with Jocelyn, I would treasure it forever. Better than anyone else, a man who's lost his wife knows how precious the time with his kids truly is.

While we are on the subject, let me tell you what I learned about my family through suffering.

Many years ago, my niece Stacey, who had just graduated high school, was on her way to Harrisburg, Pennsylvania, to meet her friend's mother. She hit a truck head-on. The life flight attendants found her unresponsive with open head wounds, but were able to resuscitate her. At first, this seemed like a blessing. In the hospital, though, she did not regain consciousness. That first day, a surgeon removed part of her brain, and she was in a coma. For 67 days, she would remain in this coma. My sister Nancy and her husband Ronnie tried to manage being there with her, and traveled back and forth. Our whole family mobilized to support them, and to be with Stacey. Sandy, as a nurse recruiter at Geisinger Medical Center near our hometown, sprang into action. She was able to act as a liaison between Geisinger and the Hershey Medical Center where Stacey was being treated. Eventually, they moved Stacey to Geisinger and we could all be closer to her. Sandy arranged other things for them, too, helping Ronnie and Nancy as they made difficult decisions and comforting them in a way that made a key difference. We stayed with Stacey every day, and on weekends we allowed friends to visit as well. Sandy held her hand, and I read the Bible to her every morning. I knew she couldn't hear it, but maybe her spirit could. We all prayed and prayed. Later tests showed a massive loss of brain tissue, and they finally decided to remove life support. It was hell on Nancy and Ronnie, and all of us.

This was the first time I discovered the tower of strength, control, and compassion which I had otherwise known as my wife. I remembered the time she had asked me to cry with her at my father's grave, just instinctively knowing I needed to do that. Seeing this side of her as an adult, I recognized fully for the first time exactly the kind of woman I had married, and I was in awe. Her capacity for love was boundless.

And then, so many years later, I found myself again at the bedside of someone else who was dying. This time it was the woman I had loved my whole life. Jocelyn and Tristan moved heaven and earth to help, and just to be with her. Jocelyn quit her job with her dance company in Portland, Oregon, to come home and help me care for Sandy. Tristan was in college for physical therapy at the time. While most professors were understanding, one was not. He had to maintain his 3.3 average to keep his scholarship. Somehow, I don't know how actually, he managed to do that while taking all the time off that he could to be at home with us.

He was there in the final hours too, holding Sandy's head so that she would not choke. He remained there, the entire time, exhausted but wholly committed to this one final thing he could do for his mom. Jocelyn was rubbing her hand. Sandy's body was emptying itself, and she was mortified that her children, especially Tristan, would be a witness to this, and have the task of cleaning her up.

"That's okay, Mom, don't worry," Tristan told her in calm tones over and over. "I'm going to be a doctor someday so don't worry."

Sandy locks her eyes on our kids, just looking back and forth from one to the other. I'm holding her other hand, but she's not looking at me. Her brown eyes, tight with pain, are locked on her babies. Somehow they are both here, holding her and taking care of her in a cruel reversal of roles. I saw Jocelyn, her unblinking eyes glued on Sandy, strong and compassionate, fiery and loyal. I saw Tristan, faithful and stoic, determined, and I was overcome. *I am so proud of you kids, so proud of how you turned out,* I thought. I was so grateful, grateful beyond words for how I knew this comforted Sandy, seeing her kids so bravely handling this terrible goodbye. The moment was holy and horrible all at once. I thanked God for them over and over.

Earlier in the day, I had been praying for healing. Now, with crushing sorrow, I prayed that she would die. I wanted her to be released from her agony. For two hours we sat like this, each minute squeezing us like a vice grip.

At last the hospice nurse gets there. She pulls us out of the room to talk to us all. She tells us Sandy's pulse is very weak, Sandy's energy is drained, and the end is soon. The nurse tells us not to worry about cleaning her up at this point. We just need to keep comforting her. I have heard enough, and I am terrified Sandy will pass while we are out in the hall.

"Let's get back in there," I tell them.

Sandy takes exactly four more breaths. I knew each one could be the last. The whole time she looked into the faces of our kids. Going over their every feature, tracing it back in her mind to the day they were born, I imagined. Finally she drew in her last breath, maybe the only breath in these whole two hours that wasn't tortured, and sighed. She looked peaceful and shut her eyes.

I said a small prayer then for my wife.

None of us moved. We all just wept silent tears and stayed where we were. The quiet room inhaled and exhaled with us as we sobbed, the light from the lamp making weak shadows on the rug. Our bodies heaved, then quieted, then heaved again. The hospice nurse hovered, holding her own vigil over us while we grieved.

Tristan looked up. "I consider this ..." he said, and his voice cracked. Determined, he went on, "... to be the finest moment of our family." He looked at each of us and we stared back, mutely, "... to be here with Mom when she died."

When you look back, time has a way of sorting through the things in your mind.

I think of what Tristan said then, wise beyond his years, and I must agree. No vacation, no holiday, nothing compares to the moment when we surrounded Sandy during the hours before she left us to go be with Jesus.

CHAPTER 33:

RAIN MAN RETURNS

After Mt. Washington, it was time to be a solo south-bounder again. Tristan drove me back down to below the Fraconia Notch trailhead so I could get back to where I had begun my little jaunt northward. We decide to have a nice steak dinner before I take off south again. Tristan is so glad to get out of his wet pants. He is rubbed raw. I'm still damp, for sure, but not doing too bad after all that. I do need supplies, because the next leg of my hike will be a few days in the woods. I've got my waterproof high-top Hoka boots on, and I'll need them for the colder weather. Tristan has also brought the gear that Jocelyn shipped to him: Fjällräven hiking pants, Smartwool 200 insulated pants, and Smartwool hoodie. I'm going to do without my Mountain Hardware coat until next week. Cold weather is in the forecast.

Goodbyes aren't so bad when you know you're going to see the person again in a week. Tristan will be back in five days to hike with me again. I've got to be the luckiest man alive with these kids. We are also talking about a complete family reunion when I get to Massachusetts or Connecticut. If that happens, I'm going to be a man on the moon on that day. No one will be able to stand to be around me.

He drives away. It never fails with either of them. A little part of my heart drives off with them as I watch them go.

I've got plenty of daylight left to get some miles in, and I'd best get going. I can get 10 miles in, even though darkness is falling earlier and earlier each day. My goal is a shelter with some water. I found it, along with two hikers I had met back in March. We had a lengthy and heated discussion about whether or not Eddie Van Halen plays the guitar part in Michael Jackson's "Beat It." The truth is, he did! With a little cell reception, I could have proved it. Bets were made, and then I actually didn't sleep well. I was just missing my old buddies from home.

The next day started out sunny, but by the afternoon storms rolled in. I hiked in the mess for a few miles, even passing up on a shelter just to squeeze in more miles. I finally pulled in for the night in a dry cabin-type shelter. I had the place to myself and there were even some resupply items there. On the next night, I slept near a hex-shaped shelter where I met Honeybee and Striker. These two were doing a flip-flop too. They hiked faster than I did, but I usually left earlier. I would keep running into them up until the day I would lose my phone at Stratton. Visiting with this lovely couple filled me with nostalgia, and I went to bed in a mellow mood, thinking about Sandy and me when we were young.

In the morning, I took off early, but by 10:00 Honeybee and Striker overtook me, as they would continue to do. That's how it is on the AT, leapfrogging over the same hikers again and again, saying a quick hi to them before you have to go off on your own. At my first break, I had just finished putting my feet up for half an hour when they stopped for their break and we chatted a bit.

Putting my feet up is a habit that I kept whenever possible just to give my old dogs some fresh air and rest in the middle of each day. While I didn't sleep in shelters, I liked taking breaks in them. I would take off my shoes and socks and sit on the edge while I cooked and ate. While lots of hikers got a version of trench foot from being wet or sweaty all day, I never did. I think my barefoot break habit was probably the reason. Maybe I was just lucky. I'm not typically a great sleeper at night, so I'll confess that many times I was able to get a solid little snooze over my lunch break.

I get to the shelter first that night, and in just minutes, Honeybee and Striker pull in behind me. I already have my tent set up, and my mushrooms are cooking over a fire.

Since they are headed into town tomorrow and I won't be seeing them for a while, Honeybee and Striker both agree to taste some, and they've turned out well tonight. My olive oil, garlic, salt and pepper make all the difference. In the end, I think the weight of the cooking supplies is still less than the weight of the food I would have to carry if I wasn't eating mushrooms. The mushrooms make up the biggest part of my daily intake, at least for the seven months when they are in season. In early March, they aren't ripe. By the end of November, they will be done for the year. Maybe there are some that get ripe in the winter months, but I don't know what they are. It's very good policy, when it comes to mushrooms, to stick to what you know for sure. Let me say, too, I know there are apps that claim to identify mushrooms, but I would never trust a picture. I take what are called spore prints. Not all the time, not when the mushroom is obvious, like chicken of the woods. However, if there's a mushroom with a dangerous look-alike, I use a spore print. To take a spore print, you hold the mushroom upright like you found it. Tap it onto a surface so you can see the color and pattern of the spores as they drop down. These are very distinct from mushroom to mushroom.

Like I said, my mushrooms are coming out perfect tonight, and Honeybee gives Striker the first little taste, and he likes them!

Luckily, I have picked more than I need, and I have plenty to share. We eat at least two pounds between us, although that doesn't make a whole lot when you have them sautéed down. They are packed with nutrients, and they fill you up and give you energy. A renewable source that I don't have to carry is a godsend on this trail, because I can eat more than anyone I know.

By Friday, October 4, I'm near Lyme, New Hampshire, and I'm ready to meet Tristan again. I hardly slept last night. I've hardly seen Tristan at all throughout this whole year (except when I was healing from my broken foot), and now I'm going to be with him on back-to-back weekends. Guess what the forecast is? Rain.

We decide Tristan's trail name is Rain Man.

Tristan loves New Hampshire, and so do I. All the mountains are high, not as high as the Presidentials, around the 4,000-foot mark. Our mornings are frosty, with a thick coating over everything when we wake in the morning. And of course, my old frostbite injuries come back to incapacitate my fingers, and I know it's only going to get worse. Now, my shoulders are actually feeling a little bit better, and I've been able to use my sticks with no problem. In the cold, though, I won't be using my sticks until the day warms up and my hands start working again.

Tristan gives me some PT advice right away in the morning, and I'm sucking it in. He recommends that I do some quad sits against a tree to strengthen the quad. That helps the muscles create support around your knees so they don't hurt so much.

The hiking is tough, but the leaves are spectacular and we are making good time. At noon the sky opens up. We are headed downhill now and can't really push our pace. When we get to a shelter, there's no one there. Tent or shelter? This is our debate. The empty shelter will give us plenty of room to dry out everything, plus we are still a little traumatized by our last rainy ordeal on a mountain. To hell with the mice, we are staying dry tonight.

We sleep well though it is pouring and cold. It feels like it should be snowing. The next day we finally got up on another big mountain, maybe over 4,000 feet, and the rain turned into big fat sleet that came in sideways and stung us in the face. My ballcap was a lifesaver. The precipitation would go back and forth, from rain, to wet snow, to sleet, and back again over and over. Battling that all day for 18 miles takes it out of you, and by the end of the day we are both ready for bed.

Tristan has to leave the next morning and head back to work, and I have to keep going without him. When we wake it's cold again, and raining, and Tristan suggests a hot meal before we separate. When we Google our options, everything is slammed with people. Luckily, farther down the road, we come upon an Octoberfest celebration at a ski slope. They opened up the slopes for mountain bikers, and we watch bikers plummet down the mountain at break-neck speeds, vaulting upward over jumps, and violating the law of gravity at every turn. People are milling around, and we have our choice of a variety of beers, sausages, potatoes, soups, pierogies, you name it. What a great way to get warmed up! It even stopped raining, and we got a glimpse of the sun.

I thanked God that Tristan had taken this job in Boston and that these moments we shared had been possible. I don't think we could have been together if he had stayed in Arizona. We will still have two more times to hike together on this trip, and that thought buoys me up like a life preserver during the times in between. He takes me back to the trailhead. He had Uber-ed to the trailhead, and now our hike ended at his car. Our goodbye was sad, because we weren't sure about when we were going to get to see each other again. It turned out to be sooner rather than later, but we didn't know that at the time.

CHAPTER 34:

CAN YOU HEAR ME NOW?

I spent the next four days plowing through the rest of New Hampshire and into Vermont. I probably needed a zero day, but in prime leaf season in New England, zero days were expensive, if not impossible. And I do mean prime. The variety of reds, oranges, and yellows was indescribable. God really is the best artist. On some mountains, at the top, the leaves would still be green, but then on the next mountain they would be all aflame. I don't know why that is. But the green looks startling mixed in with the reds, oranges, and yellows. I've never seen any art as beautiful as these mountains in the fall. I picked up one leaf and photographed it to try to capture the intensity of the red and orange spots. It was like a leaf leopard or something. All the leaves on this one tree were like this, like God's finger had been on them in a special way. It actually looked a little like blood splatter on a yellow canvas. Sorry if that's a little gross, but that's what it looked like.

The first night in Hanover, I was blessed with some trail magic which included a yard to camp in, a dinner, and a beer too many. I slept in much later than usual. On the next morning at the Thistle

Hill Shelter, I crawled out of my sleeping bag on time, but I turned around and crawled right back in. Man, was it frosty! In the end I racked up 23 miles, hoping to catch Honeybee and Striker. I made it almost to the Killington area, through some decent elevation. My shoulders felt better, and my nose was getting better unless I bumped it or wiped it, which is often now that it's colder and it runs like I'm a Labrador retriever.

I crashed that next night thinking I'd give it one more monster day tomorrow to see if I couldn't catch up with somebody. The good news was that my pack was light and I could fly, but the bad news was that this meant I needed supplies. Being low on fuel contributed to the lightness of my pack. It ran out just as my water was about to boil for my oatmeal the next morning. Close call, but no disaster. Instead of carrying my 10 ounces of water, I chugged it and drank my dose of Hunter's Hydro right there on the spot. I was feeling lucky and light, even though the rain started up again. *This is absolutely the lightest my pack can be*, I thought to myself.

And my luck continued. I ran into Honeybee and Striker getting resupplied at the Stone's Throw, a gas station and shop, just as there was a break in the rain. We ended up at the same shelter that night and bid each other a fond farewell as they hiked out the next morning, done with their hike. I put in another big day, but at the shelter a cryptic note about bedbugs and something going on with the bathroom drove me out to a nearby platform. I laid out on my tent and watched the stars blink in the crisp October air.

I get up plenty early, eat my oatmeal, and drink my coffee in the dark, optimistic about the day. Tristan's coming for another quick visit with his friend Matt, and I'm thinking about whether they are going to want to hike in the rain. But for today, the weather is perfect, and I'm ready to head up the hill.

At the top, I think I'd better check out the shelter situation for tonight. When I reach for my phone, something is wrong. My phone case is upside down, and empty. Upon inspection, I can see the strap that holds it upright is broken. Again, I want the record to show that this is not a result of my carelessness. I feel like I've swallowed a stone. Without the phone, I don't know where I am exactly, how far I am from a road or a town, or where any of the shelters are. I think I have maybe 15 miles till Stanton where I'm meeting Tristan, but now I can't even communicate with him to coordinate the details.

It's possible it fell out where I camped at night.

So, I drop my pack, and run back down the four miles of hill to the campsite and go straight to the picnic table. Not there. I was not in the shelter at all, so skip that. Next, I head to the wooden tent platform where I had slept. No phone. There are lots of wide cracks in the platform, so I squint to peer into them. I use my flashlight to check under the platform the best I can. No phone.

I run back up the hill, with my eyes peeled to hopefully see it lying near the trail. At the top, I finally have to face the disaster. It's gone. Two hikers are there at the top, anxiously regarding my pack and wondering if the hiker to whom it belongs is okay. I assure them it is mine, and that I am looking for my phone. They offer to try to call it, but I knew it had to be down the hill and way back down the trail. We wouldn't stand a chance of hearing it. They take my information in case they come across it, and I take theirs. If I don't find it, they are going to finish their hike, get in their other car they have parked at their destination trailhead, and then drive back to where their truck is parked, which will be at my next trailhead. They describe both their cars to me, so I know what to look for. They have approximated the time they think it will take for them to get there. I turn around then, and go back down the hill again. This time I walk, so I can really look.

It starts to rain.

I get back to the campsite again and spend another 20 minutes looking around. Then it pours. Now the situation is dire. Even if I do find it, it will likely be fried.

I go back up the hill, slowly, back to my pack. There were three tiny little wash-out creeks, which were running full strength this time of year, and I go down into those, feeling around. I remembered stumbling crossing one, but couldn't remember which one. I literally crawled on my hands and knees to check these out thoroughly. No phone.

I can't just leave it. I go back down this hill, carefully walking and looking one more time. This time I have my sticks, and I'm separating the ferns and stinging nettle, just in case it tumbled in there when I stumbled a bit. No phone. I sigh. Curse. Head back up the mountain. I feel depressed and completely defeated. It's really gone. I put on my backpack again and continue on. I cannot believe this shit is happening to me. I also can't imagine those guys will still be waiting for me at the trailhead at this point.

Their truck was there, but they were not. I found out later that somehow they got lost. Those guys had been hiking the trail for 33 years, one week at a time all those years. This year, they were cutting their trip short because of the forecast.

No other vehicles are there. I figure those guys have to be getting there any second, and I decide to wait for them. Now, because it's still downpouring, and I'm not hiking at the moment, I start to get cold. It's too late to put a raincoat on, because I'm already drenched. I decide to just get my tent out and wrap it around me. But that seems like a lot of work for just a few more minutes of waiting. Then I have the bright idea of just crawling under their truck. There is a puddle under there, but I'm out of the wind and I'm not getting rained on. Just as I get situated under there, a car goes by, which I could have flagged down. But I tell myself those guys will be along shortly. But just in case another car comes by, I crawl back out from under the truck.

After another full hour goes by, it's getting dark. The wind kicks up, and I do put my raincoat on finally. Thank God, a truck comes by, and I wave for him to stop. I ask him if I could maybe get a lift from him into town. It's an older guy with his preteen grandson.

"Sure, hop in," says the kid.

But the grandfather is reluctant. "Ah, I just can't do it."

"Pappy, he needs the ride!" says the kid.

The grandfather looks me up and down. "I'll tell you what," he says, "let me go home and drop off my grandson. Then I'll come back for you."

I don't know if he will or won't.

He doesn't.

It's the last vehicle I see for the night. I think I am near the town of Manchester, but I really have no idea which direction or how far. By now it's officially dark. Finally, the two hikers arrive in their car. I'm dripping wet as I crawl in. I dejectedly report that I never did find my phone. When I never called, they figured as much. They had continued to look for it, and even dialed the number a few times hoping it would ring in the vicinity. I'm so pissed over the whole thing that I can barely have the conversation with them.

They ask me where I want to go, and I don't even know. I thought maybe I had looked into an EconoLodge somewhere. The guy says he knows right where it is, and he actually lives near there. They apologized up and down for getting lost and being late, and they figured I would have gotten a ride long before they got there.

When I go in, the EconoLodge is booked. I don't want these guys to have to keep running me all over to find a place to stay.

"I'm freezing. I'm soaking wet," I pleaded. "Could I just sleep in your lobby tonight?"

That was a no.

But the clerk called the manager, and he permitted me to sleep in a version of a broom closet with a fresh towel. They only charged me $40. The stipulation was that I could only stay one night. I explained that I was supposed to meet my son, and I asked them to put me on a waiting list for the next night, if they had anything open up. During fall leaf season, on a weekend, they didn't think that would happen, but they put down my information. Maybe the rain would finally work in my favor in this case.

I went to bed wet and with no shower. But I was indoors. For that I was grateful.

The next morning I knew I had to get a hold of Tristan. At the desk, the clerk could not let me use the hotel phone or her personal phone. English was not the clerk's native language, so there was a bit of a language barrier between us. That probably did not help my situation. I really didn't know what to do, and I had no way to make arrangements. Eventually the clerk was able to get permission from her manager to let me use the desk phone for one call.

I wasn't sure whether to call Tristan or make a call to look for another room.

In the end, I decided to call Jocelyn, who could then make both calls for me. She could then be dispatcher for Tristan. She's isn't home, but I leave a long message. I have no idea when she will get it. I'm trying not to panic because Tristan has no idea where to go, and no idea why I'm not answering his calls by now. I'm second-guessing my choice. I should have called Tristan.

As I wait in the lobby, my GPS device goes off. Well, it would be nice if I knew how to answer it. There is a text message on the screen, and I manage to read it. It's from Jocelyn: *I got your message.* Relief floods me. Now we can figure things out. I have the ability to send text messages from the GPS device. Jocelyn did show me how to do it, but now I'm fumbling around, pushing buttons and just praying I don't accidentally deprogram the whole thing or something.

After a lot of tries and retries, I figure out how to text Tristan with it. I let him know where I am, and he gets it. I just have to wait there in the lobby for him to arrive. By now it's Friday at 5:00 p.m., and I think Tristan and Matt won't be arriving until 9:00 at night. The EconoLodge people really did not want me to stay there camped out in their lobby, which I can understand. But I really did not have any other choice.

Finally, at 6:00 p.m., someone calls the EconoLodge and cancels, and I get a room. I don't know who is more relieved, the EconoLodge staff or me. I shower immediately.

Tristan and Matt get there, and we are just glad we have an actual place to stay. The cancellation had been for two nights, but for some reason we had to switch rooms for the next night. It's late when the guys get there. They are hungry, and we go out for a beer and pizza. I was starving too, so I ate a whole pie. So did Tristan. We feasted and visited, and we were just happy to be hanging out together again.

I hated to ask them, but I really didn't want to get another phone. "Would you guys mind if we go back and look for my phone?" I ask.

They had planned on it.

The next morning we all had a great breakfast, got our raincoats, and went looking for my phone. Jocelyn could see the coordinates from the last place it had service, so we decided to try to track it that way. It was like a very serious game of geocaching. This is the second full day of downpour, so everything is soaked with a little thunder and lightning occasionally as well. While poor Tristan is used to the miserable conditions, I feared we would probably turn Matt off from hiking forever. Tristan, at least, is used to my fiascos by now.

When we get to the coordinates, I just know it isn't there. But they have faith in the evidence, and insist we look thoroughly. I think it's more likely I was four miles down from this area. I am convinced it isn't there, but we look. Finally, they give up, and I decide to give up too. It's time to just admit I have to buy a new phone.

We are hungry now too. We hike on. Now, when I had passed this creek yesterday, it was not the raging river it is today. While we were still half a mile away, we could hear the roar of the water. There is a bridge, but today it doesn't look safe at all. The brown water is all the way up to the boards, shooting like a jet stream underneath. When I walk up the eight steps to go over the bridge, I can see the water pummel up between the slats of the boards, making tiny geysers. The boards groan underneath our feet, and we don't spend too much time on there.

All three of us are over being out there, hungry, in the rain. Later, Matt is just jogging down a hill, and falls. Next, Tristan falls. Not too long after that, I am dreaming of a cheeseburger and break into a trot, and I go down too. As I collect myself, I notice I have broken my finger.

Nine months later, it will still hurt.

I've broken, dislocated, and frostbitten my fingers before, so this is a minor annoyance at this point. I had broken other fingers on the trail, but managed to tape them so they all healed up. With Hunter, I had even paddled the official "shortcut" (12 miles, and you still get credit for doing the miles on the trail) across a lake with a taped-up broken finger. This one, though, I will manage to damage over and over again, so it will keep bothering me.

When we finally get back, we take some showers and go to town for food. We look for a place to buy a phone. It's hard to believe that the entire town of Manchester does not have a Verizon store, but it doesn't. They decide to head back to Boston, and I decide to go south to Bennington to get my phone. I will have to walk the three miles from the EconoLodge to town in order to catch the bus at 8:00 a.m. tomorrow. That's the plan, but I have to waste a whole additional day just to get my damn phone.

They head back to Boston after dinner without spending another night. We had a great time in Manchester, which was a beautiful town with a great expresso place. We shopped a little together that afternoon too. I ended up having a pretty good night's sleep.

I'm up early. I walk about a quarter mile for some breakfast, but the restaurant isn't open till six o'clock. I go back to the hotel, and then walk back to the restaurant again an hour later.

"Are you a hiker?" asks a woman who has just perched next to me at the counter.

"Yeah, I am," I answer. The interrogation begins, and she is curious and kind.

"Wait a minute," she says, "are you a thru-hiker? I thought the thru-hikers were all gone."

"There's a couple of us left," I explain. Later I would discover that I was indeed the last thru-hiker on the trail. I start telling her that there are two people behind me, and three people ahead of me, but we are all about a day apart. This is my second zero, and I'll have to have one tomorrow to get my phone, so I'm going to be way apart from them. In the end, losing my phone would cost me three full days.

"Are you catching the bus in town then?" she asks. I tell her I am. "Do you have trail magic or a taxi coming to take you into town?"

When she finds out I planned to walk it, she volunteers to give me a ride. She paid for my breakfast, too, so I even got a little more trail magic. She had been a waitress at this restaurant and had just retired two days earlier, so she was used to hikers. I had plenty of time in town then, so I hit the expresso joint again and scored another piece of pie.

I get into Bennington late in the day, get my new phone all set up thanks to the clerk in the store, and I'm figuring out the town. By 5:00 in the afternoon I talk to some guys who recommend a place to eat and a chain of bars. I tell them I just need the food. When I go to the first bar, I have my pack with me, of course.

Now the pack is like a big sign you wear on your back that says you smell. I don't, but most hikers do. The host seats me at the bar and assures me I don't smell at all. I slide down to the end and plug all my devices in.

"Hey, are you a hiker?" a big guy asks me. Flannel shirt buttoned up and heavy boots. He's yelling from several feet away at the bar.

"Yes I am."

"A thru-hiker?"

"Yes."

"You must be about the last guy out there," he says.

"If I'm not the last, I'm right at the end anyway."

"Hey, bartender, I'm going to buy this guy a beer!" he points over at me. Now everyone knows I'm a thru-hiker. I'm thanking the guy for the beer. These two pretty girls at the bar are taking in the conversation.

"So you're a thru-hiker?" the girls say. "We haven't had a thru-hiker come through here for probably two or three weeks!"

"Well, you might have two or three more," I tell them.

"Can we buy you a beer?" one of the girls asks.

"This guy just bought me one," I tell her.

"I'll buy your meal then," she tells me.

"And I'll buy your next beer," says the other girl.

I agreed and thanked them both. They pick up their drinks and silverware and slide right down next to me. Now I'm a guy sitting at a bar with two pretty girls, and I'm feeling pretty lucky. They want to know everything. One girl, Erica, has petite features and strawberry blonde hair, and she's asking me most of the questions. Everyone referred to the other girl as Dizzy Lizzy. I don't know if that is a trail name or just a nickname, but that's what she went by. Dizzy Lizzy was wearing an elegant white hat that made her stand out and was visiting from Texas to see the leaves. Erica explained to Lizzy what the hiker scene was like, and I got to be the center of attention again.

Still not really acquainted with my new phone, I had not made any overnight arrangements. I hoped to get up early and get back to the trail. I had heard there was a shuttle to get back to the trailhead at Manchester that left at noon. I wanted to be on it. Otherwise, I'd have to get a trail angel.

Erica and Dizzy Lizzy were on a mission to find me a place to stay. Dizzy Lizzy was trying to find something at a reasonable rate, but Erica didn't think it would be possible to find anything. I had seen an overpass about a mile from the Verizon store, and truly, I could always camp there. I asked the girls if they knew of a place in town with a big yard, or a park or something where I would be allowed to camp. They really didn't think so. If I had been a month earlier, in the bubble, I would have had no problem. I decided it would have to be the overpass.

Well, they weren't having that. They kept texting and calling on my behalf, and they still couldn't find anything. Dizzy Lizzy had to go, and I hugged her and thanked her for trying.

Erica says, "C'mon. You're going with me to another bar, and we're going to find you a place." I had had two beers, but I agreed to go with her. She seemed to know everyone in this town, and kept working to find me a spot. Everyone wanted to buy me a beer. Very lovely gestures, but after one more I whispered to the bartender, "No matter what happens, don't give me any more beers! I gotta get up in the morning and hike!"

"Just pretend you're sipping, and nurse it," he advised me. I thought that was brilliant. It worked for the rest of the night. I had already had too much to drink, though, and I knew it. I had had four beers a few nights before at Hanover, but for some reason this felt even worse.

"I can't let you just stay on the street," Erica protests. We had struck out at finding me a place to stay at this bar too. She offers me her spare bedroom. I'm extremely grateful, and I accept.

As we are getting back to her place, I am not feeling good at all from the beer. I really and truly am a pathetic lightweight and can't handle alcohol at all. Funny, huh, seeing how I behaved in high school? Tonight, I feel okay as I'm walking around, but as soon as I lie down, I can feel the nausea building. I make it to the bathroom before I throw up, but I'm thinking, *Oh my God, this woman probably thinks I am trash. I'm supposed to be some kind of Christian, and look at me drunk enough to throw up in a strange girl's toilet.*

It was definitely not one of my finer moments, for the record. But I'm keeping this honest.

In the morning, instead of getting an Uber or the shuttle, Erica agrees to take me to the trailhead. She's a local, but she hasn't been on the roads up to where the trailhead is. This one road is really full of potholes and muddy, and here is Erica in her really nice BMW. I felt like there would be no end to me taking advantage of her kindness here. As we bumped along, my stomach started to remember it had too much alcohol in it the night before. I had to ask Erica to pull over so I could open the door and throw up again. I apologized over and over to her.

"Don't worry," she said, "you only had three beers."

"I guess that was one over my limit," I confessed, ashamed. "I was dumb for drinking it. I'm so sorry."

Quite literally, I was hoping that she would forget me forever.

We had to go for a long time on this back road. I told her I could walk to the trailhead from here, but she kept telling me it was okay. She was running low on gas, and finally I made her pull over. We were close to Stratton. She assured me she could get gas when she got there.

I gave her my phone number and got out. "Please just call me when you get there, so I don't have to worry about you getting home okay."

"You're the one who's throwing up!" she reminded me. "I should call and check on you."

I took a two-mile shortcut right through the woods to get to the trail. I have my app now, so I know right where I am. I have the GPS, too, so I am in good shape. I finally get to the trailhead on top of a mountain, next to a ski slope. There aren't views through the trees, but it's beautiful.

Back in the beauty and privacy of the trail, I can puke without worrying about being a terrible witness. I do so repeatedly throughout the day. That day could not have ended quickly enough. I actually got 13 miles in, but I was disgustingly tired at the end of the day. It wasn't the worst day; that would have been when I had norovirus. The day with Tristan on Mt. Washington would be the second worst. Then that day in the Bigelows with Jocelyn would be third. Those were the worst, but this one was a self-inflicted, gunshot-to-the-foot, hard day.

I got to the shelter and didn't even set up my tent. This is how you know I was really sick. To hell with the mice. Let them do square dances all over my face all night, I didn't care. I just wanted to crash.

I did get a call from Erica to confirm I was still alive, and I again apologized profusely.

"No, no, no," she told me again, "it's fine. I know you're a good guy. You just had one beer too many. That's a good sign—you don't drink much."

"It's true I don't," I admitted. "But when I do, I end up this way. You'd think I'd learn by now. I'm 64 years old!"

She assured me that I was fine, and I didn't offend her or anything. Honestly, she did make me feel a little better. Her trail magic for me on this journey was a huge blessing.

When I wake the next morning, there is no more hangover, thank God. I sleep in until 6:00, but I guess I needed it. I feel awesome, but I am starving and wolf down my usual breakfast.

I head south back toward Bennington. After a few miles, there's an immediate rush of cool air on my foot, and unbelievably, my shoe has blown out. I'm pissed. These are practically new shoes that I had bought after my "interview" with Jill. They only have 190 miles on them, which as I mentioned before means they cost over a dollar a day! Thank God for my Zip tape. I still have another day and a half before I can get downstate far enough to get a new pair of shoes.

Despite the tape, I lock in another 23 miles, a terrific day! But, after three zeros, I'll probably never see any thru-hikers after this. I've got to be officially the last hiker. Losing my phone like that and losing those days really did get me down a bit, I must confess. You'd think with everything that happened, a stupid phone would be no big deal. But it cost me three days, and that was depressing.

After two more great days, I'm just seven miles short of being out of Vermont. I'll have to dip down into Massachusetts to get the boots, then get a ride back to the trailhead to finish out the miles in Vermont. I call ahead to make sure the store has a pair of the La Sportiva's. Next, I pay a guy that I find just sort of sitting in his car on his phone to take me into town.

I get into the store about 15 minutes before closing time.

"Are you the hiker?" the guy asks me excitedly. I tell him that I am. He has my shoes all picked out and put on the counter. His name is Lee.

"Do I have time to try them on?" I asked.

Lee says, "Not only do you have time to try them, I got you a beer popped!"

Indeed, there it is sitting on the counter right by the shoes.

"I figured you needed a beer," Lee says.

People are so nice. I drank it. Just the one. I made damn sure it was just the one.

"Where are you going to the trailhead?" Lee asks as I pace around in the boots to see how they feel. "I can take you," he adds.

He takes me all the way down to the trailhead, at the Berkshire Lakeside Lodge. At this hostel, the lady has a room for me. I jumped in the shower on cloud nine. I resupply and sleep in a bed with sheets and a pillow. It was a wonderful night.

Normally I cannot put a monster day in with brand new shoes. I tell myself I'm going to put in 15 miles and make myself stop. But at lunch time, I take my shoes off as usual, and my feet feel great. I put them up to rest them as Jocelyn has told me to do.

A deer wakes me up. I feel so revived, I go another ten miles. So that's a 20-mile day and my feet feel awesome. As I camped that night, I was glad to have finally crossed the border into Massachusetts, even with all the drama. Some days, you just have to appreciate the big picture.

CHAPTER 35:

RAIN WITHOUT RAIN MAN

My first days in Massachusetts are beautiful. I start out with a nice uphill grade into Mt. Greylock State Reservation, which is the tallest peak in Massachusetts at 3,400 feet. The phone incident has cost me precious days during which all the other hikers have tromped quietly away over the mountains. For me especially, it's lonely. I'm not one who spends a lot of time feeling comfortable in solitude, and this will be a test. It turns out that the solitude is exactly what I need in order to get where I need to go in my heart and in my head. But I can't say I like it.

I'm still wrestling with a few things, I know. Fighting back from having a broken foot and those viruses helped me identify my enemy. The deep orange sunset over the lake had made me so sorry for indulging myself in anger. Again, I believed everything that did happen was for a good reason. I felt loved by God, but I also felt vaguely unsettled. There was more mess in my head to be dealt with.

The sunset on the top of Mt. Greylock looked like someone took a paint pallet and turned it on its side, just letting all the colors run. I spent the night there, though I wasn't sure if camping was allowed. I had a scary moment when I had to call Jocelyn to find my GPS again, but then I located it buried in one of the pods of my backpack. How did it get there? I have no idea. But at least it wasn't lost on the trail.

The next day is gorgeous as well, with beautiful leaves everywhere. I get a quick chat with some hikers who tell me they are planning to quit for three days because of the torrential rain coming. They tell me I should probably get out of the woods.

Well, I can't. In four days, I need to be at the Connecticut border to meet Tristan for our third weekend together. You can be sure I'm not missing it. He has a wedding in Philadelphia and will be driving by the trail. He's going to take me as his "Plus One," and then drop me back off at the trail. There probably won't be a lot of hikers at this wedding. But hey, if it's time with my son, I'm all in.

How much do I love my son? This will be my fourth time hiking through hurricane rain on the trail. No break. No rest. I love him A LOT. The problem is that it's early November. It will also be raw and cold.

By noon it started coming down hard, with a heavy wind. Luckily, I had put in enough miles during the morning to get 22 miles for the day. As soon as the rain came, so did the cold, so of course I could not use my hands well from then on. Luckily, I did sleep in a shelter that night, so I could try to dry things out a little bit and get up off the ground. It looks like I won't have to worry about finding room in shelters either from here on out.

I hike the next day in the freezing rain. There's nothing worse than putting the cold clammy clothes back on. I jumped around like a maniac to get warm. And I drank coffee and tea. Later that morning I got another cup of tea from the famous "Cookie Lady of the North," and the lovely sugar and caffeine rush afterward gave me a little boost.

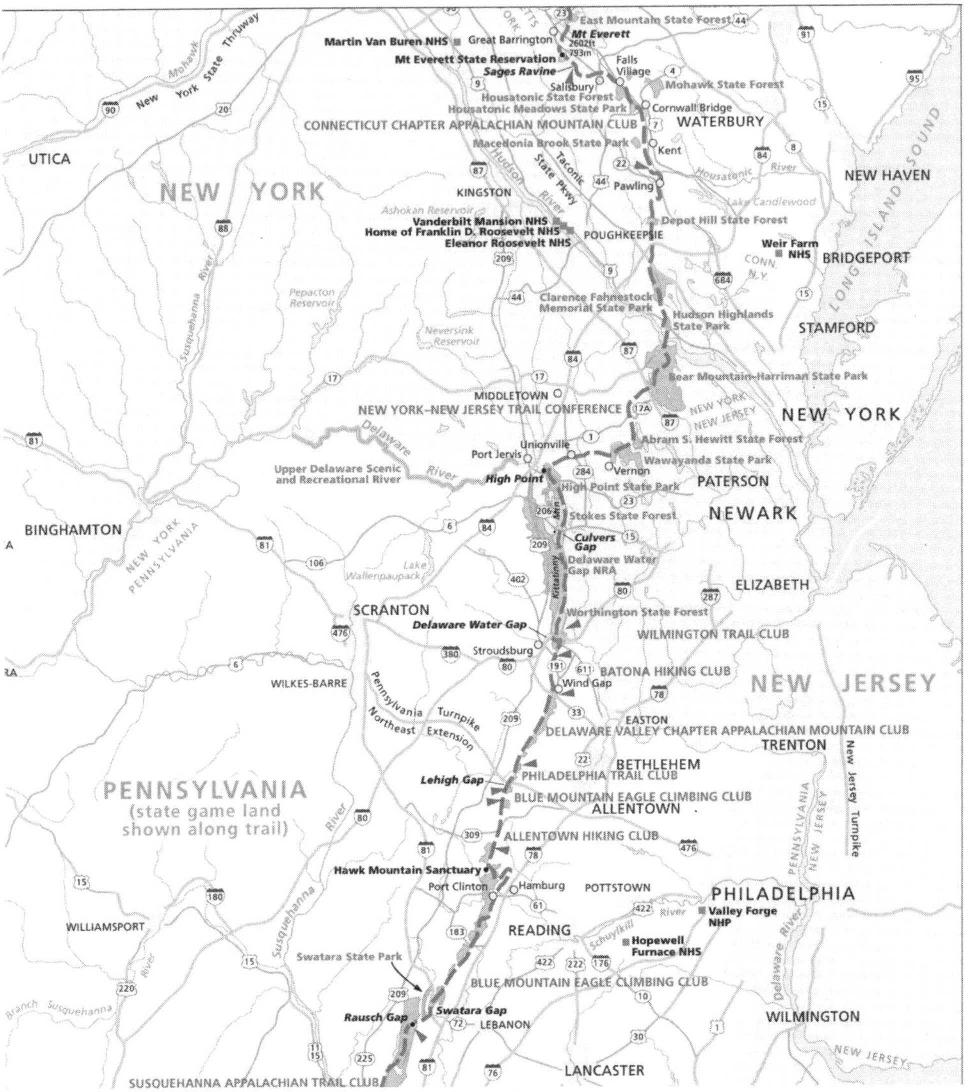
East Mountain State Forest
Mt Everett
2602ft
793m
Martin Van Buren NHS
Great Barrington
Mt Everett State Reservation
Sages Ravine
Falls Village
Salisbury
Mohawk State Forest
Housatonic State Forest
Housatonic Meadows State Park
Cornwall Bridge
CONNECTICUT CHAPTER APPALACHIAN MOUNTAIN CLUB
WATERBURY
Macedonia Brook State Park
Kent
Mohawk
New York State Thruway
UTICA
NEW YORK
Hudson River
Taconic State Pkwy
Housatonic River
NEW HAVEN
KINGSTON
Pawling
Lake Candlewood
Ashokan Reservoir
Vanderbilt Mansion NHS
Home of Franklin D. Roosevelt NHS
Eleanor Roosevelt NHS
POUGHKEEPSIE
Depot Hill State Forest
Weir Farm NHS
BRIDGEPORT
CONN.
N.Y.
LONG ISLAND SOUND
Susquehanna River
Pepacton Reservoir
Clarence Fahnestock Memorial State Park
Hudson Highlands State Park
STAMFORD
Neversink Reservoir
Bear Mountain–Harriman State Park
MIDDLETOWN
NEW YORK–NEW JERSEY TRAIL CONFERENCE
NEW YORK
NEW JERSEY
NEW YORK
Delaware River
Unionville
Port Jervis
Abram S. Hewitt State Forest
Wawayanda State Park
Vernon
Upper Delaware Scenic and Recreational River
High Point
High Point State Park
PATERSON
NEWARK
Stokes State Forest
BINGHAMTON
NEW YORK
PENNSYLVANIA
Kittatinny Mtn
Culvers Gap
Delaware Water Gap NRA
Lake Wallenpaupack
ELIZABETH
SCRANTON
Worthington State Forest
Delaware Water Gap
WILMINGTON TRAIL CLUB
Stroudsburg
BATONA HIKING CLUB
Wind Gap
NEW JERSEY
WILKES-BARRE
Pennsylvania Turnpike Northeast Extension
EASTON
DELAWARE VALLEY CHAPTER APPALACHIAN MOUNTAIN CLUB
TRENTON
New Jersey Turnpike
BETHLEHEM
PHILADELPHIA TRAIL CLUB
Lehigh Gap
PENNSYLVANIA
(state game land shown along trail)
BLUE MOUNTAIN EAGLE CLIMBING CLUB
ALLENTOWN
ALLENTOWN HIKING CLUB
PENNSYLVANIA
NEW JERSEY
Hawk Mountain Sanctuary
Port Clinton
Hamburg
POTTSTOWN
PHILADELPHIA
WILLIAMSPORT
Valley Forge NHP
Schuylkill River
READING
Hopewell Furnace NHS
Susquehanna River
Swatara State Park
BLUE MOUNTAIN EAGLE CLIMBING CLUB
Delaware River
Branch Susquehanna River
Rausch Gap
Swatara Gap
LEBANON
WILMINGTON
NEW JERSEY
LANCASTER
SUSQUEHANNA APPALACHIAN TRAIL CLUB

I kept trudging in the rain, motivated by the time I would spend with Tristan. Maybe that puts time with Tristan on the same level as a hot dog at the top of Mr. Washington? I manage 21 miles before I stagger into another shelter and crash without even cooking my dinner.

In the morning, the rain is over. I am starving. I only have to go about 14 miles to our rendezvous point, and Tristan probably won't get there until six in the evening. So I lounge about for a bit longer, delaying the inevitable squish of my feet into those dirty wet boots. It won't do me any good to get to the trailhead too early and just wait for him. Lying there with my stomach growling, I have the bright idea to make my breakfast right there in the sleeping bag, which is zipped at the moment. It's like sauteing mushrooms with a mermaid tail on, but I manage it. Mushrooms for breakfast are a delicious first for me. It is either that or carry them, and the answer to that is always obvious. Finally at 7:30, I get out and get dressed. That's so late! But, I have plenty of time to do 14 miles. I'm shooting for the intersection of the trail with Route 7A. I chug 33 ounces of Hunter's Hydro stuff and drink a strong cup of coffee. I wanted to empty my pack, so I put way more coffee grounds in my filter that morning than any human should. By the time I hit the trail, I'm buzzing with caffeine and mushroom nutrients. I'm ready to burn up the trail.

I burn it up all right. I get to the intersection, and it's only 3:00. I am at a loss. I have about three more hours to amuse myself before Tristan gets here. I decide to try to get a ride into town.

I look down. My clothes are dirty and torn by now. I still look like a drowned rat. Even though the rain had stopped, the trees were still dripping all day. The drips kind of cleaned off my face, legs, and arms, and I don't stink. But nobody in their right mind is going to think it's a good idea to put me in their car. A couple of people slow down, but after they get a close look at me, they punch the accelerator and move on. I'm not insulted in the least by this. I completely understand.

But one guy in a truck who was a contractor stopped for me. He had done the trail and wanted to hear all my stories. He takes me to a coffee shop and comes right on in with me.

The driver, Peter, and I talk for almost two hours. Other people hear us and we draw a little crowd. I start calling him Saint Peter because he was such a welcome trail angel for me. When we are done, he offers to take me back to the trailhead. I thank him when we get there and mention that as per Tristan's latest update, I would have to wait a few more hours for him. With this information, Peter decides he may as well take me all the way up to Bennington and drop me off. This way, I'll get to hang out in a town instead of at a trailhead. This sounds okay to me too, and I tell him I'll just get a ride back to the trailhead when I need to meet Tristan. Peter gives me the info of another trail angel who will give me a ride.

Tristan calls again. His traffic broke up unexpectedly, and he is going to be at the trailhead in 15 minutes. Oops. I have to ask him to come on down to Bennington to pick me up.

We stop on our way home to Pennsylvania to eat another big dinner at Wendy's because Tristan is starving. Car rides are the best, because kids just start talking to you. There's nothing else to do, so they are stuck talking, and I love it. The next morning, Tristan had to leave really early to do wedding stuff, and I didn't want to just hang around Philadelphia while he did that. So Jocey takes me to Philadelphia to be at the wedding at the normal time. As a bonus, I get a car ride with her too. I even had time to make a little batch of whiskey to share with all Tristan's soccer team buddies at the wedding. It is a fun hobby of mine, and it turned out terrific.

The wedding was beautiful with an outdoor reception. I got to catch up with all the soccer team parents again and celebrate this young couple starting out their life together. We toasted with shots of the whiskey, ate, and told stories. My night with Erica was still fresh in my mind, so I made sure I only drank one. I ended up feeling like a movie star with everyone asking me questions about the trail.

"We thought you were dead like three times!" they told me.

"Well, I'm still here," I said. "I'm all buggered up, but I'm still here!" Just being with people, relaxed and dry, and eating real food was the perfect break I needed from the trail. It restored my heart to visit with my kids, and after the three days of grueling rain, my body appreciated it too.

Tristan dropped me off at the trailhead at 7:00 a.m. I knew it would be a long time, maybe not till the end of the hike, before I would see him again. This goodbye felt more profound. I waved and watched him drive away. I guess you work really hard as a parent just so your kids can leave you and be okay on their own, right? Then why does it feel so sad when they go and do exactly that?

It was time to get back to work. I still had a little more of Massachusetts and one more New England state to go—Connecticut. I only had a few more hours of daylight, and I hoped to be in Connecticut by evening. At least my belly was full, and I wouldn't need to eat supper.

I thought the day would be easy, but it wasn't. I fell twice going uphill. I was on the north slope of a nasty climb hiking south, just boulder on boulder. The sun hadn't hit these rocks, and they were still wet. At the top, there wasn't really a campsite, but there was a flat spot on top of a rock at the very peak. I thought, *This would be cool.* The sun was already down, so I made myself a cup of tea and drank a water. This is always a mistake right before bed, but I hadn't been hydrating all day like I should. I hadn't been able to fill up until

I got to a stream that divided the two states. I didn't sleep very well because I kept having to get up, but at least I had made my goal.

I had big plans for Connecticut. At the first shelter the next day, I took my break. I was hoping to find some hikers there, but there weren't any.

I had dated a lady named Janet from Connecticut for about a year. We hardly ever argued, but she was the opposite political party from me. Now this wasn't really the reason why we didn't stay together. I actually respected her views after I sat down and considered them. Sandy and I had aligned with opposite parties too. We managed to raise two kids together, so I know it's not a deal breaker. Political differences are important, but they are not more important than relationships.

Janet had dreams of hiking the whole trail in her state, about 55 miles. I thought, *Sooner or later she's going to come through here, and this letter will be waiting for her.* I don't know why this impulse came over me, but I had no peace until I wrote it. I wanted to thank her for the time we had spent together and to let her know that she had helped me heal in some ways. I believe I had helped her, too, and I think this is why people come together. I just wanted to express my good wishes for her. This shelter had a book for visitors to sign, but it was full, so I just stuffed the letter in the back. I figured if God wanted her to see it, she'd find it. If not, then it was therapeutic for me to write. And who knows, if someone else reads it, maybe they will get something they need from it instead.

I was off down the trail again, trying to make it through Connecticut in three days. I hustled and pushed myself, and made 24 miles. Another day of great mileage! After that first bit of treacherous boulder climbing, the rest of the trail was not too bad. I made 20 miles the next day, passing gorgeous vistas, rivers, meadows, and mountains that reminded me of Pennsylvania. Maybe Connecticut had a few more hardwoods than Pennsylvania, but it was a beautiful state. Both states are rocky. The next day was like the first two—great mileage. I slept the last night in Connecticut, crossing the border into New York the next morning. That's not smokin' the trail, but it's good time in colder weather with shorter days, and I was proud of it.

CHAPTER 36:

DEFENDER OF THE TRAIL

New York would have lots in store for me.

I didn't mind the cold coming down the mountain, but as soon as I crossed the river, the wind started howling through the valley up the Hudson River. Instantly, my hands found my pockets, and my poles dangled. The wind blew them around like eggbeaters behind me, banging into my legs. I didn't think the temperature was below freezing, but the wind chill sure was. I actually stopped and pulled my raincoat out just to add another layer of protection.

Coming across, I have trouble following the trail, and I end up in a park. This turned out to be a lucky mistake. I pack a full load into my belly and probably spend a little too much time there. I have to ask directions to get back on the trail. I spend the night in a shelter, and hike out of there the next day.

It is just early afternoon when events start to go sideways again. A young lady with a young child comes around the corner. They both have backpacks, and the kid has this little, tiny one that's pretty cute. At first glance I can tell she's very upset. She's got the kid by the hand and she's moving as fast as she can, dragging him along beside her.

"Go the other way! There's a crazy man!" she tells me, tripping along.

"Whoa, whoa, whoa," I slow her down. "Tell me what's going on."

"I went to the next shelter, and there was a man there with a machete. He threatened us with it! He didn't touch us or anything, but he pulled the machete out and pointed it at us without saying a word. Then he pointed it down the trail like he wanted us out of there."

I had heard about a guy back in 2019 like this. He had actually killed people on the trail, but I thought he was up farther near the Connecticut border, and that the authorities had taken care of him. "Are you okay?" I asked her.

"I'm scared to death!"

"Listen," I asked her, "how about I walk you guys back to your car?"

She thanked me and agreed. The little guy bobbed along beside us in his little blue hat, just watching and listening. It wasn't too far to her car, about five miles maybe. I guess it didn't surprise me that crazy stuff happened here. We were literally about 40 miles from New York City, and you can even see the city from some of the higher elevations.

The more we walked and talked, I kept looking over at that little guy taking it all in. I felt so bad that his experience in the woods had to include being scared by this stupid crazy man. I started to get more upset about this situation, and I guess my protective instincts kicked in. I fell silent, thinking. We got to her car.

"What are you gonna do?" she asked.

"I'm gonna go back," I tell her.

"That guy is crazy! He has a machete!"

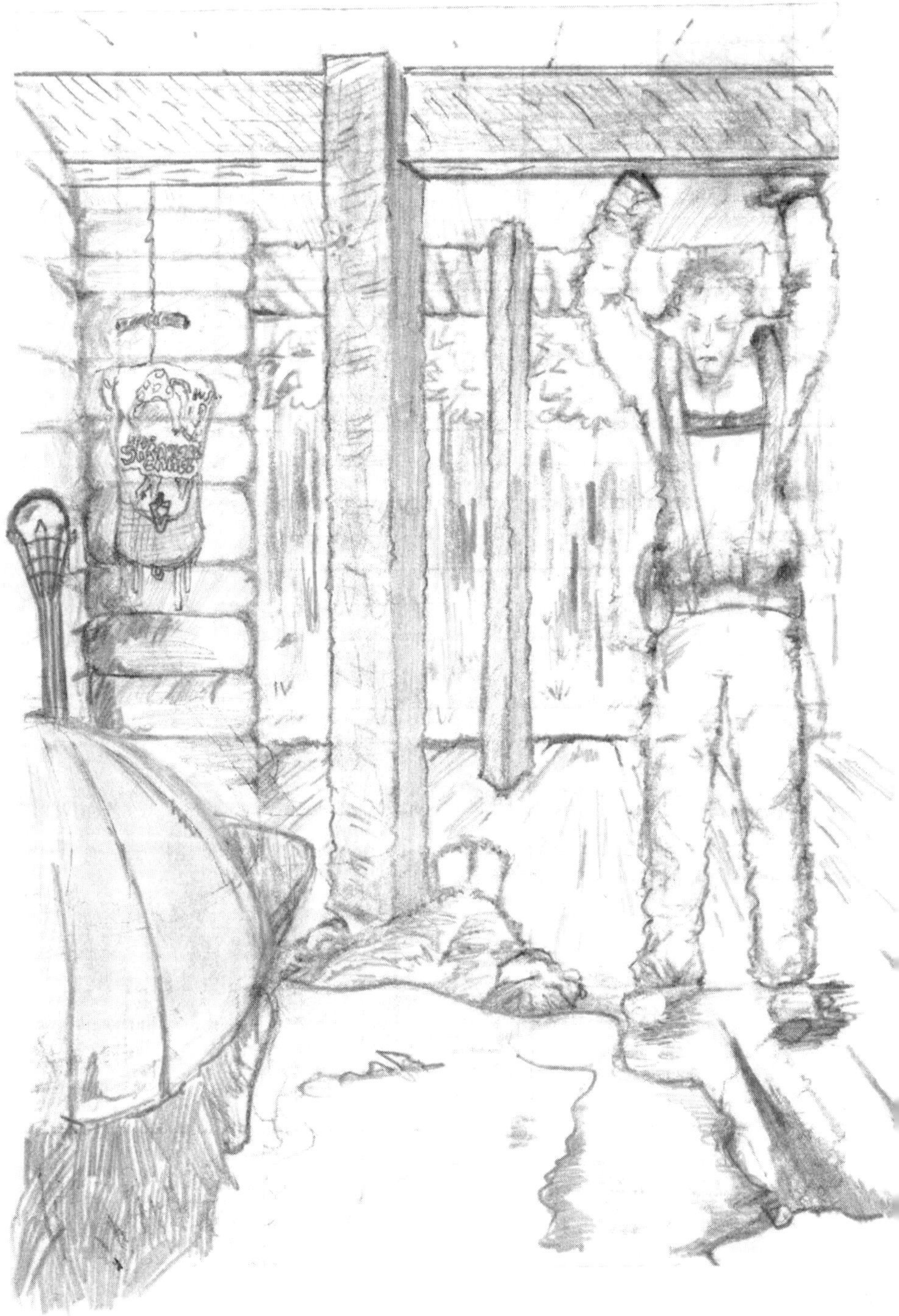

"I'll be okay," I promise. Then she thought I was the crazy one. She gave me a ride back to where I had met her, and I started back up the trail. I started putting together my plan.

I looked for something that might be a little better weapon than my hiking poles. I did have a knife, but it was a little Swiss Army knife, and I wasn't going to get anyone's attention with that. The most important part of that knife is the little scissors and the tweezers, which I think are a must on the trail. But I digress.

I come across a thick sapling of Japanese striped maple, still green. I jump up in the little tree, and keep climbing until the top breaks off. I break off all the limbs, and the remaining pole is about 6 ½ feet high. It's about 1 ¾ inches wide, and I feel like Moses with his mighty staff. I sharpen the thinner end to a nice point. Next, I take a rock and Zip-tape it to the blunt end for a little extra clubbing power. That should do it.

I think it's about half a mile to the shelter. It's not dark yet, but it will be. I figure this guy has already set up camp. What I've heard is that this guy sets his tent up in the shelter, and if anyone tries to get in, he scares them off. Well, if I could be there first this time, I was ready to meet him. I get to the shelter, and he's not there, so I get set up. My stick is real handy, leaning up beside me.

It occurred to me that if I had just met him, I probably would have been scared away too. But, because he had threatened this woman and her small child, he had crossed the line. I am ready for him. I figure he's just a blowhard, probably, and two can play that game.

I eat supper, and by now it's pitch dark. Maybe he isn't coming. I get into my sleeping bag with my stick propped up on my chest. I put my head in the rear of the shelter looking out. I figure, *Well, if he sneaks up on me, he might chop my leg off, but he won't get my head.* With that practical thought, I drift off.

I don't know how long I sleep before a thud wakes me up. *Well, he's here,* I think. I barely open my eyes, just so they are two flinty slits. All I can see of him is a silhouette, but he looks like a hiker. The thud was his machete whacking into a piece of wood just inside the shelter. As far as he can tell, I'm sure my eyes still look closed.

"I read about you," I say in a stiff monotone. "Are you my enemy?"

He does not respond. I wait about 10 more long seconds. His hand is still on the handle of the machete, dangling from the side where he whacked it.

"Yes," he says finally.

"I'm not afraid of you," I tell him. "I ain't afraid of you, and I ain't moving."

No response.

"And you ain't putting your tent in here either," I tell him, still doing my monotone voice. "There isn't room. You're welcome to stay around here, but you ain't setting up in the shelter."

No response.

"I got this staff. You got a 16-inch machete. Which one of us do you think will win? I'm ready for you."

No answer. His hand is still on the machete. My eyes are still on him, and my left hand is right by the staff ready to go. Another minute passes and probably both of us could hear my heart banging away in my chest. I wasn't scared, though. It was pure adrenaline at this point. God had my back on this, I felt sure.

Finally he pulls his machete out with one yank, and turns away, muttering curse words. He disappears into the dark.

Well, he might be gone, and he might not be. I sit up another half hour, waiting and watching and listening. At that point, I guessed I had called his bluff, and he left. I could only hope that he would start thinking twice about intimidating other hikers. I don't know what became of him, or what his deal was, but at least I stood up to him.

I had faith in my resources (my big staff) and faith in God. But I still didn't want to fall asleep and wake up with him in my face, or worse. I ended up sitting up and just watching in the woods, until I finally dozed off.

Sleeping sitting up is not good for me because of my back. I could barely move in the morning and thought, *If the guy comes back now, I'm in trouble because I can't move!* I slowly worked my way down out of my bunk, on to the floor, and then out to the ground. I did some stretches and bends that Jocelyn and Tristan had shown me from yoga and physical therapy, and eventually I started to limber up again. I did upward dog and downward dog and thought, *I am just an old dog!* I was there for about two hours stretching. I got my breakfast and was out of there by 5:15.

I decided to mutter a prayer for the guy instead of being fired up at him. He might have PTSD or some other problem. People don't just get like that without some kind of issue. Also, it occurred to me that it was actually near Halloween, and maybe this was some kind of terrible Halloween gag. I didn't know if I'd run into him at the next shelter. I had obviously chased him out of this one, so who knows?

I hiked for a few hours in the dark, a little jumpy, I guess. It was too cold for my hands to carry my hiking sticks, but I had my staff with me.

I hiked too close to a grouse. It took off and scared the shit out of me. When they take off, it's like out of dead silence a Blackhawk helicopter fires up and goes airborne right in your face. It's happened to me hunting before and I always have the same reaction. Ticker check.

Finally, it got to be daylight, and I could see around me a little better. Then I calmed down and dismantled the rock from the end of the staff, pocketed the used tape, and threw the staff into the woods. It was a beautiful frosty morning that turned into a beautiful autumn day. When I got to a high spot with a fire tower, I could see the city in the distance. I looked at all that iron and cement and chaos and commerce. I felt satisfied to be far away from it, walking through the falling orange and red leaves on my own two feet, with everything I would ever need packaged up and strapped to my back.

CHAPTER 37:

A HAPPY CREW

Jocelyn calls me early in the morning. My family is coming again, and for once, it doesn't look like it's going to rain. Jocelyn and Tommy are going to arrive around two. Then, Tristan is arriving a little later and we are going to get something to eat.

There might not be rain, but it was sure cold.

Hiking out to the rendezvous point, I walk through a meadow. There is a cow fence around its perimeter and a fire tower in the background. Leaning against the fence is a ladder just covered with shoes nailed to it. It looked like people had hiked to this meadow and said, "That's it. I'm done, right here," and nailed their shoes to the ladder. Beyond this cow pasture there is a road and then another long pasture. It makes me think of Pennsylvania.

My timing seems like it will be perfect, and I'll get to the road right when Jocelyn and Tommy get there. As I round the corner and come to the road, there is a food truck. Just right there, parked smack in the middle of nowhere like manna from heaven. It is a Greek food truck, and I get two big gyros on the spot. I know we are going out to eat later, but I have no doubt I'll be able to be hungry again for dinner. The big lunch makes me instantly tired. I just have to wait for Jocelyn and Tommy, so I ask the food truck guy if he would mind if I sack out right there on one of his picnic tables. He agrees.

I spread out my pad and everything. I had been all sweated up, so now I'm chilled and I cover up with my sleeping bag to get warm for my nap. I wake up after an hour to someone obnoxiously beeping their horn. Wasn't that nice of them to wake me up from my great sleep? I'm really thirsty, so I get something to drink, and I try to get back to sleep. I can't fall asleep again, but it's so nice to be warm in my sleeping bag that I don't mind just lying there and relaxing. I have to admit it would be nice to be in a hotel tonight, but the kids are coming to camp, and that's what we are going to do.

Tristan calls. He's going to be earlier than expected, so now everyone is going to be here at the same time. In the end, he beats Jocelyn and Tommy just by a few minutes. We plan to take the two vehicles, and park one at one end and the other about 30-32 miles down on the other end of the trail.

We take off, a happy crew. I love how it feels when we are all together. The kids interact with each other in this unique way that they don't do with other people. And Tommy has fit in with them so well. He's so relaxed and encouraging, but he can also deal with all our family teasing. Jocelyn's groin pull is not completely healed, but it did feel better as we walked. Tommy's still in really good shape from hiking about a thousand miles of the Pacific Crest Trail, and we all make good time.

We hike into darkness, and finally get to the campsite. I am hiking differently now, wearing my Fjällräven pants and my waterproof boots. All my warm gear is packed, including my puffy coat from Mountain Hardware. I thought maybe I could do without it for another couple weeks, but I decided it was too cold to do without. I was glad I had it, to be honest.

As we set up, Tristan and I decide to sleep out under the stars, and Jocelyn and Tommy set up a tent. We had done this on Mount Washington too, but the difference is that the forecast is clear and dry. We are able to see every star blinking and the haze of the Milky Way in the background. Looking up at heaven makes me feel like I'm in heaven.

We woke up early, and everyone made his or her own little breakfast. This is mid-November, so it's dark out, and yes, cold. And you guessed it, I can't use my sticks, so I had them stowed in my pack. I put the pack on, and tried to get warm. Instead of jumping up and down like I should have, I was actually trotting in circles around the camp. I don't know, maybe I was too happy having all my family with me and too cold to think straight. Of course, I tripped. And fell. And stove my wrist. And jammed a finger all up. Now I really can't use my sticks. I couldn't believe I had fallen that way. But I should have believed it; this stuff always happens to me.

I babied the finger but I couldn't tape it. We started down the trail.

"We're going to have to rename Tristan," says Jocelyn. "There's no rain in the forecast. We will have to call him Rain or Shine Man." Our laughter buoys me and I bob along. We got on a trail that took us down to a road, and there was the biggest oak tree I had ever seen. I think it was bigger than the one I had seen in Virginia. As we were taking pictures with the tree, a guy came down the road and offered to get a shot with all of us in it. It became one of my favorite pictures of the whole trail. We are all together, under this beautiful oak, and I'm making my dream happen with my family. The moment got so huge for me that I could barely hold it together for the picture.

I think when you've been depressed, and you know the heaviness and the darkness of it, the unbearable lightness of a happy moment, of joy, just hits you harder. It made me think of Sandy, and how lucky I am to have these kids, including Tommy. I was so grateful.

We pushed our pace to get to our camp with a little more time in the daylight. We wanted to build a fire and relax around it. We got our 15 miles in, and even though we are all in good shape, we were tired.

Tommy had brought freeze-dried mushrooms, black beans, rice, freeze-dried peas, and chicken of the woods. He cooked this amazing meal with a frying pan that he brought, so his pack must have been much heavier than everyone else's. It was delicious. I hated for the night to end because they would all leave the next day. We actually stayed up way later than I usually do, just talking and visiting.

The next morning, we didn't hurry out too fast. We only had to hike 10 miles to get to the car at the trailhead. We got there around 10:00, fetched the other car, and then had a nice meal at the restaurant. We were all starving and feasted. Then Tristan left, and Jocelyn and Tommy took me back up to the trailhead. I had to say all those sad goodbyes. I knew this was probably the last time I would see any of them until I finished. I really thought I wasn't going to be finishing until January, and that would mean it wouldn't count as a thru-hike because I didn't complete it before the end of the calendar year. That was going to be okay, I guess; I just wanted to have it done and get my head right. I would be all alone, except maybe on weekends, for the rest of the trip. It would be just me and the mountains, like a monk at a retreat. I looked at this prospect with respect.

While we were at the restaurant, someone had noticed my thru-hiker sticker on my pack. He assumed I was done already, and just back here for a weekend visit or something. He had done the trail as well and had finished in September. He had started the first week in March. I told him a little of my long list of delays.

"That sounds like it sucks. Hey, maybe you'll finish," he consoled me. "How long do you have to go yet?"

"I have to get down to the 900-mile mark at Shenandoah."

"I know exactly where that is. I have a picture of it!" He pulls his phone out and shows it to me. "That's your destination. I hope you make it, brother!"

"Me too," I admitted. "I need to."

I get back in the woods around 4:00 p.m., and I decide I'm not going to get too far today with only another hour of daylight left. I really don't feel like hiking in the dark tonight. I'm just going to look for a nice place to camp and settle in. And that's what I did. It was underneath a great pine tree, with a bed of needles below me. I almost didn't need my mat. The stars were out, but the next morning was supposed to be down in the upper teens, so I crawled into the tent for some warmth. I closed my eyes, but could still see the stars. I imagined I could still hear my kids' voices chatting as I drifted off.

CHAPTER 38:

ON THE BOARDWALK

Back when I had my shoulder MRI in February, before starting the trail, I had made a follow-up appointment for November, thinking I would be done with the trail by then. I still wanted to attend this appointment, because it was a consult with the surgeon about my rotator cuff. Those appointments are so hard to schedule. The most recent plan was to take a few days of rest at home and get to the appointment. But as I looked at my mileage creeping up, it seemed like there was a glimmer of a chance that I would finish before January. The encouragement from the guy in the restaurant had stuck in my head. Through Facebook, Jocelyn arranged a pick-up with my friend Gene, who would drive me home. I would have the appointment, and then get another ride back from my brother-in-law Don on the same day. These two trail angels made it possible for me to keep going without losing another day!

Truth be told, I'm not good at social media at all. I love going on it to see what people are up to, but I don't have the whole posting concept mastered. In fact, I once posted on Instagram accidentally.

"Dad! You can't put that on Instagram," Jocelyn told me.

"Put what?" I asked. "I didn't put anything on there!"

After that, Jocelyn just offered to do it for me. I guess I'm grounded from making my own posts. Which works great for me!

Unfortunately the MRI results showed that the rotator cuff had torn in such a way that the surgery would do no good. The surgeon told me that I would actually have better results just by doing physical therapy. I guess that was good news and bad news at the same time. I suffered through a torn shoulder 25 years or so before, but I had also wrecked my knee in that same fall (again, off a roof while working … at what point does a guy reconsider his profession?), and I had put all my energy into the knee situation. I wanted to have both issues corrected at the same time, but the surgeons absolutely refused. I guess it's better for your body to be able to concentrate its healing on just one area, but I thought at the time it was a time-costly obstacle for me as a self-employed contractor. Later, though, my friend Randi (who delivered the pink sparkly Crocs to me) did have two surgeries at the same time and he really suffered, so I now am grateful that didn't happen to me. In the end, though, I never took the time off to fix the shoulder, and it has plagued me my whole life. Hearing the report now, part of me was disappointed and really wanted a quicker solution that would mean complete relief. It sounded like physical therapy would be better than surgery, but it would also never completely heal it.

With that news, I headed back to the trail. Thanks to the ride from Don and his wife Diane, I got several more miles in that day and didn't have to take a zero.

I hiked into New Jersey. There was just a lake on the left-hand side, and a little sign on a rock that says, NJ and NY. That's it. I thought, *Man, New York didn't last very long.* But actually you are walking the line between the two states for quite a while, just like in the Smokies where your one shoulder is in Tennessee and your other shoulder is in North Carolina.

The day started out with rain, as the lake stretched on and on with two towns along its shore. The sun popped up around noon, like a surprise balloon. When I looked up, I saw a pole with an American flag on it, right on the trail. I snapped a picture of the flag and then a picture of me in the shadow of the flag, which I really liked.

After lunch, I wove in and out of New Jersey and New York, daydreaming about steak. And hot dogs. I cannot explain this, and I have to keep it real. For some reason hot dogs really appealed to me on the trail. By the second town, I actually considered taking my pack off and just running down to the town to get a few hot dogs. This is how a crazy person's mind can work. We all remember how it turned out the last time I allowed hot dogs to motivate my hiking. In the end, I gave up the idea and tried not to even look at the town as I walked on.

The rain picked up again, and the trail was empty. I was just a guy on a trail in the rain. It seems a little sad, but it was peaceful too.

Finally I came down a long descent, passing two or three couples and a group all coming up the hill with picnic baskets and wine to watch the sunset. Did they all realize it was raining? But a man who is motivated by hot dogs should not judge folks willing to walk in the rain for a sunset. The spot is famous, apparently, and there is a rock with a great overlook. Sure enough, it did quit raining later, so I was happy those people got the view they were after. I decided to wait on the road for a ride into town and sleep someplace dry that night.

I waited there for a while. Several cars passed me, but no one stopped.

So back up the hill I went. This was a rural farming area, but it was also a wetland. I could see how these lakes had formed between the two mountains. I came into a beautiful field and cow pasture, and then over a railroad track. Suddenly I came to a boardwalk. There was a path leading up to it on both sides which was not part of the AT, but this crazy plank walkway seemed to come out of nowhere. There were benches, and occasionally couples walking to see the sunset. Sure enough, with the clear skies, the sunset was turning out to be beautiful, and I wanted a good picture. I needed to get up higher for it to be good. Looking down the trail, I saw a tall tree with a big branch leaning over the boardwalk. Perfect. Time for some tree-climbing.

I step up on the fence rail, then jump onto the branch, and up I go, limb over limb. I shoot video and take pictures. Sam and Diane are going to love these. The elevation gives me just the right vantage point.

"Whatcha doin' up there?" came a bright little voice.

I look down to find it.

A lady with a brown ponytail and high cheekbones is down on the boardwalk, squinting up at me.

"I'm just taking pictures," I assure her. "I'm hiking the trail."

"Are you one of those thru-hikers?" Her voice has a heavy accent, but I can't place it.

"Yeah, I am."

"Could I talk to you a minute?"

Who was going to say no? "Sure," I tell her and shimmy down the branches, with a final leap to the ground that I hoped was graceful and manly all at once. She was maybe 45? Too young for me, but I'd still like to impress her. She was carrying a great big camera with a long expensive lens and a tripod.

She asked to see my pictures and we talked. She was from Lithuania, and in the end, we did exchange contact information. She was impressed by my trail photos, and told me I should be a photographer. Since she obviously was one, I took the compliment to heart. She confessed that she was not truly a professional, but that she did sell her photos. We talked and talked and I thought we were hitting it off, but it was getting dark.

She sprang up from the bench where we were sitting. "I've got to get home," she said. She had already stayed longer than usual and had quite a distance still to walk. She kept asking, so I explained the whole litany of mishaps that led to my flip-flop: broken bones, illness, the works—a total of three months off the trail.

"I've heard amazing stories from hikers on this trail," she said, "but yours is the worst one!"

"Gee, thanks. I can believe it. Everything that could go wrong, did."

"What kept you going?" she asked.

"I've got motivation," I told her with a sad smile. "My wife had cancer, and I'm doing this as a fundraiser. "

Then she wanted to know all about Sandy and what kind of cancer she had. I told her the whole story. Then she hugged me.

"I really have to go," she said. "But we will have to stay in touch."

And then she was off, and I was high as a kite, buzzing from my hug from a beautiful girl from a far-away land. Call me a cliché, and I've said it before, but a hug like that might be good for a couple hundred miles.

It's an hour after dark now, and I've got to get to someplace dry to camp. I walked maybe 20 more minutes through this maze of boardwalks, and I ended up getting on a trail that might have been an old railroad bed. I think it was a rails-to-trails deal, and it looked like a bike path. It came to a T, with a little bridge. I figure it's so late that no one is coming by here now. I set my tent up right there, off to the side a bit so people could pass if they needed to. I still had no idea where all these people were coming from. I hadn't seen humans for four days and now all of a sudden I was running into tons of people.

I was tired. I had been going a little stir crazy, so I was happy to talk to people, even if it was just to say hi as they were going the other direction. I slept soundly, dreaming of lovely Lithuanian ladies.

The next day I was trouncing through eight or nine inches of leaves, and whacked my toe yet again on a hidden rock. As I pummeled forward, I tried to trot and get my legs back under me so I wouldn't fall. This, in theory, was a good idea. But a bare branch stuck out into the space where my torso was supposed to go and stabbed into my shoulder. Yes, it hurt, but it also managed to rip into my dear Mountain Hardware puffy coat and tear two-thirds of the shoulder right off. I taped it all up so it stayed together just fine. Later I thought it wasn't looking so hot, and when I tried to re-tape the whole shebang it just went to shreds.

I ordered a new coat, and went with goose down, because it saved me three ounces. It was definitely warmer, but the outside wasn't as tough as my Mountain Hardware coat. I had to be so careful about getting it wet, so I was like a nutcase at the slightest drop of moisture in the air. I either took it off or covered it with my raincoat. Since I thought I'd be hiking into January, I'd need it. It ended up being a great purchase.

I stopped dancing on the border and officially entered New Jersey. It was time to head into a town and get resupplied. I really needed a zero, but I couldn't afford to take one. I had a niece in Stroudsburg, Pennsylvania, and I thought maybe if I could get there, I could do Thanksgiving there. Neither of my kids could be home this year, so I wouldn't be able to connect with them anyway. I will have to really fly for the next few days, down through the Delaware Water Gap, but I might make it.

CHAPTER 39:

AT WITS END

I'm near Unionville, New York, and I have heard a lot of good things about the Wits End Tavern from other hikers in Vermont. Good beer and good food, just not great on stinky hikers sitting at the counter. Well, I would see what I could do about that. I check the map, and right before I head out of the woods, I jump into an icy cold stream and wash off. Just like when I had soaked my shoulder, it takes my breath away. My whole body goes instantly numb. But I smell like Ivory soap, and I am ready. My clothes were dirty so I had jumped in with them on. They are still wet as I walk to the tavern, and I just duck into the restroom to change them when I get there.

The young hostess is reluctant to seat me at the bar.

"Well," she starts in, "I think it looks pretty full, and we have a lot of regulars here today …"

"Are you afraid I'm going to smell?" I interrupt her.

"Well, no … but anyway would you mind sitting at a table?"

"I have to charge my phone, and I can see an outlet over there by the bar."

She tells me to hang on a minute. I think she summoned the manager to sniff me out.

Pretty soon he comes over and gets into my personal space a little bit, circling me up, not aggressively, just curiously. Honestly, it made me chuckle. You know my rule on stinking.

"You can sit at the bar," he says quickly. "But you have to leave the pack." He puts his hands on his hips. "You can't have the pack in here."

"Okay," I agree. "Nobody's going to steal it out there?"

"Nah," he assures me. "This is a hiker-friendly place. You look like a thru-hiker," he adds, "but you can't be."

"No, I am."

"You don't happen to be The 'Shrooming Camel, do ya?"

"Yes, I am." Wow. My name has preceded me.

"Do you know you are the last hiker?"

"I do," I assure him. I sit at the bar, feeling pretty good. I'm so hungry, and the first thing I see is a steak. At this point I have burned through the money I raised to do the trail, because it has taken so long. But my brother has Venmo-ed me some money because he felt bad for me, I guess. I plan to blow it on this meal.

I haven't even looked at the menu, but I have seen the specials.

"I'd like to order two meals, if I can," I tell the waitress. "I'd like the biggest steak you got, and whatever kind of fish you've got." She gets me all set up. Potatoes come with both of them, and one includes roasted asparagus with sea salt. Very good. No gravy, but she gets me all the butter I want. The guy to my right, sitting there with his wife, is amused.

"No way you are going to eat all of that food," he tells me.

"Oh, I don't know about that, brother," I answer. "If you'd like to bet me, I'd take you on."

He declines. "I don't trust you hungry hikers," he says. "I heard you are a thru-hiker."

I tell him that I am, and he offers to buy me a beer. I really have to burn miles the next day, so I thank him but turn it down.

"One beer won't hurt ya," he chirps.

I had to agree with that. I order a Yuengling Lager and we sidetrack into a conversation about the brewing company, and how I live maybe an hour and a half from there.

Two girls come over then, and sit on my right. That's the side I'm deaf on and after norovirus I'm more deaf in my other ear than I even realize at the time, so I can barely hear what they are saying. They are peppering me with a thousand questions, which I have to keep asking them to repeat over and over. After a while that's pretty humiliating, but what can you do?

"What's your biggest question?" I ask. "I'll answer it before my food comes."

"What if we take the food away?" teases the one girl.

"I might bite you! I'm hungry!"

The girls laugh and have lots of questions. The wife of the man on my right is quiet, but she has some good questions too. Everyone loves to tell me what parts of the trail they've done, and what kind of circumstances they were in. Really, it was like that in all of the places I went, because I was the last hiker. At first, I hated it, like it was a badge of shame, but now I was embracing it. To tell you the truth, if I went to a bar after Vermont, I don't think I bought another beer for myself but was always treated by someone else, and I probably only bought my own food about 50 percent of the time. That was a blessing because, like I said, my finances were low at this point.

Finally my food came, the angels sang, and I feasted like a king.

The girls told me I could just nod my answers now, which suited me fine. The mashed potatoes disappeared into my mouth so fast, I was forced to order another serving of them. That fired up the guy to my right.

"Where do you put it?" he asked. "All that food weighs more than you do!"

He might be right. That was one of the questions—I had lost 28 pounds overall.

All the food was so good. I could feel my body being reenergized. I asked the waitress if they had fruit of any kind. She said they had cherries for drinks and oranges for when they serve Blue Moon. I took the orange. I'm allergic to the red dye in cherries. The bartender sliced it up for me, and I ate it skin and all. Everyone freaked out about that, but I told them it was sweet.

"Just try it one time, and you'll love it," I assured them. They all tried it. I laughed in that place from the minute the manager circled me to the very end. It was dark out now, and they started to ask where I was going to sleep. I told them I was headed back to the trail for another half hour, and then I'd camp. I told them I was trying to get the miles in so I could get to Stroudsburg.

"You're staying with us!" the girls told me.

"But I've got to get back on the trail really early," I protested.

"We'll get up!" they assured me. "We'll drive you back to the trail whenever you want."

That sounded pretty great to me. Time to go and get some shut-eye. I knew my bill would be expensive, and I went to check out.

"The guy next to you paid for everything," the host told me. "He even put the tip on."

I had ordered all that extra stuff! "No way!" I could not believe it. It choked me up actually, such an act of kindness. He didn't even know how much I really needed to conserve funds at this point. The girls saw me getting emotional and hugged me.

They lived about five miles away from the bar. They asked me what time I got up.

"You don't want to know," I told them. "But if you could get me to the trail by 6:00, I'd really appreciate it."

They agreed. I spent the night on the pull-out sofa couch, sleeping soundly with a full belly. They had the coffee pot loaded, and made me promise to save some for them. Around 5:30 a.m. they both stumbled into the kitchen. I had already eaten my breakfast, but they offered to have me eat with them, so we all had some yogurt and bagels. They got me all the way back to the trail. I had walked quite a distance to get to the bar, so it was a little drive for them. They dropped me off right around 6:00 a.m. It was dark and cold, but I was getting a good start on the day.

CHAPTER 40:

BIRD ON THE TABLE, BIRDS ON THE TRAIL

With that big meal fueling me, I could fly. I have two days to get to Pennsylvania and 49 miles to go. It will be a record breaker for me, but that's my goal. My lungs feel like they did when I was in high school. My feet and legs feel fantastic. My back, not so much. My shoulders feel awful, and my hands and jammed fingers are painful, but I'm up for the challenge. I'll be able to rest up on Thanksgiving Day. I've hiked this section before from the Sunfish Pond down to the Delaware Water Gap, in the winter when it was bitter cold with snow. This is the toughest part of the trail in New Jersey by far. Sunfish Pond is a series of boulders on the west side toward Pennsylvania. The rest of the trail was lovely, just like New York, and both of those states do a good job maintaining the trail.

I visited a guy who lived in a fire tower, and enjoyed the view of the boulders, the lakes, and the Poconos. When I got into camp, I had made it almost perfectly to the halfway mark, leaving 25 miles for the next day. My body felt pretty good, except for my back and shoulders, obviously. It wasn't even completely dark, though by the time I was set up for the night, it was. I had taken off my boots, goofed around a bit, and given my feet a break just wearing Crocs around the campfire. Most hikers do this. I was asleep by 7:00 p.m. Looking back, I wish I had gone just three more miles to make the next day a little better. I definitely could have done it physically.

They were predicting frost again for the next morning, so I was a little worried about not being able to use my sticks around Sunfish Pond.

I slept well. I was sore, but it was not intolerable. You get used to it. What I couldn't get used to was my shoulders and back, and thank God for the yoga breathing. My fingers bothered me too, but I could live with that. My pack wasn't super heavy right now either. I had only one day of food left, so if it took longer, I was going to be in trouble. My fuel tank was half full, and I know we are only talking about ounces here, but to a thru-hiker, this is holy ground. Everything, as light as possible, all the time. Especially with a buggered up back and shoulder.

In the morning, everything is white with frost, and very cold. I don't know exactly what the temperature is, but everything has a thick frost, almost like it snowed.

When I wake up, the entire inside of my tent is frost. I love my tent, and I wish they had not discontinued it, but this lack of ventilation is the reason they did. Normally, as long as I keep the door unzipped, there's no problem, but last night had been too cold to do that. At 10:30 p.m. or so I had zipped the door all the way up. By this time I am also in my 20-degree sleeping quilt, size large and tall. If you could see me, you would laugh at that size, because I am not a "large" by any stretch of the imagination. But I need the quilt-style bag because I have nervous leg syndrome, and a mummy bag drives me crazy. I can zip the sides together and cinch the bottom and top if I want a mummy bag, but most of the time I let it unzipped.

It takes me an hour and five minutes to get out of camp because my hands are so cold. I am out of hand warmers, which is stupid because I thought I had two more pairs when I didn't, and I didn't get more. Now I know I can't use my sticks all day. I just load them up in my pack. I have to do only one thing at a time, and gloves don't really help, because my hands don't produce their own heat after having been frostbitten when I was younger. It kind of pisses me off as I go along. One minute to work, and then they're burning numb. Then I have to sit there and warm them back up in my pockets, and then start again. I finally take off as fast as I can go safely. After exactly one hour, I've gone 3.5 miles, and that's really smoking the trail without poles. The pack only has some water in it, because the water sources are limited, but it's light. After another two hours I take an official break and take my boots off, etc. I am at 10 miles at 10:00, and I'm in good shape. My hands are still in agony, and I decide to take the time to make another cup of coffee. I don't even wear my gloves. I just put socks on my hands and wrap them around the cup. I sip it, but I keep it hot on the stove as I drink until it gets low. I keep adding more water so I can keep heating. If my stove fuel runs out, I don't care because I'm headed for supplies.

Lunch was all the loose food in my pack, including the gross protein bar which I never enjoy. I did enjoy the venison jerky Jocelyn had sent that was made by my brothers-in-law. Their jerky is my favorite. When I got to Sunfish Pond, I knew the pace would slow down and I still had 15 miles to go. Thank God the frost had cleared off the boulders, and I wouldn't need my back-up trail to get around them.

What I did need was a pair of hands that weren't frozen. Well, I didn't have any, so I just struggled through, taking my hands out of my pockets only when I had to. I made it through at around 3:00. I knew it would be cutting it close to get down off the mountain before daylight ended. I should probably eat, but I needed to keep going.

My sister was coming to pick me up at the trailhead, and that was the 900-mark if you go from north to south on the trail. Ironically, that same mile marker on the south to north trail was my ultimate destination in the Shenandoah's. That meant I'd gone 1,800 miles and that felt pretty damn good. I jumped in her car, happy to be warm and on the way to my niece's.

My nieces are Chrissy and Hillary, and I'll be staying with Chrissy and her husband. Hillary's husband is going to join me for the seven or so miles I'll be doing in the morning so that the day after Thanksgiving I can start on the other side of Stroudsburg. It's not many miles, but it's like a day off anyway for me, and I'm happy to have the company.

I love Thanksgiving, and I love the food. It's my second favorite holiday after Easter, because it's all about the family and the food. It hasn't been polluted by presents and commercials. It's my first Thanksgiving without the kids, except for once when I was working in Malibu, but I'm happy to spend time with family I don't normally get to see.

Chrissy had a hot tub, and she left me in there for hours while she was busy getting the food ready. What a treat that was! My bones were sore and getting in there really helped. I even played with the kids before the meal. For dinner we went to Chrissy's in-laws and I got to meet a whole pack of new people. Of course everyone wanted to hear about the hike, so I got to tell the same stories again for these folks. They all thought I was completely crazy, of course.

The food was so delicious, I just couldn't stop eating.

I loved every minute of our holiday, catching up with my nieces and nephews, and all their spouses and kids. Chrissy's husband dropped me off at the trailhead in the morning on his way to work. It went so smoothly that I had to wonder why everyone complains about the Pennsylvania section of the trail, especially the rocks. Well, I would soon find out.

For the first 11 miles, I did not have anything but good things to say about the trail in Pennsylvania. I was on a ridge with a great view and rock cliffs. That's really when the rocks began to start. I saw a sign that gave information about how thick the ice was here, originally 300 yards thick. That's a lot of ice. The edge of the glacier stopped right here. All that history with the glaciers blows my mind. No wonder all the rocks are just piled up here. They make perfect rattlesnake dens. A lot of people don't like snakes, but I think they are beautiful. I don't like them striking at me like the one in Virginia, but otherwise they are okay.

I found myself absorbed by the rock piles. Instead of hiking, you're really bouldering. The rocks are similar to the ones in Maine and New Hampshire. At least there aren't rattlesnakes in Maine, and maybe not in the White's in New Hampshire either. It was challenging, for sure. The other difference is that some rocks come straight up out of the ground to a point, thousands and thousands of them. It's so hard to get a good grip with your feet. The trail joke is that you go through seven or eight pairs of shoes on the AT, and one of them is just for Pennsylvania. I get it! You're just begging for a flat space to put your foot.

Your eyes have to be glued to the trail. Not an easy task for a guy like me who likes to look around. I did my fair share of stumbling. I passed some guys in camouflage out scouting deer or putting up tree stands for buck season which started the next day. We have over a million hunters in this state, more than any other in the whole country. These guys take it seriously. Pretty much everyone in my hometown, and in my family, takes it seriously. Where I live, the kids get a day off school to go hunting. No lie.

As a kid I had so much fun hunting with the family. Now, because I like to keep moving, I haven't shot a deer in years. But in the old days, we hunted in gangs and put on drives. First, you set up two standers, and they wait in a designated area. Then the rest of the guys, the drivers, stand about 50 yards apart in a big line, and they start walking toward the standers. That's right, you walk toward the guys with loaded guns. The drivers clap and yell and talk and make a big ruckus to flush the deer out so the standers can get a shot. Of course, I am a gifted driver of deer. A rowdy walk in the woods? Sign me up.

If you missed your target, they never let you forget it. Fathers, uncles, friends ... everyone had a joke at your expense. They would cut the shirt tail off your shirt to show you had missed one. Guess who had a lot of short shirts? I'm not particularly wild about the idea of killing anything, but I loved the comradery and the competition. When I was a kid, hunting put food on the table. For many families, it still does.

I talked to the hunters, of course, pouncing on them like they are venison backstrap steaks and I am starved, because I am starved—for conversation! A month ago I thought I would have seen some bow hunters in New England, but I didn't. It occurs to me that it will not be smart to be walking around out here on the first day of buck season with just my orange hat on. I really need an orange vest to be visible, so I don't get shot accidentally by some eager hunter. My next town would be the Palmerton area, but I have to get through these boulders to get there. I'm hiking as hard as I can.

This area was also nationally known as a popular "flyway" for hawks, eagles, and other birds of prey. The area includes Hawk Mountain. You can be walking along, and there will be a little stone hut. They are built by birdwatchers. You can go sit in these with a pair of binoculars and just watch the birds of prey fly right over your head all day long. I saw three eagles flying together right over my head, maybe 25 yards up. I was taking a break with my feet up and my boots off right in the middle of the trail, so I could see them well. I was still enough that I didn't scare them. One redtail hawk after another went over.

After that break I couldn't keep my eyes off the sky. I must have stubbed my toe 50 times.

Then I saw a golden eagle. It flew right over my head. I had always looked for them, but had never seen them except once in Alaska. Now these birds are absolutely the biggest birds I've ever seen. The wingspan is massive, and you can tell they are the terror of the skies. The eagle was so close I could see his claws, and each one was as fat as my finger. His wingspan had to be six feet wide. I was in awe.

A little further down the trail, I can see a few birdwatchers in a hut. They have cameras and binoculars, and they wave me over.

"Are you a thru-hiker?" they asked. "We can see the triangle on your chest."

And then we went through the whole thing again, that I was the last hiker. They had seen the golden eagle too. We talked for about 10 minutes, and I asked about the trailhead at Palmerton.

"It's seven miles," they said, "but it's a rough seven miles."

"Well, it's been rough," I agreed.

"It's gonna get even worse," they warned.

Terrific. I bid them goodbye and just a little bit further I ran into a family of Asian descent. They all had cameras and daypacks, but they were also collecting mushrooms. I couldn't wait to talk about mushrooms with them.

I had a hard time with the mother and father because of the language barrier, but I was able to get some information from the kids. The daughter spoke very good English, and I asked her about the mushrooms. I showed her the ones I had collected.

She showed me hers, and I felt I had to warn her about our "Angel of Death" mushroom that looks just like a white mushroom that is safe to eat in Asian countries. She said she had lived here long enough to hear about the Angel of Death mushroom. She showed me the mushrooms in her pack, and they all looked safe. I make it a habit to mention this to anyone whom I recognize as Asian, because the last six fatalities have been Asian people mistaking this highly poisonous mushroom for their native one. We talked for quite a while because this young girl wanted to do the Appalachian Trail on her own someday. Her parents seemed pretty apprehensive about this, but I tried to encourage her. Really, if you stayed in the bubble, you could find people to stay near every night. You had to be smart about it, but plenty of single women do it. I showed her a picture of Moonshine, but I don't think the parents were sold.

I said goodbye to my new friends and got a hug from everybody.

I ate another Snicker's bar, but I had to get off the hill before the parking lot cleared out of the day hikers. Hopefully one of them would be my ride into town.

The last descent toward the trailhead was pretty steep and rocky. Jim Thorpe, originally known as Mauch Chunk, might be the prettiest towns on the trail, despite the evidence left behind from its mining history. You have to take the good with the bad, I guess.

When I finally get to the parking lot, it's still daylight, and there are plenty of cars. I sit and wait with my backpack on a big rock, and hope and pray that a hiker will come out who can give me a lift to town so I can buy my vest. After 10 minutes, two ladies are headed down the trail, and they look like real hikers. I can just tell by the way they are walking.

When we get acquainted, I find they are none other than the famous trail angels Jinx Hikes and Yard Sale. These two encouraging and funny ladies are former hikers who still love hiking today. I met up with them later at Trail Days, including Yard Sale's husband Crazy Hair. They own the Lookout Hostel on Route 309 where I would get to stay later. Right now, of course, their hostel is full of hunters.

Jinx Hikes will provide trail magic for me later on down the road. The two of them must have spread the word about me, because it seemed like every hostel I went to from that town on knew about me before I even got there. It was like I had celebrity status, with the dubious honor of being the last guy on the trail. At the same time, the "fame" of being the last hiker increased the people who followed me on social media, and then the donations for Sloan Kettering also went up. That was so encouraging to me! The AT world is kind of a small world after all. Those ladies helped me out more than they knew, just by spreading the word.

But before all that, they gave me a ride into Palmerton, so I could buy the orange vest. It would be suicide in the woods the next day without it. The first place we stopped was sold out, and the next place was sold out too. They had nothing in orange at all. Finally we stopped for a bite to eat in a place called Bert's Restaurant that also had rooms really cheap at $35. It was definitely a louder bar, but it would work for the night. Best of all, it was warm and dry. I decided to stay there, and catch a ride to the trailhead in the morning.

I had a great breakfast there. When I peeked in the "Hiker Box" that places keep to provide free supplies for hikers, there was some orange. It turned out to be a jacket with sleeves, all in orange. Bingo. My Filson wool hat is orange too, and I've had that a long time. I sleep in it. The orange color was pretty dirty, so I actually kept it on my head while I showered the night before, soaping it up like it was hair to try to clean it up. Now I was ready for hunting season for sure.

CHAPTER 41:

DRAGGIN' HORNS

Wearing my new orange jacket and clean hat, I get a ride in the pre-dawn hours to the trailhead. Predictably, it's full of cars because this is Pennsylvania, and today is the first day of buck season. Today is a very bad day to have a set of horns.

I barely take one step into the woods, and I already hear shooting. It's not even daylight! Hunters can get a little too excited sometimes. Thank God for my jacket. I head up a steep ascent, right outside Palmerton. This is some of the hardest hiking in the country, right in this spot. It's rocky, full of house-size boulders stacked one on top of another. I don't even know how trees grow here, to be honest. You're kind of on top of the Lehigh Tunnel, which everyone has to drive through to get from Northeast Pennsylvania to the Philadelphia and Reading areas. About an hour into the hike, I can see people dragging their freshly killed bucks out of the woods. Pretty soon I see an older guy with a buck, trying to drag it over some huge boulders.

"Hey, buddy, do you need a hand?"

"Man, I could sure use one. Did you already get your buck?" he asks. I am wearing all this orange, so I probably look like I'm hunting, not hiking.

"No, I'm just a hiker, but I can give you a hand. I am a hunter, but right now I am hiking the Appalachian Trail."

He seems to have a fresh realization that he is on the AT.

"I don't know," he says. "My family is way over on the other side of the hill. About four or five miles away."

"I can help," I tell him.

"Can you carry my gun while I try to drag him?" he asks. I look at him; he's definitely gray, thin, and has a few more years on his bones than I do. There's no way he's going to get this deer out of here, over four miles of this terrain. It's not a huge deer, just a smaller 8-point, but he isn't going to make it.

"Tell you what," I offer, "I'll run ahead and put my pack at the road we are gonna cross up here in about a half a mile. Then I'll come back and drag the deer while you carry the gun."

So that's what I do.

When I get back, the guy hasn't moved. He did try to get it over the boulder, but he couldn't get it. I held his gun for him. We used my rope so we could both get a handle on this deer, and together we struggled to get it over the boulder. I bet it weighed about 120, maybe 100 field-dressed, but it was a tough job and it wasn't working.

Finally, I said, "How about this? You take your gun. I'm going to take his legs and tie him around my body so I can climb it with him on me."

Well, that worked. I tied his feet around my shoulders, and I held up the deer's back legs, and put my butt right in its carcass. In this way, I could walk up and over, and we got it out of there. It was maybe one of the worst spots on the trail even though there was no elevation, just up and down boulders. I got him to the road, and it felt good to give this guy a taste of trail magic.

He called his family to come and get him and thanked me. I headed on my way.

I ended up dragging two more bucks on this day. Up and over rocks, just until we could get to a nearby road. One was gut shot and bled all over my jacket as I hefted it fireman-style over my shoulders. I really wasn't crazy about smelling like deer guts the rest of the day and could not wait to get into a stream and wash off.

I was exhausted, but I felt strong. My lungs felt great. There were still plenty of guys in the woods, so I didn't want to strip down and get shot, or be observed. So, with my clothes on, I headed for the water.

My first contact put a hold on that right on the spot. The water was freezing. I thought maybe the next stream would be warmer, but it wasn't. I never did get in to clean the clothes. I was sweated up dragging the deer, but as soon as I stopped hiking, I was freezing again. I just couldn't do it. I ended up boiling water and using a bit of soap to clean my clothes, and myself, at the end of the day. I washed my undershirt in the creek and hung it to dry.

It was so nice to see people, and I talked to everyone for a few minutes to see how they were doing and ask if they had seen anything. As I hiked, I had seen a few bucks sprint by, and I could tell them about that. As a kid, it's all any of us talked about all season. And, if you shot something, your buddy next to you helped you lug it out. I hadn't had the best mileage today, but that was fine.

When I first crawled into my sleeping bag, after washing everything, I was freezing. But it was so cozy and warm in there, and I was so exhausted from hauling deer, that I slept like a sack of stones.

I woke up plenty early. I had to put on the wet clothes in the freezing cold of a raw November morning, and that hurt, I can tell you. Once I started walking, I was fine. I had four heating pads in my mittens, one on top and one underneath for each hand so I could use my sticks, and that helped a lot.

I'm hearing shots again, as soon as its daylight. I vow that I cannot help anyone drag deer today, because I have to meet my friends, Matt and Lisa, at the end of the day. They are hiking in from 309 to meet me, and they've promised me a steak dinner, which always inspires my feet to fly.

After about a half hour of hiking, I come across this guy alone with a trophy buck. I mean, a nice one. I admired his deer, and we chatted. I could tell he really wanted me to help him drag it. My clothes had just started to really dry, and I was plenty warm, dang it.

I helped him anyway.

Matt calls me. They have gotten a late start, and they aren't going to make it quite halfway. I'll have to go a little farther to meet them. This is probably for the best because the trail I have just been through would be pretty tough for someone who was not a practiced hiker. We pick a rendezvous spot and plan to hike toward each other.

I see another hunter, a young guy, with a buck. I chat with him. He's young and he's doing fine so I don't help him. Then there's another guy, and the terrain is bad again. He's not directly on the trail, and we are getting close to a power line. We are several hours into the day now, and there's shooting everywhere. It's like a firing range. Now this hunter does not have any orange on! He is wearing a buckskin baseball cap.

"Man! It's hunting season!" I tell him. "What are you doing out here?"

"I don't hunt," he said.

"You got a hat that's the same color as a deer," I explain. "Some poor hunter is going to shoot you and then he's going to feel like shit for the rest of his life."

I cut a sleeve off my jacket. "At least put this on your hat," I beg him.

He did. And he thanked me. I don't know if he took it off 20 feet down the trail or if he kept it pinned to his hat.

I was able to meet up with Matt and Lisa, cozied up in front of a nice fire on the trail. We hiked out together, and they treated me to a juicy steak dinner at Thunderhead Lodge. I spent the night at the Lookout Hostel, which you remember was owned by Yard Sale and her husband Crazy Hair, whom I met up in Palmerton. I had the place all to myself. I resupplied, did laundry, showered, and called the kids.

The next day I am back at the trail near Route 309 and heading south. I come upon a grandfather and his grandson struggling with a deer. Neither one of them can really handle it. The rocks aren't too bad here, and it's a small doe, but the two of them just can't manage it.

"How far do you have to go?" I ask.

"Half a mile," says the grandfather. Looks like I'm off again.

I got the grandson to give me a hand. We could do it together pretty quickly. We got two big sticks and used my rope and got it right out of there. We got ahead of the grandfather a bit. He was gray and thin, taking his time over the rocks, and I could tell the whole morning had taken it out of him. He had come out without a gun, just spending his morning to help this kid get his first deer. My father-in-law Sam was the same way. When Tristan got his first deer, I'm not sure who was happier, Tristan or Sam.

They already had it gutted, and I asked the boy about the heart. He didn't know if they had it out or not, so I reminded him not to forget it. The grandfather probably had it covered, but by now he was a distance behind us and I was starting to get into my dad mode.

I left them then, before the memories got too strong. I was sure they would be able to get the deer on the tailgate. I needed to get 15 miles in today.

Looking back, I think it was a good change for my body, to do a different kind of exercise instead of just churning out the miles. My left arm is still completely useless, but I still have good strength in my right arm. My body was finally starting to feel pretty good otherwise. My healed foot feels great, my knees, ankle, everything from the waist down. My back always hurts, but I was used to it.

After a quick meal and nap at the Allentown Hiking Club Shelter, I run into some hikers, real hikers. I can tell because they have packs with sleeping gear in them. These guys don't have a lick of orange on them either. They were not in favor of hunting, but I assured them that would not keep them from getting shot by accident.

I cut a piece of the other orange sleeve for both of them. I still had about a vest left at least. They both fastened the long pieces to their hats. The one guy just sort of tucked it under his hat like a fancy tail, and the other guy had it going up and over and down the back like a skunk stripe. Hopefully, it was better than nothing.

The rain had started, but I put my raincoat on too late. Trudging along, my wet clothes stuck fast to my skin and rubbed around under my raincoat. I kept it unzipped, as the temperature was warming up.

A bang cracked through the trees. Close. Maybe 300 yards in front of me. When I got there, a hunter was gutting a bear. I helped him get the bear on a sort of cart that he would use to drag it. He was headed all the way back toward 309 in the opposite direction than I was. There was a road about 200 yards away. I figured I could help him that far at least.

Dragging a bear is not like dragging a deer. They weigh more, obviously, but they are like dragging a piece of blubber. They get snagged on everything, roll away from you down a bank, and are generally a pain. This one was about 350 pounds. It was nearly impossible to move and I was sure glad we had the cart, and only had 200 yards to go.

After that I am so tired that I am dizzy. By now the rain is sheeting down, and I'm cold. I had left my pack where I had encountered the bear hunter, so I didn't have that to weigh me down on my walk back. I retrieved it, and finally came upon the Eckville Shelter at about mile 13, which was not as far as I wanted, but this shelter was a blessing. It was enclosed, dry, warm, and a real building with a door that shut tight. I hung up all my clothes and burned a candle underneath them in the building all night. I didn't know if it would help dry them, but it was a nice sight. Best of all, I was not bothered at all by any mice.

It stopped raining in the night. At 1:00 a.m. I went out to take a leak and the stars were out. The air was already turning colder. Back in my warm sleeping bag, I slept well. I didn't have a pillow, because all my clothes were wet. I've tried the blow-up pillows, but I just can't keep them in the bed. They pop out every time you roll over so I gave up on those things. Now Hyperlyte makes a soft terry cloth bag that you can put your clothes in, specifically to use as a pillow. But, I had forgotten it at home the last time I was there.

I was not excited about putting the wet clothes on in the morning.

CHAPTER 42:

LA LA LA (PORT CLINTON)

My lack of excitement was well warranted, but it turned out the candle did help take the worst of the moisture out. The rain is gone, but it is cold outside now. All the mud puddles are frozen, and so am I. I hike fast in my base layer, a little Smartwool T-shirt that has 1,800 miles on it now and is worn through, especially over the shoulders where the straps go. I also have on my alpaca hoodie, which also has holes rubbed through on both shoulders. I've worn both of these all day, every day. Hey, they've done their job.

I'm headed for Port Clinton, where they have the big ice cream challenge, and I'm excited to try it. For this challenge, hikers are invited to eat a whole block of ice cream. If you can do it, you get a free shirt. As I hike, I'm warming up. I'm feeling a little sore from dragging the bear, but in ten minutes I can forget all about that. It's a stunning, sunny morning. The deer are running all over the trail, but I'm not hearing any shots. I'm kind of relieved not to be sidetracked by dragging these dead animals around all over the place. I've got a hike to finish, and I haven't put in a great day since Thanksgiving.

The mileage might not be that great today either. My goal is just to get to Port Clinton and spend the night somewhere there. I'm flying and take a nice long break with my feet up at a shelter. I didn't even snack, so I could do better with the ice cream.

By 2:00 I arrived and scouted around to find the place with the ice cream challenge, so I could get the T-shirt. Wouldn't you know, they closed with the end of the hiking bubble? I was having hot dog flashbacks. Maybe someday I can get back here and try it then.

The next order of business is to find someplace to stay, and I can't find anything. It's cold. I'm not hiking right now, so I feel the temperature. I start asking people, and a guy gives me the name of a hostel called the Cozy Cottage at Shepherd Valley with Phil and Julie. When I call, Phil is able to pick me up. These two are so nice, and I highly recommend their hostel. It's on a gorgeous farm with animals running around. My little room was clean and cute, and they invited me for dinner and breakfast. They had heard of me, and knew I was the last hiker; probably Jinx gave them the heads-up. I got all cleaned up and charged up. They were a lovely family.

They provided a great breakfast, and I didn't want to leave. If I could have taken a zero to rest with them, I would have. Phil tells me that before I get back on the trail, I have to stop at the barber shop at Port Clinton.

I take him up on his suggestion, and am I ever glad that I did. He drops me off there and introduces me to the owner. I had bought a hoagie for my lunch the day before, so I ate it outside before going in. Meanwhile inside the Port Clinton Barber Shop, the owner and a guy named Harold Seaford were having their usual morning conversation. Within minutes, Harold picked up his guitar and started singing. There are all kinds of musical instruments there, and hikers are encouraged to pick up one and start playing. Sometimes pedestrians just come by to listen to the music. Now the hikers had been gone for a while, but they knew about me and knew I would be coming through. I wouldn't have stopped there if Phil hadn't told me, so I almost missed it.

After I ate the hoagie, I left my pack outside and went in. They made a spot for me right next to Harold and he played on and on. The barber played too. The story goes that they give guitar lessons and one of their students was Taylor Swift. That's the story and I cannot confirm or deny it. Her home is right down the road, so it could be true.

I had dreams of going over 25 miles this day, but I couldn't leave the barber shop. I was in awe of Harold's talent at his older age. He could sing anything, and would just look right into your eyes and sing away. People shouted requests. Sometimes Harold played them, and sometimes he did not. He played fun songs, country and western style, or folk style, a variety like you'd hear around a campfire. The two stylists were there cutting, and maybe ten or more spectators were there too. Most people are there for the music, not for a haircut.

Harold, sitting right next to me, asked me to sing the next song. I told him I couldn't, but I would sing along with him. Of course everyone was rooting me on to do the solo. I told Harold I'd practice with him, so I sang with him twice, and then it was time for me to go for it. I totally locked up, all I could remember was the chorus, "La, la, la, la, la" forever. We all laughed and clapped, and I made an idiot of myself, but it was a great time.

I got my haircut there, and three hours later I finally left. So much for my 25-mile day. Sometimes life is more important. I kept telling myself over and over that I was a lucky guy to experience this, and that was the most important thing. Some people never get to be in a place like this, but I did! A guy from the shop gave me a lift for the few blocks to the trailhead.

My mind stayed on the barber shop as I headed down the trail, with the "La, la, la, la, la" echoing in my head with every step. I wondered briefly if those hikers I had met had ever looked up "Beat It" to see if Eddie Van Halen was playing guitar. I bet I was doing almost four miles an hour, singing and hiking, with some mild elevation and stunning views. I decided to go on after dark to make up for lost time. Even at night I was speeding along. I took a break only to eat Snickers bars, beef jerky, and peanut M&M's. Finally by 10:00 p.m. I had put in 18 miles, at least half of it in the dark. That is a respectable day.

It's cold, but I'm sweated up. I heard there is a creek here, and I intend to get in a rather deep hole. I try not to think about it. I take my clothes off and jump in before I can stop myself. My breath goes immediately, and I leap out pretty quickly. Sadly, I had forgotten I had my headlight on. It clattered off my head and down to the bottom of the deeper hole. I was going to have to go back in after it, which hurt me, I can tell you that. I took a minute to get my breath back under control and to try to get fired up again for the shock.

I managed it. Except for my hands, I was really okay. I was naked except for a pair of wool socks and my Crocs, but the trail was deserted. I used my little trail towel to dry off and snuggled directly into my sleeping bag. I had a Patagonia long underwear set on, just to keep my skin off of my sleeping bag, and it felt pretty cozy. My alpaca was still kind of sweaty. It didn't stink, but I didn't put it on. I put on my Smartwool hoodie and flipped the hood part up over my wet hair. I had eaten some of that Wild Bill's beef jerky that I love, so I was not hungry really, and I fell asleep in no time.

I was already dreaming of my breakfast. Oatmeal with Mudwater mixed in and peanut butter tastes pretty gourmet when you're hungry. I just can't get enough of peanut butter. Some people dream of glamorous hotels; I dream of peanut butter.

When I woke, it was still freezing cold, but my breakfast was all I had imagined.

And then I hike, and hike some more. The cold gets me going faster and faster, and I know I can put in huge mileage days through this area. My body feels pretty good and my brain likes the 25-plus mile days. Very satisfying.

I pass through Camp Swatara, and I imagine it just bustling with kids everywhere. It was empty now. Same thing with the William Penn Shelter. This shelter even had windows up on the second floor, but none that looked out over the rambling Amish farms below it. I wasn't ready to camp yet, so I passed on through. I was near Route 81, so I was able to get a guy to agree to come pick me up for a trip into town, but then at the last minute he had a family situation come up. He canceled.

I was walking along by a stream then, after it had gotten dark out, and I tripped a little on a rock. It was the kind I've already told you I stubbed my toe on a million times. I stumbled forward, and tried to trot my way out of it, but it didn't work like that. Instead, I fell forward, and a branch sticking out into the trail caught me right in front of my left sleeve. Of course this felt terrific on my shoulder, but it also managed to rip the seam of the sleeve, up over my shoulder and clear down around the back. Another coat casualty!

My little tumble also catapulted me over the bank, into some massive poison ivy vines (I would discover later) wrapped around a tree, and into a little stream. When I finally collected myself, I noticed the sleeve dangling halfway down my upper arm, attached only by about a fourth of the seam under my armpit.

I climbed back up onto the trail and proceeded to curse for a good 15 minutes about ripping that dang coat. I loved that coat!

By the time I made camp, it was bitter cold again, and I was wet. I used Zip tape on the coat sleeve and managed to reattach it pretty well. It would rub a bit under the arm, but I got it to hold together. Ready for the day to end, I slept.

The next day brought more of the same—cold temperatures and a bit of a detour. I got to talking to Jocey and paused to take a break. When I got going again, I went the wrong direction. I caught myself after a bit, did a little more cursing, then headed back the right way. I passed through a historical section called Yellow Springs Village. The highlight of my day was a surprise meal from Jinx. She brought me homemade bean soup and cookies that were still warm from the oven. That was heaven in my mouth. The salty soup tasted so good, and the sweet chocolate cookie was a perfect finish. I think my mood improved considerably after her visit.

In my tent, in the dark and cold again, I slept encouraged knowing that the next day I would get to see some old friends and make a new one.

CHAPTER 43:

OLD FRIEND, NEW FRIEND

It's a bright and sunny day, but the temperature never gets out of the teens, with a high of 18. That's dangerous for my hands, and it was single digits in the morning. That means no sticks all day.

As I was hiking along, I passed these beautiful reservoirs. I couldn't believe it. I've lived in this state, not too far away from here, and never hiked this area near Harrisburg. No one has even talked to me about it. At one point, I was up on a ridge with a view of both mountains, and I climbed a tree to get a better picture of this incredible area. It was truly wilderness. No sign of a town or even a road.

Then I saw him.

A magnificent 10-point buck, with a distinctive dropped tine that I had spotted clear back near 309. That time I had been several feet from him, and I could see that crazy dropped tine curving around almost like it went into his mouth. It was the same deer, right here, just feet away from me again. He walked with a limp. His dropped tine was on the right, as I was looking at him, just bedded

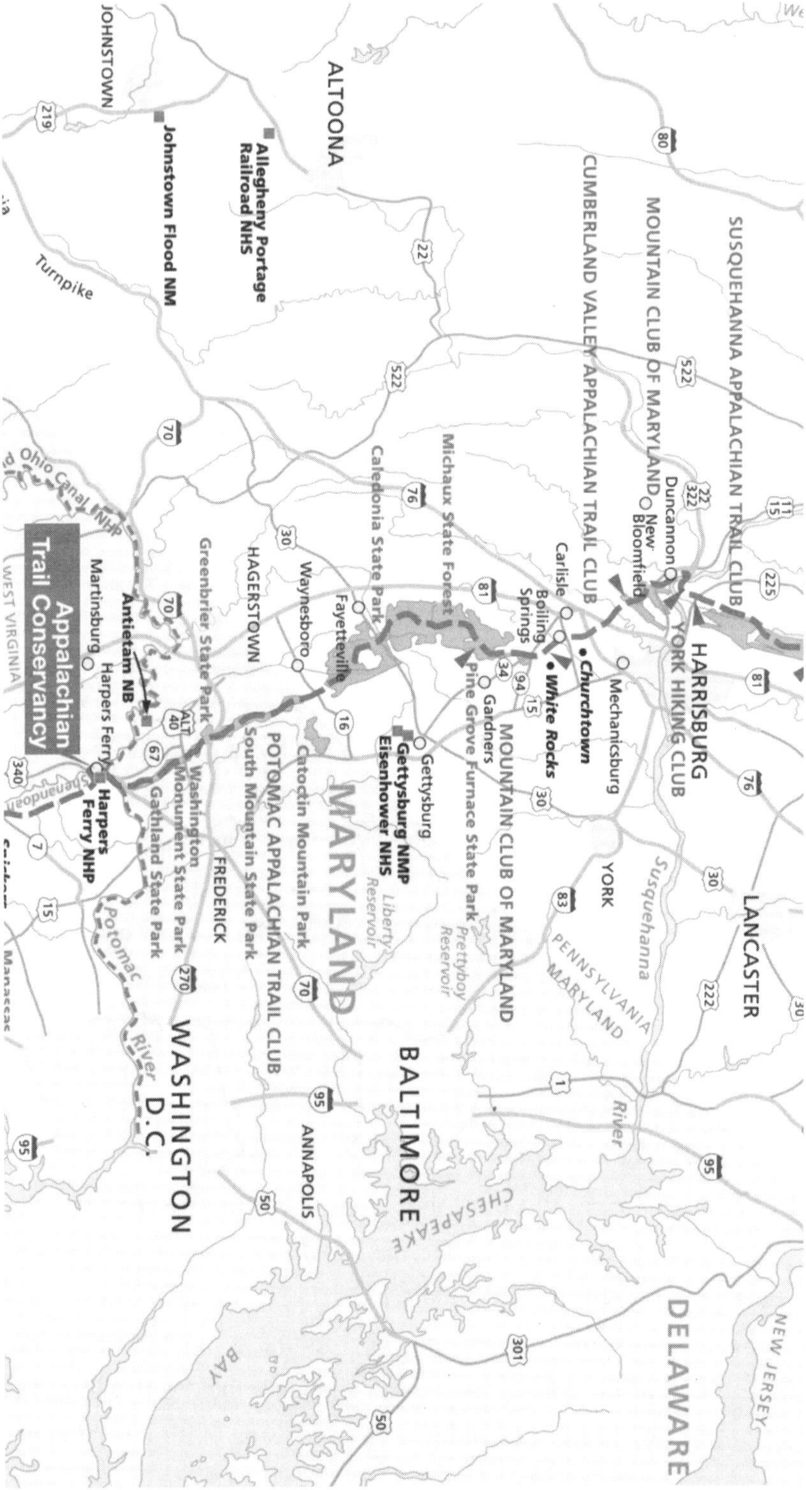
JOHNSTOWN
ALTOONA
Allegheny Portage Railroad NHS
Johnstown Flood NM
Turnpike
SUSQUEHANNA APPALACHIAN TRAIL CLUB
MOUNTAIN CLUB OF MARYLAND
CUMBERLAND VALLEY APPALACHIAN TRAIL CLUB
YORK HIKING CLUB
HARRISBURG
Duncannon
New Bloomfield
Carlisle
Boiling Springs
Churchtown
Mechanicsburg
White Rocks
Gardners
Pine Grove Furnace State Park
MOUNTAIN CLUB OF MARYLAND
Michaux State Forest
Caledonia State Park
Fayetteville
Waynesboro
HAGERSTOWN
Greenbrier State Park
Gettysburg
Gettysburg NMP
Eisenhower NHS
Catoctin Mountain Park
South Mountain State Park
POTOMAC APPALACHIAN TRAIL CLUB
MARYLAND
Liberty Reservoir
Prettyboy Reservoir
YORK
LANCASTER
Susquehanna River
PENNSYLVANIA
MARYLAND
BALTIMORE
ANNAPOLIS
CHESAPEAKE BAY
DELAWARE
NEW JERSEY
Ohio Canal NHP
Antietam NB
Martinsburg
Harpers Ferry
Harpers Ferry NHP
WEST VIRGINIA
Appalachian Trail Conservancy
Washington Monument State Park
Gathland State Park
FREDERICK
Potomac River
WASHINGTON D.C.
Shenandoah

down in the ferns. He had come so far, and survived the season I think because he was so far back in. Who was going to come in here after him with all these rocks?

He was resting. I imagined him taking in deep breaths, filling his lungs with the element that his body most craved. That breath would allow him to run from a hunter and live another day. When he found water, he would drink it in like a deep sense of peace. It would fill every void in his body, from his mouth to his tongue to his throat and on down to his stomach. The deep wilderness sheltered him, called to him, saying, *Come here. Hide in me. Find peace in my moss, in my mountain laurel. Lay in my ferns, I will cover you. If you want to hide, even if it's just for a little while, hide in me. I have work for you to do, but for now, take cover and rest. Eat, drink, and breathe for I have rescued you again. Take your rest, then live like you might die tomorrow.*

I was rooting for that deer. He looked at me, and I shut my eyes because my uncle always told me that if you shut your eyes, they won't run. I thought of Psalm 42 which starts out, *As the deer pants for the water brooks, so pants my soul for You, O God. My soul thirsts for God, for the living God. When shall I come and appear before God? My tears have been my food day and night, while they continually say to me, "Where is your God?"* (42:1-3 NKJV). I wanted to crawl right into those ferns with that deer. Then, maybe I could go back home with every ounce of this trail filling me up to satisfaction.

I needed to get going.

Jocelyn hasn't had any luck getting a ride for me, so she posts on Facebook and Instagram to see if anyone can provide some trail magic. Sure enough, there were responses from a ton of people. Most of the responses that Jocelyn got were from people at work, of course. They couldn't come until after five, so I would be hiking into the dark and trying to find the road. I would manage it.

I finally got past the DeHart Reservoir to get to Clarks Valley Road. I had hiked for miles and miles and couldn't even see the dam that created it. If you didn't know any better, you'd think you were in Maine even though you are relatively near Route 81. It was another rough day with lots of New Hampshire-style rocks, but I made 22 miles. I felt more than satisfied with that. It was just stunning terrain, and it became one of my favorite parts of the trail.

I beat my trail angel to the road, and I have to put on all my clothes as I wait to stay warm in the dark. He gets there about 20 minutes later. He takes me (I am 10 miles from the Susquehanna River) to my friend Kristen Van Horn's home. Remember how my teacher gave Sandy and me the book *Walking with Spring* by Earl Shaffer, which inspired us to want to do the trail? That was Kristen's dad.

My trail angel drops me off at a bar. I go in to have a drink and a burger, and Kristen meets me there. We end up going back to her place. I take a shower and charge all my devices. Kristen cooks us another meal, and we catch up on our lives in the meantime. Even though she and her sister were friends with Sandy and me, we haven't kept in touch. It's crazy to think that high school was 50 years ago.

I also give a call to "Trail Magic Natalie." She is famous on the trail, and almost every account you read of a hiker doing the trail includes her and her kindness. I make plans to hike to her place the next day. It's a long way, 30-plus miles. I feel like I can do it if I can leave well before daylight. I wake up around 3:00 a.m., and Kristen gets me to the trailhead at the Halifax area around 3:30 a.m.

Because I'm planning to get to Natalie's tonight, I don't have too much in my pack at all. I have ham steak from the night before, peanut butter, a protein bar, oatmeal, and beef jerky for lunch, so I can really move today. I'm ready to fly.

First thing I do, I get lost. I manage to find the trail again, but it means lost time. It's still buck season, but I'm there at 3:30 in the morning so there aren't any hunters in the woods at the moment. By 5:30, I start to see the flashlights. I'm going as fast as I possibly can. The 30-mile day will be a personal best, and another lifetime goal off my list. According to my conversation with Natalie, this part of the trail is my best chance for getting it done.

At daybreak, I'm already hungry, so I take out the ham steak, which is about 1 ¼ inch thick, and as wide around as a plate. I break off a 3" by 6" piece, to start. At this rate, the steak will be gone well before the day is over. I take my boots off just for the moment, especially since now I am in the waterproof winter boots, and eat. But I don't stop for long.

I get to chat with a few hikers, but I don't come across anyone who is dragging a deer, thank God, or I would have been held up. I take my second break around 9:00 a.m., and I already have about 12 miles in. I'm ahead of schedule, and I want to stay that way.

By now I'm down below Harrisburg and closing in on Mechanicsburg, Pennsylvania. I take my next break, even though I don't feel like I need it. I just think to myself that it is probably a good idea. Again, more ham steak and shoes off. I have one more bite left, and I save it. I feel like the salt in it is helping me, and it tastes awesome. At this break there isn't really a great place to eat, but there is a nice water source. I also down a Snickers bar. And it tastes pretty good. So then I eat another one with a cup of coffee. That takes some time, so maybe I am there for about 20 minutes on this break. Of course I drink some of Hunter's Hydro drink. The double caffeine kicks in and I'm off and running. My back and shoulders aren't feeling too bad today at all. It's like my whole body is just charged with blessing and purpose. I'm wearing my gloves made of possum fur, and the mitten covers, so even though the temperature is in the 20s, my hands aren't bothering me.

I'm down below Carlisle, and my goal is to get below Boiling Springs. That's the farthest place south that Natalie can pick me up.

The big round bales of hay dot the mustard-colored hillsides like giant resting beasts. The sky is bright blue with big, puffy, white clouds billowing upward. I can feel the sun on my gloves and on my whole body. It's like hiking through farm fields for several miles, and I can just fly. It looks different from the fields at home. These fields are long and open and the soil must be so rich. It feels soft underfoot. At home the fields are rocky and chopped up more.

I'm walking and thinking all day. This is close to where Sandy and I drove to drop Jocelyn off at her dance practices, before Jocelyn became a professional. We brought her down here every day of the week except Sunday, a 2 hour and 20-minute drive every day. Jocelyn just loved it down here, and we were happy to do it.

Once in the Boiling Springs area, I am amazed that all the time we were bringing Jocelyn down here I never visited this place. I wish I could spend a whole day here! There's great fly fishing in this clear limestone stream with trout of every variety and a well-stocked fly-fishing store in town. Natalie has asked me to call when I get here, and let her know when she should meet me at the next trailhead. I'm really flying, but I hate to tell her a time that is too early. When I call, she's already at the trailhead! She went early!

I actually walked past the trail on the other side of the lake, but then I figured it out using my phone, which cost me a bit of time. So then I really hurried. I'm averaging about 3 ½ miles per hour without my breaks and my total was 31.5, definitely a personal best! I got to the trailhead, but it was a little confusing. I got all the way out to where I thought she was, but she wasn't there. Then I saw a van down the road, and when I went to ask for help, it turned out to be her.

"Is this The 'Shrooming Camel?" she calls out.

"It's me!" I call back. "Is this Trail Magic Natalie?"

"It is!" she says. She looks like a welcoming mom, with happy brown eyes and broad shoulders. She's been following and commenting on Instagram, so it felt more like a reunion than a meeting for the first time.

She lives back in Mechanicsburg, so that's where we head. It's a little way back up the road, so we have time to chat. Her husband is not feeling well, so he doesn't hang around with us too much. Natalie offers me a hot bath with Epsom salts, and I thought that sounded amazing. She said dinner would be ready in under an hour, so that gave me plenty of time to soak.

I showered first, and then climbed in the tub with a whole container of Epsom salts. I felt like the luckiest guy in the world. I could smell supper and my stomach was sure ready for it. I ate triple servings of everything. She and her husband asked me dozens of questions, wondering how I knew Jinx and some other folks from the Lookout Hostel. It was so kind of her. She just takes in these hikers and spoils them rotten. That kind of royal treatment is so appreciated when your whole body is just shot from all the miles under your pack—all the hills, all the rocks, and all the nights on the ground.

When I wake up at Trail Magic Natalie's the next morning, she's got a massive breakfast waiting for me and I stuff some extra cookies into my pack. The plan is to have a quick visit with my old pastor Gary and his wife Cindy, who live back in Boiling Springs, take a zero there, and get resupplied. My visit is a bit of a surprise for him, but I also didn't plan to get so many miles in.

When I get there, Cindy is home but Gary is at a meeting. I go with Cindy to REI near Camp Hill and she buys my supplies for the next week; I am just covered in trail magic these days. I had broken my sticks falling again when I slipped on some ice, and the REI guy replaced them for free. I hugged him on the spot.

"I can't believe you're giving me new sticks!" I told him, "I've already gone like 2,000 miles on them." I showed the broken ones to him. I love that place! I dearly love my sticks, a pair of graphite ones that are super light. I have had all kinds of sticks in my life, but these are special.

Cindy ended up getting me an electronic hand warmer that would prove to be extremely important before the trail is all over. Then we visited a coffee shop with a great lunch.

Pastor Gary and Cindy made me a huge meal for supper, and we had a great time catching up. They had played a huge role in comforting me and the kids during and after Sandy's illness and death. Their support was unending. Texts, visits, arranging meals, all of it. Cindy would come over and spend the night just to help Jocelyn and me care for Sandy during the night. We had other friends too. I couldn't list them all. I was emotionally shot at the time, but looking back now, I can see how God used those people to bless us.

Now, Pastor Gary is a funny guy with a dry sense of humor, which I love. We used to call him again and again and say, "We're so sorry. We need you to come over." He would call us his "highest maintenance parishioners." That would always crack Sandy up. And then she'd tell him she'd call him tomorrow. Cindy loved Sandy like a sister. I will never forget their dedication toward us. We had so much going on at the time.

When I woke up at their place, it was very cold again. I'm already grateful for the hand warmer. The trail looks like it's going to be easy, with gentle rolling hills. They dropped me off at the trail, and they cried as I walked away. That choked me up too. I just love being loved. I actually called them an hour later.

"Good grief. Cindy's still crying," Gary told me.

CHAPTER 44:

SPARED

I get 26 miles in, despite a later start. The morning was still rough. I had to hike a bit in the dark, and it was cold, but not terrible. It got above freezing later, and I was able to use my new sticks. I still found some mushrooms, too, even though they didn't look great. I hadn't packed a lot of food, because I knew the next place I could get off-trail was down around Waynesboro to resupply. In the end I didn't have to eat my supplies because I was able to get so many mushrooms. I just hiked along, more and more alone, with plenty of time to think.

Looking back, I know I was saved the first moment I uttered the sinner's prayer in Pastor Harding's church as a ninth grader. I know that. But I also know I never really made a change in my life until I studied the book of Ephesians in Sunday school with Nick Kindt. But even through all that, I never really dealt with how my words had killed my father. That I could be so evil, so cruel, was too awful to accept. I knew God forgave me, but I could not forgive myself. I buried it way deep down, down wherever it is that people hide things even from themselves. I did a good job of it. If something came up that reminded me of it, I just pushed it further down.

If I'm honest, the whole time I felt like God was leading me to do this hike, and I wanted to do it, but my thoughts were dominated by all I had been through—how my wife suffered, everything that happened in Providence, and especially what I had done to my dad. And you know what, if I had been able to keep hiking during the bubble, I would have been surrounded by other hikers and never been forced to reflect the way that I did. I was in the wilderness alone most of the time, especially for the last two months, and it was not a happy solitude. I often came across the dead ash trees, with their bark stripped away and their pale bones broken and leafless, getting more hollow by the day. It kills me to admit this, but they looked like I felt—worn out. This life was so hard. Why couldn't one of those trees fall on me? Back home, they would all say Steven died doing something he loved, and I would be with Sandy again.

Don't get me wrong, I constantly felt the presence of God and saw Him in His sunsets, in His sunrises, in the power of a hurricane, in the power of a tornado, in the beauty of a moose walking by me, or a golden eagle flying just feet over my head. I felt God. I saw Him. But I was still empty and tired of having to work so hard to keep my head on straight.

The day itself was fine. The visit with Gary and Cindy had left me on a high, and I was also buzzing a little because I had just met my long-time goal of hiking over 30 miles in a day. So I started off on fire, just eating up the trail after checking in with Jocelyn and Tristan. It ended up being another monster day.

It got cold that night, very cold, and I dreamed of Sandy dying again. When I woke up, I was not in a good place. After counseling, I could sometimes take the thoughts captive like Paul says in 2 Corinthians, but this night I just could not.

It had been almost two months since I had been with any of my thru-hiking friends. My mind was sick again, and my heart was in pain. I felt that no one was thinking of me out on the trail, and worse, that no one was contributing to Sandy's cancer fund. Satan saw his opportunity to hit me. The lies he tells can make more sense than reality sometimes. And then almost before you know it, you aren't in reality anymore. You go to a place that's pretty dark. The next day it's a little darker. Pretty soon it's midnight, and it's dark as hell, and you can't see shit. Nothing in your life that made sense before makes sense now.

I could only see darkness, and not just because it was the middle of the night. I couldn't tell Satan's lies from the truth, and I could feel the spiritual warfare all around me. I had Ephesians 6:10-20 and Daniel 10:10-14 playing on repeat in my earbuds. Now, I had listened to the whole Bible five times, but skipped the book of Job every time because I knew what it said, and I didn't want to hear it. I didn't want to hear reasons, or comfort, because I knew I didn't deserve it. Job was not a murderer, but I was. God had allowed my wife to die, and that's all I could think about. I knew I was in a bad spot. I said prayers but nothing seemed to help.

I was thinking, *I am under attack, just like it says in Ephesians, just like Job.* I managed to sleep a little more. When I woke again, the world had turned to ice. It had to be in the teens or maybe even single digits. There was a thick beard of frost on everything. All the little mud puddles were frozen, and little icicles hung off the rocks. I had my hands in my pockets, and had to keep them there. No hands, no poles. No poles was no good, and my back was really feeling it. As I mentioned before, at 26 I had fallen three stories off a roof and landed on a car, breaking it in three places. My back, not the car. Of course, I had just stocked my pack, so it was heavier than normal. At least using those little warmers from Cindy kept my hands halfway usable. I started hiking with my hands in my pockets, just letting my poles drag behind me from the straps over my forearms. My back lets me know that there's punishment for favoring my hands. After maybe five miles, my damn boots come untied.

No way was I going to expose my hands to tie them. It would take another hour just to warm them up again.

The passages from Ephesians and Daniel about spiritual warfare are still rattling around in my head. And slowly, like light just coming into the forest at dawn, I am beginning to realize that my current state of mind is probably Satan coming for me, after having such a good day the day before. In my head I can see the darts of the enemy coming for me, and I know it's time to put the blame where it belongs so I can snap out of this, like I did when my foot was broken. I can envision the archangel Michael, just as the angel Gabriel describes him in the Daniel passage, clashing swords with the enemy, the blows of metal on metal ringing out all around me.

But I keep tripping on the bootlaces. Finally I think, *Okay, that's it, I have no choice.* I can see a stump up ahead that will help me execute the whole maneuver. Remember, with the messed-up collarbone, I can't slip out of the pack without setting it on something. Well, the stump is too high. I look forward, nothing. I look back, and there's a shorter stump. I heave myself back there, poles clacking along and grumbling. This stump is lower, so I decide I'm not going to take the pack off. I'll just haul my foot up on it and tie it there. I brace for the cold I'm going to feel taking my hands out of my pockets, turn around to face up the trail, and hoist up my foot on the little stump.

A deep crack erupts from somewhere to my right. There is snapping, more cracking, and the banging of wood on wood. Branches whoosh through the air. Completely helpless, I just hunch up, paralyzed, but managing to take one step back. The entire woods crashes around me and in front of me, in layers of sound that last for a long moment. Then there is silence. Some residual snapping. Even the birds are suddenly quiet.

I look up. A massive dead ash tree, at least three feet in diameter, has fallen right onto the trail. The ash has taken out three other live trees with it, and the trail is obliterated for at least 50 yards in front of me. The tall stump, where I had originally planned to remove my pack just seconds before, is completely crushed by the dead center impact of the ash tree.

I would not have had time to run.

I would have been killed precisely as I had thought I wanted.

But suddenly, I am glad. I am grateful. To my surprise, I want to live. Guilt washes over me. I had been wallowing in self-pity, forgetting about all my wonderful friends and family who had cared for and supported me and disregarding the beautiful children God had given me. The magnitude of what had just happened collapsed me to my knees, by the stump, sitting on my feet. I just looked in shock at the destruction. I should be dead right now. My heart should not be beating right now.

Another limb that had been hung up snapped right beside me. The sound brought me back to my vivid imaginings of the sword fight happening around me as Michael battled to keep me from Satan's blows. Had God pushed the tree down so I would see that He was protecting me? Did Satan push it, and God got me out of there just in time? Oh, what does it matter? All I know is that my heart should not be beating, but it is. It is.

I didn't deserve it. For the five years it had taken for cancer to finally claim Sandy, and the next six years I had spent angry about it, I had been blaming God. Worthless to the core, I hadn't done a lick of good to anyone all that time. I deserved to get crushed by a tree and had even asked for it. Why had He spared me?

Because I love you, said the Spirit to me, full of gentleness. *Let's start over.*

Like the day I had cried with Sandy at my father's grave, I wept until there were no more tears left. *Thank you, Father. Thank you for being faithful to me. Thank you for being faithful to Your Word. Your promises to me are wonderful. Your Word is great. I'm sorry I listened to Satan and all of his lies! Thank you, thank you, for keeping me alive.*

About half an hour later, I finally raise my head again and view the chaos of downed trees around me. I notice, as if they are suddenly reattached to me, that my hands have been out of my pockets this whole time, and are now very numb. But they aren't in pain right now, and I am filled with the anticipation of making a fresh start. I'm ready to make up for all this time that I've wasted being self-absorbed and having this massive pity party for myself.

I've got to get going again. So I do.

I'm thanking God the whole way, and then at some point my thinking shifts. Satan had done a pretty good job of screwing with me. I started muttering accusations at first, but then I got louder, bitching and cussing at him. He is the enemy, not God, and I need to focus my anger where it belongs.

You're such an asshole! I yell. *You're a liar and my enemy! You murdered my wife! C'mon, give me what you got!* I start playing back all my accidents on the trail, the falls, the illnesses. *You meant these for bad, trying to get me to quit! Well, I'm not! You mean this for evil, you son of a bitch, but God turned every one of these broken bones into healing.*

God had healed my bones, and in just an hour, God has healed my heart as well. I have scars for sure, but I am forgiven. I am whole. My voice rises to a fever pitch.

I know where you are going, Satan, and I know where I am going when it's all over. Your days with me are over. Even if God allows you to nail me with something, I'm holding on. God will turn it to good, even if He kills me. You lost, you f-----g asshole, you lost!

It feels so good to let this all out, swearing and yelling and challenging Satan to the fight. I go on for maybe an hour in this way, cussing like a drunken sailor.

Then something taps me on the back. Satan is going to take me up on the fight!

I turn, ready to swing.

Unless Satan wears a cute blue cap and trail-running shoes, it isn't him. This poor young girl had been following me and had taken in my whole tirade. Now she was bawling her eyes out!

She says, "First of all I want to give you a hug!"

I'm still just getting through deciding I shouldn't fight her. I let her hug me.

"I listened to the whole thing. I was scared to death you were a crazy man, but then I could tell you had something terrible happen."

I said, "Yeah, did you see that tree back there, it almost fell on me!" I told her the whole story, including my confession and reconciliation with God.

She said a little prayer for me right there on the trail.

I didn't get her contact information, but that's okay, I'll see her in heaven. She was already late for work, but she told me she was so glad she had run into me on the trail. She ran on. As I watched her trot away with her blue cap bobbing along, I marveled again at the everlasting mercy of God.

That afternoon, I finally listened to the whole book of Job. That is a long-ass book. I knew it had answers for me, but I also hadn't been ready for them. Now I was.

CHAPTER 45:

NOT TOO CRABBY

I plan to get into Maryland today, but this border area is tough hiking. It will be especially rocky in the beginning of Maryland, kind of like the Palmerton area. But it is beautiful.

On this day I pass the scenic Pine Grove Furnace State Park. It has a cool history lesson and I ate lunch there even though it was pretty early in the morning. I also passed some people who were just there to walk around. This park includes the remains of the Pine Grove Iron Works, and some of the chimney stacks are still standing. You could tour the whole little area that was full of the remains of this village.

I got to Quarry Gap Shelter. This shelter is the coolest shelter I've ever seen. It had … well, décor. It was like Sandy had decorated it, actually. They had a Lucky Charms elf, flowers, and hanging baskets. The floor was painted, and there was chinking in between the logs. There were two shelters with a bathroom in between them. I didn't even have to go to the bathroom, but I went in it because it was so pretty. I so wished this shelter had been at the end of my day, but it wasn't, and I had to move on.

I leave this shelter thinking, *All those hikers who complain about Pennsylvania trails and shelters should apologize.*

By now there are snow flurries. I'm wearing my possum gloves. I mentioned them before but didn't tell you why they are special. They are made by Zpacks. I've had this brand for a few years, and they are so lightweight, but so warm. It turns out that possum fur is hollow, and that's why it insulates so well. I had trapped as a young man for years, but I never knew this. I highly recommend them. You can use your phone with them on and everything. I even wore them in the rain. On super cold days I put a handwarmer on the top and on the bottom, with the mittens over top. This combination makes the cold tolerable for me.

I'm hoping for another 25-mile day, so I have to get going.

The snow and the wind pick up as I come out of the gap. I'm warm so far, but it's cold enough that I'm hiking as fast as I can go, over three miles an hour. My pack isn't terribly light either; I finished off the jar of peanut butter in two days, but I have a lot of other food in there.

After a solid 26 miles, I make it to the Tumbling Run Shelter. I was hoping for farther, but it's not easy-going in this section. It was cold and dark, and I decided it was time to call it. I know I'll have to get off-trail sometime tomorrow to resupply. I don't need laundry so much, because it's been so cold, and that will save me a good hour and a half and I can get right back on the trail again.

The morning dawns pretty cold again. My useless hands can't push the buttons on my phone so I can't check in with my kids. I put in my air buds, and just like when I had norovirus, I hope Jocelyn will call me instead.

She does. I ask her if she can help me find someplace warm off-trail tonight. Even if there is a hostel on the trail, it's probably closed. Even if it were open, it will be hard to get a ride there. This is how it's going to be from now on, but hopefully Jocelyn can search something up for me. I really need to get into a town to get my devices charged up. My headlight is dead from hiking into the night. My charging battery is dead, too, because I've used it all night to keep my hands warm. I've also left my phone on all night, so I'm able to use it to get around in the dark but it soon dies. Without a phone, I'm pretty helpless, I can't tell exactly how many miles I've gone, or exactly where I am. I text Jocelyn through the GPS and she doesn't respond for a while. After maybe 14 or 15 miles I came to Raven Rock Road, which is in Maryland, and hoped to hitch a ride into a town, but that doesn't work out.

I took a right turn then, onto a road, just hoping. I've left my GPS on so Jocelyn can see where I'm at. Thank God, after I went about four miles, I came to a little town called Smithburg with a restaurant called the Dixi Diner. It was like a diner right out of the movies, in the middle of nowhere.

Jocey was able to get me a Holiday Inn hotel room through the kindness of my cousin Shane who generously spent his reward points on me. While I ate and charged all my devices, the waitress at the diner was able to get me a ride to the hotel. I just checked in, threw my pack down, and went nearby to a grocery store to restock. Afterward, I thoroughly enjoyed a warm shower, just letting the hot water beat on my cold body, and especially my shoulder. My shoulders were killing me this night, and I finally took some Ibuprofen, which I hadn't had since I broke my finger in Connecticut with my kids. I can usually avoid it if I use the CBD oil, because that really helps. I crawled in bed, warm with a full stomach, and fell asleep in minutes.

In the morning, I get to a nearby diner at 5:00 a.m. and drink a ton of coffee with a huge breakfast: four eggs, two pieces of sausage, four pieces of bacon and two pieces of French toast. I will probably regret the French toast later since norovirus has killed my ability to tolerate gluten. At 6:00 a.m., another trail angel gets me back to the trailhead. I am unbelievably blessed.

I've given my buddy Dawniller a call. We used to work together in Tanglewood and go out together, and it was a lot of fun. He said he wanted to do some trail magic for me when I got to Harpers Ferry.

I had decided this would be my finishing point heading south. Next, I would drive back to where I left off with Jocelyn and Bob at the 900-mile mark, and head north again to finish at Harpers Ferry. I had been there in the early '80s with Sandy. The Shenandoah and the Potomac Rivers meet here in this pretty little manicured town, almost like going back in time to Civil War days. It will be a good place to call the end.

I've got close to 40 miles before Harpers Ferry. The way I feel now, I can smoke through that by noon tomorrow. It's crazy to report that there were no incidents at all. I was right in Harpers Ferry at noon the next day, just like I told Dawniller I would be. I actually backtracked to a parking lot across the bridge so I could see the beautiful view from there. Right then, Dawniller pulls in.

I thought we were eating in Harpers Ferry. We had done a job in Fredericksburg before, and used to come over to Harpers Ferry after work to eat, or kayak or hike. But this guy Dawniller, with his Guatemalan grin behind his mustache, is always up for a good adventure.

"I got a surprise for ya, Uncle Steve," he tells me.

I am not his uncle, obviously.

He ends up taking me out of Harpers Ferry to the bar Avery's Grill, a place we used to go weekly with the whole crew while we worked a job here for six months. One guy, Rusty, was 100 percent bullshit all the time. His goal was to start trouble whenever possible.

On our first day on the job, Rusty comes up to me and says, "So you're the son of a bitch who took my job away from me?"

I didn't know what to say. "Oh, man, I'm so sorry," I squeaked. And then he walked away without cracking a smile.

"I'm probably the only one you can trust," he told me later. Which wasn't even remotely true. I loved working with that guy. He made the day fly by. Chris and Tom also worked there with us. These guys, and Rusty, are true artists at what they do. It makes you proud to work with them.

Dennis was one of the carpenters on the crew. He is the one who told me I had to try the soft-shell crabs on the menu. I've never had the soft-shells, but Dennis was promising me they were better than anything I'd ever had in the whole world.

"I doubt it's going to be better than steak," I told him, with visions of juicy charcoal-grilled beef sizzling in my brain.

Dennis guarantees they will be.

He is right!

After that first bite, I had a whole new favorite meal. They all knew how to eat them, but I didn't know the first thing. I caught on quick. I will admit it takes a long time to get filled up because you have to work for your meal, but that's okay when the company is good. It was expensive, but it was good eating.

Dawniller's surprise for me is that we are going back to Avery's Grill, and it was like a little homecoming. Everybody knew us from our old Saturday night routine. I filled up on Maryland crabs in Old Bay seasoning, remembering the first time we had them, and all the good times. Thanking him for my ride and the amazing meal, I bid my old friend farewell at the hotel doors.

SECTION V
NOBO (AGAIN)

---

*I have fought the good fight, I have finished the race,
I have kept the faith.*
2 Timothy 4:7 (NKJV)

CHAPTER 46:

COLDER

My ride early in the morning is my brother and sister-in-law, Don and Diane Rider. They came all the way down from Pennsylvania to drive me from Hagerstown over to the 900-mile mark on the trail on Skyline Drive. I'll be heading north from there, to end finally at Harpers Ferry. Now, imagine two threads running north to south, crisscrossing over one another on the top of a mountain ridge; this is the Appalachian Trail and Skyline Drive. In fact, at one time the road was actually the trail. Now imagine there are roads running sideways across these threads. These are the access roads to get on and off Skyline Drive and the trail. Some are bigger roads, some are smaller. Don and Diane are going to get me on one of these access roads that leads right into the 900-mile mark of the trail.

But first, we are going to spend the night at my good friend Steve Smith's son's house in Front Royal. Now that sounds complicated, but it isn't. Steve Smith was my friend from the Sunday school class when I was assigned to report on the church of Ephesus. He passed away from a heartbreaking battle with pancreatic cancer about 18 months after I lost Sandy, and his whole family has been so support-

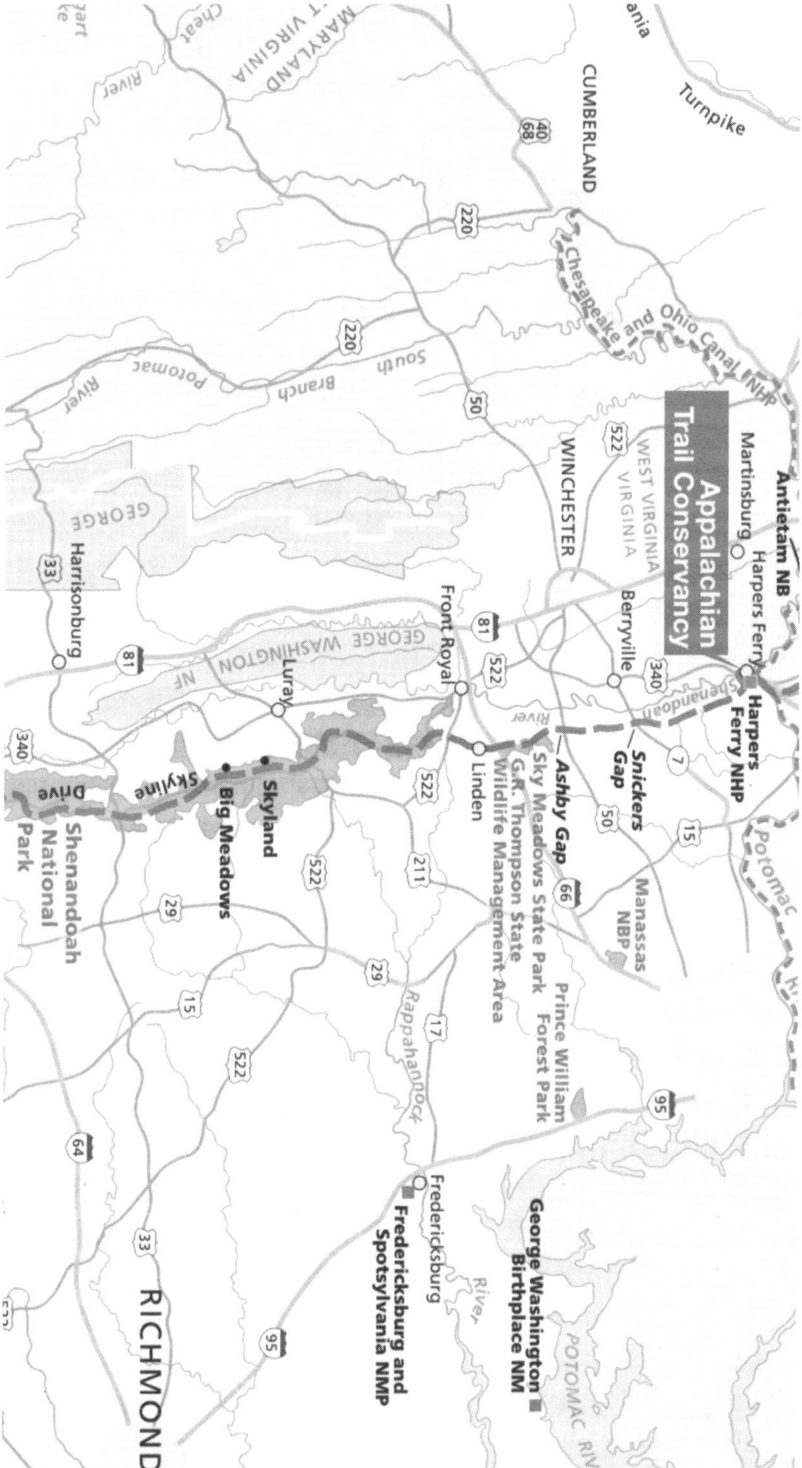

CUMBERLAND
Turnpike
MARYLAND
WEST VIRGINIA
Cheat
River
Chesapeake and Ohio Canal NHP
Antietam NB
Martinsburg
Harpers Ferry
Appalachian Trail Conservancy
WEST VIRGINIA
VIRGINIA
WINCHESTER
Berryville
Harpers Ferry NHP
Shenandoah
River
Snickers Gap
Ashby Gap
Sky Meadows State Park
G.R. Thompson State Wildlife Management Area
Manassas NBP
Prince William Forest Park
Potomac
South Branch Potomac River
GEORGE
GEORGE WASHINGTON NF
Harrisonburg
Front Royal
Luray
Linden
Skyland
Big Meadows
Skyline Drive
Shenandoah National Park
Rappahannock
River
Fredericksburg
Fredericksburg and Spotsylvania NMP
George Washington Birthplace NM
POTOMAC RIVER
RICHMOND
40
68
220
50
522
81
340
7
15
66
211
29
17
95
33
64

ive of my hike. His son Brent has this beautiful cabin in Front Royal, and it's pretty close to the trail.

I'll say this, Steve's death did not help my mental state after losing Sandy. If there was ever a couple that Sandy and I wanted to hold up as a model for our marriage, it was Steve and his wife Phyllis. They seemed so peaceful, so united, so calm. And then he died. It crushed me. God was on a real roll when it came to rescuing the faithful. I hope that sounds as sarcastic in writing as it does in my head. Steve's death really pulled the trigger, so to speak, for my breakdown.

I was headed to this cabin with mixed feelings. Good, fond feelings, but sadness too, remembering Steve's life and his legacy. It's snowing as Don, Diane and I pull up the road. The trees are holding on to each flake against the gray sky. The empty cabin is nestled in the woods like it is waiting for us, waiting to see what we will do.

We get into the hot tub. The snowflakes fall all around us, melting instantly when they hit the water, but resting lightly in our hair and our eyelashes. It's so cold, and the wind is blowing. I stay in for a good long time, just willing those extra minutes to erase the wear and tear on my muscles from all those miles.

We wrestle the cover back on the hot tub, and freeze ourselves doing it.

And then I sleep, warm and at peace, as the snow comes down, down, down.

In the morning, we wake to a white world. It is winter all right. I think, *Well, there goes my 25 miles a day.* Diane had brought me all the stuff I needed from Jocelyn, including lots of food. I have about 150 miles to the finish line.

When we try taking the access road to the 900-mile mark, we find it is shut down. The snow was so heavy and wet that it stuck to everything and had pulled down trees all up and down Skyline Drive. Authorities had closed that access road and Skyline Drive.

The only access roads still open that could get me to Skyline Drive and the trail were just north of the 900-mile mark, or else much farther south of it. Closer was better. I was going to have to make do with as close as we could get from just north of the 900-mile mark. Don and Diane dropped me off about 1,500 feet lower than where I needed to be up on the trailhead. Everything was a pristine white. I could see that the top of the mountain was white, too, and it was probably much deeper up there where I was headed. They bid me goodbye, and I headed off in the snow, hoping for the best.

There were tracks in the snow. I assumed someone had walked their dog. Those tracks actually helped a lot for a while. I finally bumped into the dog-walker, and we chatted. I asked him about the conditions, and he thought heading out into this was a bad idea. He said that it was going to get miserably cold, approaching the zero mark, and I should probably go back and wait a week.

I noted that he was making it through okay.

He agreed. "But at the top you'll never get through the drifts."

I thanked him and went on. I was too close to quit now. For a while I had thought that there was no way I was going to make this a thru-hike, and then with my high mileage it became possible. Now I didn't know. It didn't look good, but I just didn't know.

One of the things Jocelyn had sent for me was my ice clamp-ons. I almost didn't throw them in the pack, but thank God I did. I used them almost immediately. The guy was right; I hadn't counted on the drifts. By the time I got to the trailhead and started hiking south toward the 900-mile mark, it felt like the drifts were just on the trail and not beside it in the woods. I tried to walk off the trail for a while to avoid them, but it didn't really help. I had to keep shifting back and forth from one side to the other. At that elevation, the wind was really whipping and the snow had turned from slush back to powder. It just kept getting deeper. At the top of the hill, my hiking sticks were in snow up to the second bracket. Over my knees. I finally got to the top.

I had hoped the snow would be all blown off up there. It wasn't.

I've hiked in other snowy situations, where the ground would be bald except for the occasional drift, but not here. In fact, it seemed like it piled up on the trail. Any other tracks in the snow were long gone, and it would turn out that I would not see another footprint in the snow for seven more days. My mileage was suffering. I had hoped for 15 miles, but there was no way.

At about 3:00, the temperature bottomed out at 19 degrees, and the wind was at least 35–40 miles per hour. I had to put my raincoat on over my coat. I had my Fjällräven pants on over my insulating pants, and my insulated boots of course. I wore my alpaca socks. I had my mittens with the warmers over my possum gloves. I started to worry about, you know, getting in trouble here. So I vowed not to use the battery-charged warmers in the mittens unless I really had to. I decided to make it my goal not to use them except in the early mornings when I had to use my hands to break camp. Prior to the warmers, breaking camp had been such an ordeal in single-digit temperatures.

For just regular hiking, I was able to use the extra disposable-type pocket-warmers I had packed and tuck those in my mittens. Using my sticks was now non-negotiable. I couldn't have made it without them. I only had enough of those pocket-warmers for six days, though, doing that. I didn't use any on my feet; maybe I was working so hard to get through the drifts that they stayed warm.

I kept thinking, *We are in the south. This snow can't last.*

By the time darkness arrives, I know I had strained my legs going through the drifts. Tristan is now in Arizona, and I'd better give him a call before I do something permanent to my legs. I leave a message and ask him to let me know a time that I can call. For the most part, I keep my phone off now, just so I can conserve battery in case something terrible happens and I am stuck up here.

But Lord, wasn't something terrible already happening? Somehow I never put my current circumstance into that category. In my head "terrible" meant like, in the movies. A battle for survival in life-or-death circumstances. You know, a man vs. nature ultra-drama. Turned out, I was closer to a life-and-death drama than I imagined.

The fact that they had closed down part of Skyline Drive nagged at me. That was not a good sign. And there were trees down everywhere.

In the end, the snow was so deep, I had to go off-trail often. Sometimes I just walked the Skyline Drive and that meant I had to keep my phone on at least airplane mode, so I could keep navigating.

Tristan calls me over his lunch hour, which is three hours later for me. After I describe my situation, he knows exactly what I did. He explains that I probably strained my groin, and some other tendon, lifting my legs high to get over the drifts.

"It would be best to get off the trail to rest the legs," he advises.

"Well, I can't," I explain. "All the roads to the trails are closed."

"Can you just take a zero day?"

"In my tent, I can."

"What about getting further down in elevation, where the snow is not so deep, and then do a rest?"

In the end he also described a different way of walking that might help. Instead of lifting my legs so high to clear the snow, he suggested keeping my legs straighter, like a toy soldier, and kind of pushing the snow forward. That's how I walked, and it did help.

That night I camped out. It was so cold. My sleeping bag is a gem, so my body was warm at least. My plan for my face includes wearing my Smartwool gator up over my mouth and cheeks, and then I pull my Filson hat down over my eyes so all that is sticking out is my nose. My nose freezes, but that's how I breathe. What really sucks is that I can only lie on my right side, but no one can do that all night. After a while, I force myself to sleep on my left side for a little while, even though it kills my back and my shoulder. I had to wake up to take a leak, unfortunately. Everything was crystal clear. I figured it had to be morning, but when I checked, it was only 9:00 at night. Just being out for that little bit was absolutely freezing, and I scurried back into the bag as quickly as possible. Like an idiot, I had left my bag unzipped and open, which I never do, but this time all my body heat had escaped from the bag. Since I had just frozen my balls off going pee, it took forever to get my bag warmed back up again. I thought, *That's it. I'm never drinking anything again.* I didn't get much sleep that night.

Thank God I didn't get cold toes. I don't know what I would have done. The temperature the next morning, according to my GPS, was one degree. One. The wind chill had to put it way below zero.

I wake up at 5:00 a.m., but I just could not get out of the sleeping bag. I waited till 6:30, near daylight. I decide to cook in my tent. I was wearing every stitch of clothing that I carried, and finally managed to bumble through my breakfast. Packing up was hell. I put the electric warmers on in my pocket. I would work a little, then warm up my hands. Pack up something else, warm up my hands. Over and over again. When I was finally ready to exit the tent and I tried to unzip, I got a surprise.

The whole tent was completely drifted over. A side caved in and some white powder got inside as I unzipped.

I wish I had a picture of it, but I was inside. The drift came up the left side, about two feet high, up and over the top. The other side had less snow, but the fine powder collected in the upper dips in the canvas. I guess I should have imagined this was the case. I had bumped my head while packing up and thought that it felt a little more solid than normal, but then dismissed it. I never worry about my tent. It's been in 80-mph winds and stayed intact. It's bulletproof. I didn't know about my new hiking poles, which serve as the tent poles. They had to bear the weight of all the snow.

I thought I'd better push it off, so like a dumbass I started pushing out from the bottom. I tried to unzip again, and I quickly realized I didn't really get it off the top because it caved in on me again. Well, by this time my hands were frozen and I had to take a minute and sit there while they warmed up. I just thought, *How in the hell am I going to fold up this tent in this snow at this rate?*

I had to dig around in the snow to find my stakes, but I finally get them pulled. One was frozen in the ground, so I took a bunch of the other pulled-out stakes and used them like a tool, pounding them with a rock around the frozen one. I looped a piece of rope around it and used it for leverage to finally get it free.

Good Lord, it took me until 8:30 to get out of that mess and get back on the trail.

I probably hadn't gone more than 10 miles the day before, but I knew I had to be close to the 900-mile mark, maybe half a mile? I couldn't figure out where it was exactly. And I really didn't want to get my hands cold again searching through my phone. I just walked until I saw something I recognized from being there with Jocelyn and Bob. I knew the 900-mile mark was close to a road, so I could confirm I had made it.

Now I had to turn around to get back to Route 33 where Don and Diane dropped me off and go the rest of the way north to Harpers Ferry. I made it back north on the same trail in half the time because I didn't have to break through new snow. Ten miles in, ten miles out.

I got back to the road where Don and Diane had dropped me off thinking I would hitch a ride, just to get off the trail for a bit. The road was just a silent white expanse, with no sign at all of any human activity.

I decide to keep going north on the trail to the next access road, Route 214, about 37 miles away. There was a little path where someone had been walking, so I stayed on that path. But when the snow got deep, the tracks stopped, and I was back in the drifts again.

It didn't take long for me to get tired out in these drifts. I was still walking as Tristan described, pushing the weight of the snow aside and keeping my legs straighter. If there was a place where it was really bad, I would take a swipe with my stick to break up the drift before shoving it with my leg. It was already 4:30 and getting dark. I considered camping right there in the middle of Skyline Drive. If they do open the road though, and try to plow, they are going to plow me right over. My white tent will be virtually invisible. Off the road, I'm going to get snowed over again but that's what I decide to do. The temperature is cold and the wind is blowing, and it's still snowing a little. Later my GPS confirmed I was at zero degrees again. I wolfed down a Patagonia meal. I could not eat enough. These go down so nice, but it comes back to haunt you later, I'm afraid. They are full of nutrients and calories. With the shivering, I knew I needed the calories. I had bought more olive oil, too, but I guess the mushrooms were over. I could eat them frozen, but I couldn't find them in this mess. I ended up adding some olive oil and a giant scoop of peanut butter to the Patagonia meal just to add even more calories to it.

I kept breaking off twigs, trying to find some sassafras for tea. I did finally find a small tree with two leaves. One leaf was straight, and the other was a mitten, so I could identify it. I pretty much destroyed that poor little tree, but I got enough bark to make myself tea for a week. That felt amazing to drink, and it made me tired. I just kept thinking, *I only have a few more miles until I can get off, and then I'm going to eat myself into oblivion.*

Full and safe and warm-ish in my tent, I tried to relax. The wind was just whipping against the tent. A big stick actually snapped off, and crashed down onto my tent, scaring the shit out of me. Luckily it did not tear it. In the morning the stick was snowed under, and I don't even know where it went.

I woke up at five again, and tried to get little things ready without wasting too much of the battery on my headlamp. I ate breakfast in the sleeping bag again. I also unzipped my tent a little bit, and as I unzipped the screen part, it sagged down into my burner. The corner of nylon vaporized in the flame in one quick black puff of smoke. Well, luckily the bugs weren't going to be a problem for the rest of this hike anyway. I guess that's why you aren't supposed to cook in your tent.

The guys at Trail Days said that if I sent the tent back, Hyperlite would put a new screen in it for me. I should have known better than to cook in the tent, but I was freezing my ass off here. At this point, desperate times called for desperate measures.

Crawling out and packing up was the same ordeal as the day before. But I got back on the trail and was hiking by 7:00 a.m., so that was an improvement. Time to make up for lost time.

It was a beautiful day, actually, it just refused to get warm. The world was so crisp and white. I was pushing my legs like Tristan told me. On one step, hidden down under the snow was a big rock, and I hit that sucker just right. I told you I stubbed my toe a million times, but this time I did something to my toe that I could feel was different. The jarring aggravated my groin muscle. I felt like I couldn't go on anymore.

I got to an area that had a shelter and took a break. I had only gone about six miles, but I really couldn't walk well, and I decided to camp right there. I had been battling this snow and the paralyzing cold for all this time, and I really needed to get out of the woods. I would need food in the next couple of days, anyway. But for now, this shelter would have to do.

After this, it has to get better.

I talk myself off the ledge here a little bit. *I'm okay here. I really am.* I've got two jars of peanut butter left, beef jerky, coffee, one more Patagonia meal, oatmeal, three Snickers bars, a protein bar, and my hydration powder.

Most of the shelters I'd passed were just full of blown-in snow. But this shelter was dry inside, so I got everything out of my pack and aired it all out. I took time to rub my legs down really well with CBD oil, as well as my shoulder and groin, and it helped a lot. I really needed to give my groin and toe a rest. My brain kept trying to slide into the ditch here, but I kept talking myself back into a positive place.

There are some good hours of daylight left on this bright winter day. Like so many of them do, this shelter slanted down on the side, and I put my legs up by jamming my feet into that slanted part. I thought resting like this would drive me crazy, but it wasn't as bad as I had imagined. I stayed in my sleeping bag, and I knew it was also a good time to check the weather. For that, I buried my head in the bag and used my phone so my hands stayed warm. I still had battery power, but it was time to get to town for sure. I had one full battery left. The GPS battery was in pretty good shape. I only turned it on and off in the morning and evening so I could be located.

The snow has not shown any signs of melting, and the weather is showing no warm-up for at least two more days. The snow is still frozen fast to the leaves, to the mountain laurel, and the rhododendron. Even the west sides of all the trees are covered and white. The effect of this was remarkable. When I looked ahead up the trail, the forest was black with tree trunks. When I looked behind, they disappeared into a sea of white.

The snow was not powdery anymore. It was crusty hard, splattered into the woods with broken limbs everywhere. I really thought this wind for three days in a row would have blown off the snow from all the leaves and tree trunks, but it hadn't. That snow was plastered on there.

I had been melting a lot of snow for water, because obviously no water is moving up here. I didn't want to burn up my fuel, though. At first I was breaking off icicles from the rocks and chewing them up. Then I tried breaking them up and putting them into the big pot that I cook mushrooms in, melting them that way.

In terms of volume, it takes nine packed cups of snow to melt into one liter of water. But that really uses up the fuel. I decide to build a fire. All the twigs are covered in ice, so that isn't the greatest scenario. But I am able to find dead sticks and whack them on the side of the tree to dislodge the ice, and then I can use them.

It really is the perfect opportunity to take a zero in the woods. Well, not a complete zero. It is not raining. It is cold, but I have the best sleeping bag, and I'm managing. My mind stubbornly drifts off now and then to a dark place, but I keep dragging it back, just like I dragged all those dead deer over the boulders. I'm remembering scriptures, just to keep my thoughts on track. I don't want to run my phone down by having it read scripture to me, and I don't have my little Gideon Bible either. I just pour over the verses I have memorized over the years, and that gives me about 5,000 to work with. I'm in pretty good shape in that department. They encourage me.

I get thinking again about Daniel and Ephesians, and acknowledge, *This is Satan again, trying to discourage me.* Oh well. When I feel myself getting worn down, I'll just pray more. I'm not going to waste the lesson I learned when I was spared from being crushed by the ash tree.

I did a lot of thinking this day. I thought back over all the people I had met on the trail, wishing again that I had written down every name, and kept all the contact information. The posts I'd made in the past became like stepping stones, leading me from memory to memory. But I didn't post everything. Everyone was already so worried I was going to die out here, and I didn't want to add any fuel to that fire. As long as I wasn't worried that I was going to die, that's all that mattered. The only time I really felt like I might actually die was my episode with norovirus in the woods. Everyone's worry then felt pretty legitimate, because I was sure feeling it too, lying there naked on the logging road, too weak to even use my phone.

So today was not the day to be worried. If I ran out of food, I'd be hungry. Route 214 was 37 miles away, so I just had to get there. I was going to be okay. And really, to be out here in this pristine moment in the sunshine and snow was something that many hikers don't get the chance to do. A lot of people like winter hiking. If it weren't for my hands, I probably would too. There are no bugs, and no leaves to impede your view. I did climb a few trees on my second day for photos, but the snow on the one side of the tree made it difficult. Obviously I did it without my pack on, and I just had to watch my shoulder as I went. I know it sounds crazy that I would climb trees in this situation, but I feed on that different perspective, and it's just natural for me.

Lying there I was looking at the tree right in front of me, wishing I could climb it.

But not today. Today I am resting my groin and my toe. I'm feeling lucky again, glad that the tree fell in Pennsylvania, changing my perspective. I still don't have peace exactly, but I'm praying. God seemed to be silent, so I would stay patient. I'm thinking, *If there were no snow, this end of this trail would be done in a week. But now it will be a few weeks. What am I going to do if I get to the end of the trail and I still don't have the peace I'm looking for? Was it all for nothing? Sure, it would be fulfilling for me in many ways, but really, did I get the healing that I wanted and needed so badly?* I believe I had come to understand the spiritual warfare happening, the battle for my mental health. I also believe I had changed dramatically, maybe even down to the chemistry in my brain, in the time after

Sandy's death. The Steven Wright from 2014 who was buoyantly happy in his faith and his life, died with his wife. That's sad to think. I was gradually becoming someone else, a little more battered and weathered, but I hoped joy was possible for this new guy too.

Lord, what am I going to do? I'm getting depressed because I need an answer to why Sandy had to die so painfully, and why I had all these things in my youth. Why did it feel like you weren't there? Why can't I come to terms with this? I'm going over these verses in the Bible, and I don't get it. Do you want me to fast? I don't know how to do that and hike at the same time.

I slept with all this on my mind. I had dreams. Not nightmares. In one, I dreamed of the story in the Bible where the disciples have trouble casting out demons, and I was in the story. I asked God why I could not cast a demon out of somebody. I said, *You gave me power to do this, but I couldn't. What did I do wrong?* In the dream, Jesus said to me what He says to the disciples, *This kind does not come out unless you fast and pray.*

I woke up. I didn't think God had necessarily sent me this dream. It might have been my Patagonia meal. But it did make me think that God wanted me to fast. Back in my 20s, I had experienced a dramatic spiritual warfare experience after fasting and praying for a week, so I knew the power that fasting and scripture could have. I had fasted on occasions after that, too, but I couldn't imagine how it would be possible to fast while I was burning up calories hiking, so I just had to dismiss it and go back to sleep.

CHAPTER 47:

HUNGRY

When I get up in the morning, it's still very cold. Maybe not zero? But cold. Because I'm in the shelter, I don't have the tent to completely pack up. I just roll up the pad and eat. I'm out of there in a half hour, which makes me glad. My first steps tell me that my groin is better, thank God. My toe still hurts, but it's tolerable. I'm going to take it slow. I actually have cell phone reception. Who knows where it's coming from? I'm able to call Jocelyn.

Unbelievably, a snowplow goes by. That means the roads are open! In about two more hours, there's even a car coming the other way. I'll be able to get out of here.

I flag the guy down, and it's a park ranger.

"What's the scoop?" I ask him. "Are the roads opened up?"

"Not really," he told me. "We have our snowplows out down here, but up where you're headed, the roads are not open."

So I guess that's good news, at least some roads south of me are open. He says I've got to get all the way up to the 37-mile mark for it to be open. I asked him if I could catch a ride with him.

"I'm sorry, buddy, I just can't do it," he tells me. He notices I'm a thru-hiker. "My God, man, where are you going?"

"I'm just going to Harpers Ferry now, and then I'm done."

"You're quitting then? When did you start?"

"March."

"Oh my God, it's a thru-hike?"

I tell him my whole story, talking for about a half hour. It is nice just to talk to a human.

Since it is plowed, I decide to walk on the road for a while. It crisscrosses the trail anyway.

I can feel myself getting hungry. I take a break and make a fire, just to melt snow and eat. I end up blowing an hour and fifteen minutes to do this, but it can't be helped. As I'm digging out my food, I realize that somewhere, somehow, I've lost my last Patagonia dinner packet.

With resolve, I leave my pack and go back to find it. I walk the road for a mile, but I worry that the wind might have blown it, so I head into the woods. In the woods, the snow has completely drifted over where I've walked, and I realize I am never going to find it. I go maybe 300 yards, breaking trail all over again before I give up. This isn't good. I just stand and stare at the ground for a full minute. What the hell is wrong with me? How could I lose that?

In bitter disbelief, I turn around and stomp back.

No more cars pass me. I can see a truck going away from me. It's the ranger again. I flag him down and tell him what has happened, and that I had looked for the packet. I knew it shouldn't lie there for a bear to get, or even just as litter. He tells me he will go in for it in a few days. I paused, picturing the ranger beaming and saying *No problem, buddy. I've got an extra one right here for ya!* But of course, he didn't.

I get back to my pack, processing the idea that I won't be eating dinner tonight. By now I have a partial jar of peanut butter, two Snickers bars, one day's worth of beef jerky, and no protein bar or cashews. With irony I think, *Well, I guess I'm going to fast after all.*

I say a quick prayer. He took it out of my hands, didn't He?

I do have some food, and I think I should eat it, I prayed. *I need to keep my strength up so I can go these miles to where I can get off the trail.*

So, I'm not going to starve. I'm just going to be very hungry. There's a difference. I ration myself to one scoop of peanut butter each day, along with a torn off piece of beef jerky.

I had not asked the ranger if it was okay to stay on the road. They were using the road to cut down the trees that fell over. I stayed on the road for a little bit, and then I went on the trail when it was on the south side because it seemed a little better. Today temperatures had risen into the 20s, so that helped. I still have some battery left in my hand warmers, so I am saving it for the morning because otherwise I won't be able to break camp. After tomorrow, it will run out, so I don't want to use it at all today.

My stomach's growling, and I think, *Here I go. I'm fasting whether I want to or not.* I'm not playing music, I'm just hiking and thinking, reciting scriptures over and over. I just try to mediate on God, thinking about the things I'm still upset about. In the end, though, all I could think about was eating. I'm not a very good faster, I guess.

It's a wrestling match in my head, just like Jacob with the angel, for the rest of the hike.

I know I can get off this trail when I get to mile mark 37, where Route 211 crosses the trail and Skyline Drive, so I really need just to focus on getting there.

However, I get to a spot where I start thinking I can take a shortcut to the small town of Luray off to my left. I know I can go just these five miles downhill, and I'll be out of this. So I go off the trail and head right down through the woods. Still wearing my clampons, I get pretty far, and the snow is only about eight inches deep. My pack is definitely lighter now, too, because all the clothes are on me, and there's no food in it. The snow seems better here. I don't think it's melting, but it's packing down better. I go as far down as I can, and take a quick video to post later. But the wind is really blowing, and you can't understand anything I'm saying in it. I come upon a ridge, maybe a 20–60-foot ridge, as far as I can see to my left and right. I can see the town down there, but I can't figure out how to get off the ridge.

Then I get the idea that all I need is a tall tree, and I can climb down it and get to the town. I just knew there was a big burger waiting for me down in that town. I walked the ridge, and I never did see a branch or tree that would work. I turned my phone on, and it came on for a second, but then blinked off. Dead.

I finally have to give up on the ridge. Another valley is heading into it, and I can't get down to the town. I have to climb back uphill to the road.

Now my stomach is pissed off. I keep telling God, *I don't know what you're doing here, but I'm going to keep believing.*

I walk by some little camping area, maybe a nice summer retreat or something in a beautiful area. But there is not even a place where I can sit to take a break. There are picnic tables but the snow is as deep as the seat. I end up lying on top of the picnic table and melting some snow to make some coffee. With the leftover water I make a super strong version of Hunter's Hydro drink.

I get a good buzz from that caffeine. I have one Snickers bar with a bite out of it and one more scoop of the peanut butter left. I look at these items and try to make a smart choice.

I go with the Snickers bar. The peanut butter will be my supper even if I have to saw off the neck of the plastic jar so I can get my hand in there to get the last little bits still clinging to the sides.

There's still no traffic. It has to be close to passable by tomorrow, and I can hitch a ride out of here.

I get to another shelter. I don't get the tent up. The shelter is dry, and I just set up in there for the evening, trying not to think about my hunger. I think about trying to kill a squirrel, or a deer—they are so tame up here. All I had was a stupid little Swiss Army knife, and I doubted I could kill anything with that. I did try to kill a squirrel with a rock, but I missed him twice and then gave up.

The next morning I think, *I've got to get some food.* I did cut the peanut butter jar in half, and I licked every last drop out of there. *I'm really fasting now, Lord. You've got to give me an answer. Help me understand the reason behind it all.*

God's timing and mine definitely don't agree, but I keep walking, trying to trust Him.

I come around a corner, and there is a stream running. My SteriPEN is still plenty charged, and now I can fill my water. When I bend down to get it, I decide the stream might actually be big enough to have trout in it. I take off my pack and walk down a little way, and the holes are getting bigger and bigger. Now the edges are frozen, and in places it is frozen all the way across. The water is definitely running underneath, and I can see some fish under the ice. I start to get a little excited.

I grab my hook, jigs, and line from my pack. I used to carry the pole, but I gave it up as too much to carry and I didn't use it enough to make it worth it. I attach the little jig to the line and head back to the fish. There are about six little brook trout under there, and one of them is going to be my supper! Looking at them, I actually think about damming up the area, breaking the ice, and then scooping them out. But I'll be wet. I'm going to try fishing them out first.

They don't like my jig. I try again. Nothing, and my hands are getting cold. With sudden inspiration, I get into my garbage bag and rip off a bit of the old Patagonia meal bag. It is silver on one side and a reddish color on the other, like a worm. I poke that stupid little scrap on there, and I catch a brookie. I pull him out, gut him with my Swiss Army knife on the spot, and eat him right there. I eat the head. I crunch the bones. If you have never been hungry enough to do that, then you will never understand how good that brookie tasted.

I throw the hook in again. I catch four more and put them right in my pocket. None of the others will bite, so I walk back to my pack. I get out my stove, and I have a nice sit-down meal. These little guys are like sardines, so small that they all fit together right in my tiny titanium pan. I boil water in the pan and cook the fish in the inverted lid with olive oil. I have three teaspoons left, and I blow about half of it to keep them sizzling, keeping the rest just in case. I really should not have been using my fuel, but I was celebrating.

Encouraged, I walked on. As I began a small descent, the snow disappeared. But then the trail turned uphill again, and the snow returned. Just 500 feet in elevation seemed to make all the difference.

I went back to praying. I prayed that God would excuse my little fish dinner while I was fasting, but I figured He wouldn't want me to starve for real. I kept praying, but still heard no answer. I got to the next camping area, and again I have no idea how many miles I have gone. I maybe could have read the mile markers to figure it out, but I guess I didn't think of it.

I was by no means full, but I did sleep better that night. At least I didn't have hunger cramps. I thanked God there was something in my belly. My supply was now down to a teaspoon and a half of oil, salt and pepper, and garlic. I dreamed of Snickers bars.

I stay on the road as much as possible now. The snow is only four inches deep, but I'm still wearing my ice clamp-ons. At first I took them off on the road, because I didn't know if they were slowing me down. But out of nowhere I would come to an icy patch and just go for a ride. Whoop, right down. I couldn't stay off the road, because the snowbank was there. But there were big stretches of this black ice, and I ended up just keeping the clamp-ons on. Mine were the kind with the teeth, not just the wire things, and I was so glad for them. They really gave me traction, and I don't think I could have done it without them.

I didn't sleep in a shelter or a tent that night. I went back into the woods a little bit, put my mat out beside the trail, and cowboy camped. I gazed up at the stars, so far away and icy cold. The tent really only blocks the wind, and I didn't need it to do that tonight. I did a lot of praying, and I felt close to God, I really did.

I woke up in the morning super cold, but it was going to be a beautiful day. When the sun came out, it hit the trees that were all frost covered, and they glittered like they were made of glass. The whole world is so fragile and so perfectly made when you see it like this. My stomach was roaring. I wandered off the trail to see if I could find another stream with more brookies in it. It was either that, or else I had to get off this trail somehow.

I decide to go back and see if they have opened up Skyline Drive yet. I've meandered quite a distance off the trail by now. I have to hike quite a while before I see the trail again, and the road alongside it. It looks bare, but there are still those treacherous spots of black ice.

A vehicle approaches slowly up the road. He's going south, but I flag him down with probably more enthusiasm than is necessary.

"Did they open the road up?" I ask.

"No, I'm just the inspector. Maybe today."

"Hey, I've been out here for eight days," I tell him, "and I've got to get off-trail."

"You went through that blizzard!" He is as shocked as I am hungry. "I see you're a thru-hiker."

"I am. Is there any possible way I could use your phone?"

"Sure," he said. "Don't you have a phone?"

"It's dead. Everything's dead," I tell him. I explain that my GPS was the only thing I have left. "I texted my daughter, but I don't know if she got it. I should be better at using it, but I'm not, and I have not gotten an answer. I just don't know if it went through."

He takes my phone and charges it while I use his phone.

I can't get hold of Jocelyn, but I leave her a message. I tell her I'm going to walk, but if she can find a way off the trail, I'd appreciate it. I let her know I have to keep my phone off, but she could text me a yes or a no about getting off-trail through the GPS. I explained that I was talking to a ranger, and they expected Skyline Drive and the trail to be open tomorrow. There's a place where the road to Shenandoah crosses the trail, and someone could meet me there.

I tell her that probably by mid-morning, I can be at that intersection.

The ranger let me charge my phone in his car for maybe 20 minutes, and that was such a blessing. I was able to get up to about a 20 percent charge.

I keep the phone off the whole time after that, until I get to camp at night. I'm able to get hold of Jocelyn, and she had gotten my message and has some folks lined up. They just need to know a pick-up point and a time.

She even had found me a place to stay. What a kid!

"In Luray, at the Open Arms Hostel," she tells me. "It's the owner who can come for you if you would like to stay there. Or you can go to a Holiday Inn, and Shane can get you a room there all the way up at Front Royal."

I decide to stay at the Open Arms Hostel. That turned out to be a great choice because it was close to the trail. The people were so nice. I got to meet a guy there named Cam, a section hiker who was tall and lanky, and about my age. He was headed southbound and had hiked through the area I had just been through. He was taking a few zeros at the hostel, because he could not get back on the trail either. Luckily, he had gotten off at the right time.

That night before I got off the trail was pretty rough. My stomach was going nuts, cramping and growling all night long. I literally dreamed of bacon. I dreamed of hot dogs. I dreamed of hot dogs wrapped in bacon. And then I dreamed of the bacon wrapped around a hamburger. I could not wait to get a piece of bacon the next day.

I camped out again, under a beautiful clear night. Even without the protection of the tent, I can manage the cold, and it makes packing up the next morning easier for my hands. I lay in bed and wondered what in the world my fast had accomplished. I didn't think I had gained any insights or answers. But I resolved to be patient. One day I would find out the reasons for everything and be content. All I had been able to think about was food; I wasn't sure that was too holy.

Looking back now, I think the "fast" did me good. It made me trust Him. I never did feel like I was in any danger—I was just hungry. I like testing my body to its limits, and I had done that. Hopefully though, there would be no more sushi for me on the trail. I'm going to have the steak.

CHAPTER 48:

A PURPOSE

It's very cold in the morning again. I still have a last bit of coffee, and this is the last of my fuel. I have used three full containers of fuel. I had been able to give the ranger my garbage, and now my pack is very light. I'm eating icicles as I go, chomping on them, so I don't even have water to weigh me down. I keep thinking I will pass a car and get a ride to the meeting point, but I never do. When I finally get to the road around noon, the trail has just opened. Perfect timing.

I make the call to the Open Arms Hostel, and the owner comes to pick me up. Happiness. She takes me to the hostel, but I beg her to take me to town.

"I'm absolutely starving," I confess.

"I can't right now," she answers. Just then Cam comes down the steps. He looks so well rested and well fed. I want to be like Cam!

"I'm going to town if you want to go," said Cam. "We'll just walk."

"Sure," I said, "I just need to get there quick." Cam's long strides strike a hot pace, and we get there in no time.

Man, I ate and ate and ate. I got two bacon cheeseburgers first, with two orders of fries. Then I got a vanilla milkshake.

I had not showered, and I was there walking around town. I didn't think I smelled too bad, because it had just been so damn cold. I had walked down the hill where the hostel was; I had taken my raincoat off for the first time in eight days. I figured I had to stink, and maybe I just didn't know it.

"Do I stink?" I asked Cam, just to make sure. He said that I didn't. I couldn't believe it.

When we got back to the hostel, I asked Cam if I could go first in the shower. I just let that hot water run and run over me, getting me completely warm and relaxed. I just crashed then, for a lovely nap. I had planned to make phone calls, but they would have to wait for later.

When I woke up, it was time to head back into town to get some supper. My favorite thing!

I had no trouble eating again at the Chop House in town. My brother called and said he wanted to buy me a steak, and that was fine with me. I told him he'd better get a 100-dollar bill out, because I was going to eat two! I guess everyone had worried about where I was since I hadn't been able to make contact. I only ate one steak, and a piece of fish as well, with some appetizers and a piece of pie. They also had Mitchter's Small Batch Bourbon. I got a shot of that, which was really good, and I sipped it through the meal. It has to be one of the finest whiskies ever made. My nephew bought me a bottle once and I fell in love with it. I saved the last sip for after the last bite of food, and it burned all the way down, just the way I like. The bartender was fun to chat with, and he called the manager over.

"You gotta hear this guy's stories," he told the manager. The manager and I chatted, and she followed me on Instagram then.

"You know we are going to have a Christmas parade?" she asked me.

"No, I didn't. The owner of the Open Arms Hostel has been busy doing something; maybe that's what she's been working on."

"Yeah, it's starting now, and you'll hear it go by."

Sure enough, I could hear it. So I bid the folks at the restaurant goodbye, got a hug from the waitress, and headed out to the street. I walked uptown, looking for the owner of the hostel, imagining she would be there somewhere. I found her doing a fundraiser for the arts, and I contributed to her fund. Since Jocelyn had lived the life of a ballet dancer, struggling mightily to live on the meager money it paid, I have a soft spot for the struggles of artists.

The parade was lots of fun. I got lots of Tootsie Rolls and mini Snickers bars—perfect! Like a little bit of trail magic. When the first handful landed at my feet, these little kids ran out to grab them all, and I wanted to tackle them. I guess starving on the trail can turn a guy into someone who begrudges little kids their candy? I'm proud to say I caught myself and no small children were harmed. I did get my fair share of candy, though—don't think I didn't.

The owner of the hostel gave me a ride home from the parade. On the way, we stopped at the little theater to unload her van.

"Are you taking a zero tomorrow?" she asks me.

"Nope, I've got to get right back on the trail," I tell her. "I practically took a zero today, because I got picked up at noon."

In the morning, I got to town early to get one last big breakfast. I was back at the hostel in time to catch a ride back to the trail with the owner at 8:00 a.m. Cam and I piled in the car. At the trailhead, he headed south, while I went north.

I start up the trail, and with what seems like a few steps, I reach 2,100 miles. I just sit there and look at the sign. Only 100 more miles to go. I can hardly believe it. Now under normal conditions, with me hiking my best, this would be over in just a few days. It wouldn't be that easy, but it was definitely doable now. For the first time, I seriously thought, *I don't want this to end.*

Now, just because I love being in the woods I had casually indulged myself in thinking about how fun it would be to stay on trail longer. But now, the thoughts running through my head on this hike felt overwhelming, and I needed more time to handle them. As I stared at the mile marker, I thought, *Wow, this is incredible.* I had started the journey as a man who didn't really want to live, who walked around hoping that a tree would fall on him, even as he walked out his dream of hiking the trail. Now, I did want to live. I wasn't sure I completely understood what I was supposed to do with the rest of my life, but at least I wanted to live and find out. In these last hundred miles, I prayed that God would show me what He wanted me to do.

I wanted to make a difference.

I wanted to fulfill my mother's prophecy over me, *"All my life I prayed to God that one of my sons would change the world. You are that son. You are going to change the world. Do you hear me? You are going to change the world."*

Could I?

I could feel a little part of me beginning to take those first steps of belief. Maybe I could.

I felt glued to the spot. I sat down. I had only hiked maybe a mile, but I sat down for quite a while. Finally, a peace washed over me. I hardly recognized the feeling, but it was there, flowing like cool water through my whole body. That's what the fast had been for, that feeling, right there. I thought again about how I hadn't wanted to live, and was amazed at how far I had come. I was a man who thought he was a shitty witness for the Lord, who had nothing left to bring. I had done plenty of things that Satan was quick to point out were shameful. But now I was a man who was looking at God, and not at that asshole Satan who wants to ruin my life. I thanked God for showing me who my enemy was, not by speaking to me in audible words, but though the Holy Spirit guiding me toward understanding and using a falling tree to do it. I was a lucky, blessed man, *with a purpose,* whatever it might be.

Again, like it did when I looked at the lake with Jocelyn, the gratitude overwhelmed me. The tears came again, just streaking down my cold face, and it felt good. *This feels good,* I thought. *This is what healing feels like.*

I finally stood and looked at the snowy trail ahead of me. *Just a little farther, friend. Onward.*

The snow starts getting slushy by the afternoon, and I am glad I have my clamp-ons on. At least I'm in the woods, and the road has been opened up. Every time I have to cross the road, I am glad for the clamp-ons all over again, because of the black ice still coating most of the surface. It's actually beautiful out, and I feel like I could run into another hiker. But all morning, I do not. I call Cam just to see how he is doing, and to see what the snow is like in the other direction. He is doing great. In the Skyline Drive area, you have reception several times a day, which is pretty nice.

I go around 10 miles to some overlook and take a nice break. On this road there are dozens of overlooks. Elsewhere on the trail they don't really cater to overlooks in the same way. I got my share because I am a tree-climber, but they don't really work to get you the great views if you don't climb trees. I cannot lift my left arm over my head at this point, but I don't need to. It is pretty easy climbing even without doing that. I have to take my pack off, though, to climb, and so that is kind of a hinderance. I definitely need a stump to get the pack on and off.

Because I didn't get the super early start, I'm just hoping for a 20-mile day today. It starts to cloud up, though, despite the forecast for clear skies. Before you know it, I'm in a rainstorm. The upside is that the rain might melt some snow. I cover up my down coat with my raincoat immediately to keep dry.

I don't mind getting wet when I plan on it, like hiking in the morning in the summer. Those of us who are early risers have to walk through weeds that will just drench you. And you wind up eating spider webs too, at least until later in the morning when other hikers get out to break them up in front of you. It's so nice to see someone coming from the other direction, because you think to yourself, *Thank God I don't have to eat any more spider webs.* I bet I've had as many as 20 spiders on me at one time, just from blowing through their webs. When I hike with Jocelyn, she walks along with her sticks flailing around in front of her, like she's writing jerky cursive letters in the air. I don't even know if she uses them to walk. I only have one hiking speed, fast. Letting Jocey lead also helps keep my speed down, though she isn't slow by any means. Sandy often said I'm like a hummingbird on crack. I don't know much about crack, but maybe. Now Sandy was a fast walker in general. I did not enjoy walking with this woman. I swear she felt like it was a race every time. I don't mind running but don't like walking fast. Hiking is different. I like hiking fast. But, on trail, I am also a stop-and-smell-the-roses guy, so maybe that's an odd paradox. Hurry up and stop, hurry up and stop.

This is how your mind drifts when you're hiking alone.

I'm always looking for mushrooms. A lot of people complain that on the Appalachian Trail you have to have your head down to watch your footing, and you can't enjoy the views. I guess that's true. But even if you could look up, there aren't any. Just kidding. There are some, but it's called the "green tunnel" for a reason. If you want beautiful views, you just have to look for them. You don't have to see 50 miles in the distance for a great view, you just have to see seven, or 10, or 15 feet into the woods, and the views are incredible. Tiny mushrooms pop up, pushing leaves and sticks out of the way. I like to get down on the ground with my camera, level with the mushroom and see it the way an ant might—this little fungus just working to get to the surface. My other favorite view is the really soft moss, the little buds that come up out of the green.

I find some of this beautiful moss showing up through the snow during this rainstorm. Each little bud popping up out of the snow seems to have its own little story. I spread my hand over the moss. There is snow all over, but not on the moss. Is it warm? When I lightly pushed down and across the moss, it felt like petting a dog. Those little buds moved softly under the palm of my hand. As my hand left, they snapped right back to attention. The life was just bursting out of it, even up here at 3,000 feet in the cold. This moss was finding a way. Everything was dead around me, but this moss was alive, just like me.

Everything reminds me of the miracle of life now, instead of death.

I didn't make it to 20 miles, just 15. I camped at Gravel Springs Hut where I could spread stuff out to dry. In the morning, the rain had turned to snow, and the wind was blowing. I had slept with my head in the far end of the shelter, so when I woke up at the usual time in the dark, the freshly fallen snow was a little surprise. When I checked my phone, I saw that there would be a couple of cold days to come. Well, all right.

I can see now, there's an end to this. My phone now predicts that in about four days it's going to be 50 degrees out. That will be absolutely dreamy.

I'm booking down the trail, just hoping to get miles in without getting hurt today. It would be impossible without ice clamp-ons. Maybe that's why no one is out here. I'm hovering right around the 3,000-foot mark, give or take a few hundred feet. After I get a few more miles in, I can see two hikers coming with a dog.

It was so nice to see humans. We sat and talked for a while. They wanted to know everything about my hike, and the guy had done the AT 22 years ago. I didn't ask him why he did it, because everyone has a reason. I usually do ask people, but this guy had so many questions that I just didn't get around to it. I think there's such a fun perspective when you talk to a couple, and one spouse has done the trail but the other one hasn't. The wife was a camper, but had zero desire to do the AT. There's a difference between a thru-hiker, and a day hiker with a tent. I think you do have to be just a little crazy to do a thru-hike. You're giving up a warm bed, civilization even, for like six months. And that's if everything goes right. These two had a funny relationship. She kept busting on her husband in a way that reminded me of Sandy too.

I enjoyed talking to these two, and I said a quick prayer for them as we parted.

As I went, I was still bobbing along from memory to memory of Sandy and I hiking together and her busting on me just like that wife had done to her husband. In all honestly, I knew Sandy didn't really want to do the trail after we had kids. After we had been married maybe 27 years, she had really lost her desire for roughing it. Once Sandy even said that her idea of roughing it was a Holiday Inn with a black-and-white TV. But it had been fun to talk about it. And it had been fun to talk to this couple and hear their banter. She had said she just wanted a steak dinner after a good day's hike, with a glass of red wine, preferably dry, on the side. That's something Sandy would have said.

By the end of the day, I had a tough 15 miles under my belt. I camped at a nice spot right beside the trail. After looking at the weather, I decided to lay the tent on the ground and sleep on top of it, instead of inside it. If it got bad, I would just crawl under it like another blanket. It was a beautiful night. Wintertime stargazing is the best. It's so crisp and black, and the stars seem extra bright. It gets dark at five, so there are more hours of gazing.

Although it's super cold again in the morning, I have a nice bed of snow under me and with my insulated sleeping pad I don't feel it a bit. The sky and stargazing were well worth it. My hands aren't too bad this morning for some reason. I get my breakfast and I'm ready to go with my headlight on. I'm not worried about it running out, because I know I'm getting off at Front Royal and I have plenty of charge left.

I have 25 miles to Front Royal. I think I can get in 18 today, and then have a short day the next day. I get sidetracked by the beauty, but I'm making good time. It's different from any other section because it was a park for so long, and doesn't particularly go through wilderness all the time. I mean, it was wilderness when they first made it, but you can see that the views on both sides over time have been built up by small towns and rural communities. I think they did a good job preserving this area. It isn't spoiled at all. I love seeing the squares of farmland patched together like a quilt. There is no snow in the valley, anything under 2,000 feet, so the farmlands are all green and brown.

I ran into a few day hikers on the trail. One person was a backpacker and planned on spending the night. We had a nice talk, and he was so happy for me that I was hiking the trail. He had dreams of doing it years before and said now he would have to wait until he retired. He might have been 55 or so, and would have to wait another 10 years or so I guess, and then he would be my age. I think I reinspired him, and I wished him luck. His name was Mountain Man.

That put a big smile on my face. I told him about how, when I was a kid, that's all I wanted to be. I had wanted to quit school in third grade and be a mountain man, and then again in fifth grade when I was so much more mature. He shared all the details about how he got the nickname. He really regretted not doing the trail as a young man, before life got in the way. I agreed with him there.

"At least I am doing it now," I conceded. "Trust me, you haven't missed your window just yet. But, if you think your body is going downhill, you'd better quit your job and go do it."

He laughed, kind of.

"It's worth it," I assured him.

"It's a deal, brother." He laughed for real then, and we shook on it.

I bid him goodbye and good luck and told him I'd be praying for him to do the whole trail.

He gave me a thumbs up, and then he switched his hands to "I love you." I signed the same thing back.

That's how it is on the trail. You meet people with the same mindset that you have, and you immediately click with them. It doesn't seem to matter whether they are young, old, Democrat or Republican. You've got one thing in mind: being in nature. Letting God speak to you through the mountains, and large rocks, and trees that you can't get your arms around, sometimes not even with two or three people. It's just something special, this world we've been given. I could tell you story after story of the different scenarios where people have met and connected, but then this book would be a thousand pages. No one would read it, and I couldn't afford to publish it. So I'll let it go at that.

I have a lot of hiking yet to do, and a lot of pictures to take. And I did get a lot of great pictures on this day. The sun was brilliant. So even though it was cold, my hands didn't seem to be so affected, because of the sunshine just soaking into my body. I think my core temperature was rising. All I had on was my alpaca hoodie and my Smartwool T-shirt. That was all I needed. If my hands got cold, I could just warm them up by tucking them under my armpits. Now, doing this made me gasp for air every time, because I have such damn cold hands. But then it only took a few minutes to warm back up and I would be hiking with my sticks again.

I made nearly 18 miles. Seventeen-something. That would make for an easy day into Front Royal in the morning. I didn't really want to take a zero day, but they were calling for all-day rain and high winds, especially in the mountains. It's still cold, very cold, but I guess we are going to have a warm up after that. They were not calling for rain until later in the morning the next day, so I cowboy camped again. Part of me felt like I wouldn't be able to sleep out like that for much longer, so I'd better enjoy it while I could. I didn't want to be at a shelter tonight. I wanted a ridge with a great view of the sky all around. I wanted to see all the stars.

And they put on quite a show. I found a cliff area, with a nice 30-foot flat spot. No overhanging trees, and plenty of space before the cliff started. I saw one magnificent shooting star go across, while all the rest winked and danced in their spots. I had never seen a lone one like this. And then, on my last night on the trail, I would see just one more that was even more spectacular than this one. This last one left a trail, and I was just thanking God that I got to witness it. I felt like it had to hit the earth somewhere, because it went above me all the way to the horizon.

We are almost there, reader, at the end of the trail. Almost.

CHAPTER 49:

THE CHURCH

It's still brutally cold, and I keep thinking the forecasters have it wrong. This is weather for snow, not rain. Sure enough, by 10:00 in the morning or so, the temperature had climbed from 20 degrees up to about 35, and then it started to rain at about noon. By that time, I was able to get a ride into Front Royal.

I had left messages with several people in an attempt to get a ride. I get down to the road, but still no takers via phone calls. So, I stick out my thumb, and a guy picks me up almost right away.

He was a former hiker too, with lots of questions. I get into Front Royal at a fairly early hour. He tells me all the hostels are not running anymore, so I should use this hotel that he recommended. I prefer the hostels, but okay. Front Royal must be on the larger size, but I didn't remember it with any detail. It looked familiar to me, and I think I was once there with Tristan.

This fellow also took me to his favorite barbeque place. It was a great menu; they had roasted chicken, brisket, or pork, and he liked all three.

"I bet you feel like you could eat all that," he joked.

"I guess you just talked me into it, brother!" I ordered all three on the spot. I figured I could keep the leftovers for myself the next day, since I was taking a zero. The sides were baked beans, French fries, or potato salad. So I got all three, plus a beer.

Well, there were no leftovers, in the end. The only thing I didn't finish was the beer. It tasted good, but it was early, and I was way too full to finish it. The guy did not stick around to watch me eat all three. He took off after a quick picture of my meal all spread out in front of me. We made plans to connect later that night. This was a Saturday, and the next day would be Sunday, so I asked him for a church recommendation.

"There's all kinds of churches here," he said. "You're in the Bible belt, buddy. I don't go to any of them."

"How come?"

"I don't know," he muttered. "My mom bitches at me every day about not going to church. I just got out of the habit, and I decided Sunday was my day."

We talked about it a little more, and then he left.

I just kept exploring. I found four different churches. I decide to take a chance on one of them, because I read that it started earlier in the morning. Then I could make my escape back to the mountains. It was called Williams Chapel CME Church.

I woke up and had a big breakfast with coffee. I thought I had read the service started at eight, but when I showed up there were just a few people coming in, the musicians, I think. I walked up to the door, not dressed very well, obviously, because I'm headed straight back to the trail after the service. My sweater has those big holes worn through at the shoulders where my pack has rubbed them away, and I'm wearing my pack. I thought I could just get a ride to take me back to the trail afterward.

As I get there, a very large black guy comes sprinting across the parking lot to intercept me.

"Hey there, what are you doing, bud?" he asks a little aggressively.

"I'm just seeing if I can go to church here," I explain. Maybe I looked a little like a terrorist? The guy was not convinced yet, but he was trying to be a good Christian.

"Oh, oh, okay, I see."

"I know I don't look too good, brother," I assured him. As I talked, he seemed to become less alarmed.

"Yeah, you are welcome to join us; why don't you just go for a coffee and come back? It won't start for another hour."

So I did. I thought this church seemed pretty good. The other woman walking in was black too, so maybe this church would have more of an African American vibe. By the time I had another coffee, I was ready for some lively worship and looking forward to it.

I came back still wearing the backpack. I thought no one would want me to have that in there, so I took it off and stowed it in the back of the church. I sat down about halfway up. My clothes were clean, but full of holes, and I can imagine what the congregation was thinking as they saw me. As the folks rolled in, I could see it was an all-black church after all.

The music was great, with great preaching, and a lot of amens. It was awesome. They were all curious about me, and I had to give the abbreviated version of my story over and over. I really lucked out, because it turned out there was a church dinner afterward and I was invited to attend.

"You don't know what you're doing, inviting a thru-hiker to a dinner," I warned them. "I'll eat everything you got!"

"We're planning on it," they assured me, so I went and ate with them. They had more coffee, and after about 20 minutes they had the food ready: ham sandwiches and baked beans, the works. I ate it all. I got to talk to the pastor, Tonia, for a little bit. I signed up for their newsletter, and they kept in touch with me. I loved the service, and I loved the people. A long time after I was done with my hike,

I had a bad day. I just felt that I had let God down and needed a prayer. This little church just came to mind, and I actually called Tonia. She picked up right away. We texted a little bit after that, too, and she sent me Bible verses to encourage me as well. I just thank God for this little church that He sent me. Everybody in the church treated me so kindly, like a true brother, and they got me a ride to the trailhead too.

CHAPTER 50:

FINISH LINE

I get to the trail a little before 2:00. The trail, and all of Skyline Drive, is open, so I start hiking to Harpers Ferry again. A sign appears. It reads, "You are entering the roller coaster. Enjoy the ride."

I thought, *Uh oh. This could put a bind in my 20-mile day I have planned.*

There is still a little snow, and it's flurrying. I'm not wearing my clamp-ons anymore. This sign made me laugh then. I thought, *One more hard thing, huh? Well, okay then.* I am looking forward to this ride. I love roller coasters.

They couldn't have described it better. These were those little up-and-down hills, like the kind of roller coaster where you go like 50 miles an hour and almost feel like you're going to fly out of your seat. Up and down, up and down, and then you come to a steep banked turn, and the G-forces have you smashed into your seat. That's how this part of the trail was. There was a fairly big up, and a fairly big down, but the in-between part was the fun part. I wasn't winded at all, running on adrenaline. I could see the end, and it was making me sad, actually. I told myself, *Calm down. Don't fly. Don't get hurt.*

When I got to the end, I had some great pictures and some great views, but no other people. They might be up on Skyline Drive now, or in the park, it's such a nice day. Cold, snowy, and sunny all at the same time. I was using my possum gloves and my sticks today, and they felt fine too.

I didn't plan for this to be a high-mileage day, but I was flying and couldn't help it. I got to a spot they called the "Bear's Den." I believe there are three of them on the whole trail. It was a fancier sort of hostel, with a slate roof and copper gutters. I would enjoy being here to volunteer if they ever needed any help. I met Fern here, a young lady on the petite size, slender with wavy brown hair and glasses. We had such an easy time talking, and I wished I could take a zero day just to talk more with her.

The owner was awesome too. I had lost my really good headlight the night before, and he gave me a spare which I still use to this day. They run a tight ship at Bear's Den. I had a pizza for supper, which was hot and juicy, and I had a nice shower. I was busy talking poor Fern's ear off until it was time for bed.

I said goodbye in the morning, walked down the road, and started hiking. But unlike every other day that I had done this, it would be my last full day and night.

I learned my most important lesson on the hike during those last 13 miles in general, and especially on that final evening. I was overflowing with emotion. I was so amped up on adrenaline, I couldn't sleep. I went through all the pictures I had taken and could remember every detail about every one of them. I had climbed 75 trees to get the best pictures. Out of all the training, all the work, all the stops and restarts, I had made it. My pack had over 7,000 miles on it by now.

I had decided that I was not going to end my hike until God spoke to me in some way. I figured I could keep on hiking until I got to Key West if I had to. I felt like Jacob wrestling with God.

Jacob wouldn't let him go until God blessed him. I had actually told God that. But I also never liked Jacob in the Bible. I thought he was a weasel. I liked Esau a lot better and identified with him. But God comes right out and says, "Jacob have I loved, but Esau have I hated" (Malachi 1:2-3; Romans 9:13)! Even so, Jacob was a weasel all right. I can't deny that.

Anyway, my family would have shot me if I had told them I was planning to keep going.

I'm playing back all those videos and pictures, remembering how depressed I was when I broke my foot, or when I got COVID, or the norovirus, when I "separated" my collarbone, or when I dislocated my left shoulder. I busted three fingers, one of which will continue to hurt a year later. Every time something happened to me, I was bitching at God, *Why the hell would you let this happen to me? I know this is Satan, but can't you stop him from hurting me? I don't know how much more I can take.*

I'll tell you a secret about myself. I always could count on my body, my whole life. It was fast, strong, and it has served me very well. I was a good athlete, a good carpenter, a good roofer. If we needed money, I would just work harder, and it never let me down. I probably abused it, to tell the truth. But it has been through all these injuries that I found my answers from God. God's clearest communication to me wasn't when things were going right, it was when I was injured.

Like most sleepless nights, I finally fall into good sleep during the morning hours, so I do not get up in the dark like usual. I wake to a cold morning with glorious bands of pink, orange, and red streaking across the sky. I think, *This is my last day of hiking.*

Nine months and nine days.

I ate a huge breakfast and hit the trail by 7:30. My pack was feather light, empty except for a Snickers bar. A light pack meant I could fly, and man did I ever. I couldn't control my feet. God had healed my body, and somehow also used those broken bones to heal my brain. I think on the trail God was trying to teach me the lesson: *Your body isn't going to get you out of this one. You gotta trust in Me. You gotta leave your wife's death in My hands. You even built her tombstone with your own hands. You never gave her to Me.*

So I gave Sandy Wright to God that morning when I was walking to the finish line. It was a big release. I want her back, but I can't have her. I'll have to go to her now.

And that did it. After 2,200 miles, that was the release I needed.

There, finally, was the peace in letting go, not just of Sandy, but of the words I had said to my dad, and even all the hardships I had let myself think He didn't care about.

With my prayer answered and peace in my heart, I knew I could finally go home.

I wanted both: to go home and to stay on the trail. It had been the most terrible and the most wonderful thing that had ever happened to me. *I want to live.* Even thinking it to myself seemed surprising and new. Like an old dirty blanket, I was washed clean again and ready to start over. I was finally able to forgive myself, and release Sandy to God.

I am anxious to see my kids. Jocelyn and Tommy are coming down to meet me. I cannot wait to get into Harpers Ferry and see them waiting there for me. My feet are flying. My nose on the other hand is sniffling as I fight back little tears. I know I have to slow down or I will get there way too early. To be honest, I don't really know how early but I can't help it, so, what can you do?

The crisp dirt and leaves crunch in a little rhythm underfoot as I walk the high ridge northward. My mind keeps cycling through the many things I have been through on the trail, knowing I needed them to get my lesson learned. Now, with every step, I am thanking God.

There are two bridges at Harpers Ferry, one coming up from the south over the Shenandoah River, and one crossing into Harpers Ferry at the northeast end over the Potomac. I come across the southern bridge into town, not really knowing where I am because I have never been on that part of the trail before. Walking out of Harpers Ferry just across the second bridge across the Potomac River will be my finish line. Three weeks earlier, I had come down from the north to the start of that bridge over the Potomac and purposely avoided looking at anything besides the guardrail. I wanted everything to be a complete surprise, and it sure is. Walking down the ridge and onto the southern bridge, I can see the icy Shenandoah. Water breaks up over the shallow ledges, and rushes downstream in eddies and deep swales. Once in town I pass old historic buildings. Their faded stones are so pale. This town looks like a set from a movie.

I head just a block north off of the trail to the Appalachian Trail Conservancy office which won't be too far from the spot where I'll be meeting the kids. The white grout laces the gray stones like thick icing and the building is rather squat. I am 40 minutes early, so I decide to go in and look around in the shop. As soon as I walk in, a ranger sees my thru-hiker sticker on my vest.

"Are you The 'Shrooming Camel?" he asks.

"Yes. Did someone call you and tell you I was coming in?"

"We've been waiting for you," says the ranger kindly. "You just made it."

They usually close the trail before today, the 21st of December, but this ranger admits they were keeping it open just for me.

I say, "Do you mean if I had waited one more day, this would not have counted?"

"You're right," he says.

I can barely process that.

"We were hoping so badly that you would show up today," he continues, "otherwise this was it. We were willing to stay till now just to make sure you got this. We heard about everything that happened to you and wanted you to make it."

Of course I get choked up. You can't make this shit up. I am so blessed, and so grateful.

"I can't sign the book right now," I tell him. "I have to go down and walk across the bridge. I haven't got there yet."

"Well, get going. Don't be too long down there because we've got to close up."

I assure them I won't delay.

"You've got an hour," they tell me.

I get to the bottom of the hill outside the office, talk to a few people, and pretty soon Jocelyn calls to let me know they are in town.

They pull in within minutes. They surprise me with two additional family friends in tow, all of them bundled up against the cold. Tears, tears, everywhere tears, and I am high as a kite. The trees are bare, and the path is asphalt in places, gravel in others. It is a typical gray winter day, unless you are about to finish the Appalachian Trail. Then everything is magical and glittering with promise. I laugh and cry all at the same time, tripping along the steps, the walkways. We strode together across the bridge over the Potomac to the edge of the tunnel from Sandy Hook where I had stopped my southbound trip. To be honest, I can't remember what any of it looked like, I can only remember how I felt.

It was the best feeling of my whole life.

We piled into a car and headed back to the ranger station, where I finally signed the book, and the champagne corks started popping. There are big moments in a life: the births of your children, your wedding, maybe graduations. For me, this day would rank right up there with those other momentous memories.

Reader, I misinterpreted some of the Bible. I believed that it clearly said God would never give me more than I could handle. I believe that's not just a bad interpretation now, but it's a bold-faced lie. I know that will shock some people. All these years, I thought it came from the verse that says: *No temptation has overtaken you except such as is common to man; but God is faithful, who will not allow you to be tempted beyond what you are able, but with the temptation will also make the way of escape, that you may be able to bear it.* (1 Cor. 10:13 NKJV).

But God isn't talking about trials and tribulations there. He's talking about temptation and sin. I hope my misinterpretation has not ever caused anyone a problem. I think my misunderstanding cost me a lot of pain. If you're thinking you can't handle something, like me, and you're thinking it means you're weak, you're wrong. I believe God gives us things that we can't handle, specifically to make us trust and lean on Him. I did not know that until this hike, until I was at the point where I could not possibly do it on my own. Think about it. Rationally, with everything that happened, I should not have been able to finish this hike. But I did it through the power of God. I prayed: *I can't do this. Please help me. I'm weak. I'm in pain.* I hiked in a lot of pain over this trail. And my help came from more places than God. Each of my kids also helped me tremendously, because they knew how important it was for me to finish. Even beyond the help I got from my kids, I could not have done this without the prayers of my friends and family covering me. I was overwhelmed with gratitude. I realized that each and every person had been literally the hand of God helping me and supporting me.

It's true I deceived my family by not fully revealing what was going on and what I was doing. Essentially, I lied to them. I told them I would quit if it became too much or if I thought of hurting myself. The truth was I had no intention of quitting, no matter what happened. I just figured I could plow through anything.

But I could not handle my wife's death. I could not forgive myself for what I did to my father. With that pastor at the altar, I knew God forgave me, but I couldn't forgive myself. And it took me all these years, all these broken bones, and missed opportunities, to figure out that it wasn't about accepting it, it was about letting it go. And I finally did. I suppose I'll be hard-headed again sometime before I'm dead. God will have to teach me some other hard lessons. But I thank Him for this lesson. I thank Him for the life He has given me. I pray that He will use me again in a mighty way.

You might be reading this and thinking, *This guy was messed up.* You would be right to think that. But I'm recovering. I've got a better attitude. I'm definitely not 100 percent. I still get depressed some days, but I catch myself. I do not allow myself to think of Sandy's death for more than about 10 minutes at a time, and I can do that. I can let it go. Then I can get up, and I can thank God for the wonderful life we had, and all the blessings we had. Now I don't think about her suffering and dying. I focus on what a wonderful life we had together. I'll see her again in heaven. Even her death is a beautiful thing because it was a release from this lousy freaking cancer. She has a brand-new body, and it is young and beautiful. She was a stunning young lady, and I believe she is a stunning young lady again with her loved ones in heaven. I thank God.

As soon as I became a Christian, my biggest thing was that I wanted to be a good witness, an ambassador for Christ. Sometimes I was more like a traitor, not an ambassador. I was a poor witness, not a good one. So, look at my life. I left it open for anybody to see. Is it a parable? I am not in any way an example of how to do something. I'm more like an example of how not to do something. I am like the foolish man in the story that Jesus tells. I have a life that has a lot of windows you can look into. You can see what I am, what kind of a man I am. Sometimes the glass is faded, and the vision you see is wobbly and curvy, and you can't make out what it really is. But sometimes things are crystal clear.

Good man, bad man, you make your decision. I hope you do see one thing: a man who loved God with all of his heart. God is truly the most important thing that I've ever held on to. I believe He lives in my heart and still has something good to work out in me. I believe He will use me. Maybe, just maybe, the prophecy that my mom uttered over me when I flunked fifth grade, *You are the man that is going to change the world for good,* can be true after all. I plan to spend the rest of my life finding out.

THE JOURNEY DOESN'T END HERE

If you've walked these pages with me, thank you. My hope is that you've found something real here: hope in the middle of brokenness, comfort in the face of loss, and strength to take the next step.

SPEAKING

I share my story of grief, healing, and hiking the Appalachian Trail at festivals, retreats, schools, churches, and events nationwide.

If you'd like me to bring this story to your community, reach out:
theweighticarried@gmail.com

STAY CONNECTED

theweighticarried.com/steven-c-wright
Instagram: **@steven_c_wright**

On my website, you'll find:

- Bonus trail stories & behind-the-scenes reflections

- Updates on upcoming events & speaking engagements

- The Campfire Membership → a monthly newsletter of raw stories, photos, and video reflections delivered straight to your inbox

KEEP THE STORY MOVING

This book will travel farther with your help:

- **Leave a review** on Amazon or Goodreads — your words help others searching for hope discover this story.

- **Share it** — pass your copy on, or gift one to someone carrying something heavy.
- **Invite me to speak** — stories come alive face-to-face.

A FINAL WORD

The Appalachian Trail taught me that healing doesn't happen all at once. It happens step by step, mile by mile, in both the peaks and the valleys.

Before she died, my wife said:

> *"If you let a dream die, a part of you dies with it."*

My prayer is that her words help you **dust off a dream, carry your weight with courage, and step toward the light.**

See you down the trail.
— Steven C. Wright